UNIVERSITY OF
GLOUCESTERSHIRE
at Cheltenham and Gloucester

Oxstalls Library
University of Gloucestershire
Oxstalls Campus, Oxstalls Lane, Longlevens,
Gloucester, Gloucestershire GL2 9HW

WOMEN IN THE AGE OF ECONOMIC TRANSFORMATION

The world is going through a period of radical change. This is self-evident in post-socialist Europe with the disappearance of centrally planned economies. However, policies of liberalization and privatization are also sweeping the less developed world. While traditional theory predicts beneficial results from these changes, the practical outcome is less certain. Whatever the overall effect, it is clear that some citizens will pay a higher price than others.

In **Women in the Age of Economic Transformation** the authors deal with the impact of structural change on women. Each chapter summarizes the changes that have taken place in a particular economy. This is developed further by an empirical analysis of the effect on women. The authors discuss the evidence of gender bias and reach some telling, if unsurprising, conclusions. It seems that, regardless of the type of change involved, women suffer more in the transformation process. The editors conclude that this is unlikely to be random; rather, it reflects the social and political condition of women. Addressing these issues is thus essential if the burden of economic transformation is to be distributed fairly.

Nahid Aslanbeigui is Associate Professor of Economics and Finance at Monmouth College, New Jersey. She is particularly interested in the areas of women in development, history of economic thought and economic education.

Steven Pressman is Associate Professor of Economics and Finance at Monmouth College, New Jersey. He specializes in macroeconomics, poverty and public finance.

Gale Summerfield is Associate Professor of Economics at the Monterey Institute of International Studies. She has written extensively on the impact of economic reforms on women in China.

WOMEN IN THE AGE OF ECONOMIC TRANSFORMATION

Gender impact of reforms in post-socialist and developing countries

Nahid Aslanbeigui, Steven Pressman and Gale Summerfield

London and New York

First published 1994
by Routledge
11 New Fetter Lane, London EC4P 4EE

Simultaneously published in the USA and Canada
by Routledge
29 West 35th Street, New York, NY 10001

Typeset in Garamond by
Ponting–Green Publishing Services, Chesham, Bucks
Printed and bound in Great Britain by
Biddles Ltd, Guildford and Kings Lynn

British Library Cataloguing in Publication Data
A catalogue record for this book is available from
the British Library

Library of Congress Cataloging in Publication Data
A catalogue record for this book has been requested

ISBN 0–415–10422–X
ISBN 0–415–10423–8 (pbk)

Cover illustration: Copyright © 1994 by Bidjan Assadipour

To the 100 million missing women

CONTENTS

CONTENTS

Asia

Latin America

FIGURE AND TABLES

FIGURE

TABLES

ix

FIGURE AND TABLES

FIGURE AND TABLES

CONTRIBUTORS

Eileen Appelbaum, formerly Professor of Economics at Temple University, recently joined the Economic Policy Institute in Washington, DC as Associate Research Director. From the summer of 1987 through 1991 she was a Guest Research Fellow in the Labor Markets and Employment section of the Wissenschaftszentrum, Berlin. She has acted as consultant to the Office of Technology Assessment of the US Congress on several volumes, including *Programmable Automation Technologies in Manufacturing* (1985) and *Trade in Services* (1988), and is co-editor of *Labor Market Adjustments to Structural Change and Technological Progress* (1990). She has published numerous articles on the labour-market experiences of women, including the effects of technology on women's jobs and the reasons for the expansion of part-time and contingent work arrangements in the USA. She is the author of, among other works, *Back to Work* (1981).

Nahid Aslanbeigui is Associate Professor of Economics and Finance at Monmouth College. Her main areas of research are women in development, the history of economic thought, and economic education. She has published articles on these topics in journals such as the *Southern Economic Journal, World Development, History of Political Economy, Review of Social Economy*, and *Journal of the History of Economic Thought*. She is currently writing a book on A.C. Pigou for Macmillan's Series on Famous Contemporary Economists. She was the co-winner of the 1985–6 Henry George prize awarded by St John's University and the Robert Shalkenbauch Foundation.

Walter M. Bacon, Jr., received his PhD in international relations from the University of Denver in 1975. A former President of the Society for Romanian Studies, he has published extensively on politics, foreign policy and civil–military relations in Romania. His most recent publications include the entry for Romania in the *Encyclopedia Americana* (1992) and a chapter on 'Security as seen from Bucharest' in Daniel N. Nelson (ed.), *Romania After Tyranny*.

Scott M. Fuess, Jr., is Associate Professor of Economics at the University of

Nebraska – Lincoln. His research is primarily in labour economics. He is the author, or co-author, of articles published in the *Journal of Political Economy*, *Economic Inquiry*, *Industrial & Labor Relations Review*, *Journal of Labor Research*, *International Journal of Industrial Organization* and *Economics Letters*. Results of his research have been reported in *The Economist*, *Fortune* and the *Los Angeles Times*. Since 1988 he has served as an Associate Editor of the *Quarterly Journal of Business and Economics*.

Gisela Geisler is Associate Professor of Anthropology at the University of Durban-Westville in South Africa. She lived and worked in Zambia through most of the 1980s. Her anthropological research focuses on gender dynamics in rural households, the relationship of gender dynamics to agricultural production and state policy, and the effects of structural adjustment policies on rural communities. She is the author of several reports and numerous journal articles on these issues.

Karen Tranberg Hansen is Associate Professor of Anthropology at Northwestern University. She has conducted extensive research in Zambia since the early 1970s on colonial culture, urban work, gender and household dynamics, and development issues. Her many publications on these issues have appeared in professional journals, and she is the author of *Distant Companions: Servants and Employers in Zambia, 1900–1985* (Cornell University Press, 1989) and editor of *African Encounters with Domesticity* (Rutgers University Press, 1992).

Richard P.F. Holt teaches economics at the Martha and Spencer Love School of Business at Elon College in North Carolina. He did his graduate work at the University of Utah and the University of California. His main research interests are in international labour cooperation and post-Keynesian economics. At present, he is working on a book evaluating the effects of post-Keynesian thought on economic science.

Bun Song Lee is Peter Kiewit Distinguished Professor of Economics at the University of Nebraska at Omaha. His research interests are rural–urban migration and fertility in developing countries. He has completed various research projects on how rural–urban migration affects migrant fertility in Korea, Mexico and Cameroon. Articles based on this research have been published in the *Journal of Development Economics*, *Population Studies*, *Demography*, *Social Biology* and other journals.

Bozena Leven graduated with honours from the Central School of Planning and Statistics in Warsaw, Poland in June 1980, receiving a Master's Degree in economics with a minor in political science. She received a PhD in economics from Cornell University in 1990. Dr Leven has served as a consultant to the Ford Foundation International Affairs Program and has published on the economic condition of women in Poland in *The Journal* *of Economic Issues.* She currently teaches economics at Trenton State University.

Patrice C. McMahon received her MA in international affairs from George Washington University, and is currently a doctoral student in the Political Science Department of Columbia University. She was a Fulbright Research Scholar in Poland in 1988–9.

Friederike Maier is Professor of Macroeconomics at the Fachhochschule für Wirtschaft, Berlin. Her research focuses on labour-market developments, labour-market policy and social policy, with special reference to the situation of women. She is the German expert in the EC-Network on 'Women's situation in the labor market'. Her recent publications have appeared in the *Cambridge Journal of Economics, Frauen in Deutschland 1945–1989*, edited by Helwig and Nickel (1993), and *Zeitschrift Für Sozialreform*.

Verónica Montecinos is Assistant Professor of Sociology at the Pennsylvania State University, McKeesport Campus. Her undergraduate degree in sociology is from the Catholic University of Chile. At the University of Pittsburgh she received an MA and a PhD in sociology and an MA in political science. In 1988, she was granted an Andrew Mellon Predoctoral Fellowship and spent a semester as a fellow at the Kellogg Institute for International Studies at the University of Notre Dame. Since then she has published on the politics of economic policy-making, and on the institutional dimensions of regional integration.

Louis G. Pol is Peter Kiewit Distinguished Professor of Marketing at the University of Nebraska at Omaha. Previous to his present position he taught at Memphis State University and the Roy Crummer Graduate School of Business at Rollins College. His book *Business Demography* was published in 1987, and along with Richard Thomas he published *The Demography of Health and Healthcare* (1992) and *The Health Care Book of Lists* (1993). Over the past several years he has been involved in a number of projects in Iasi, Romania. In 1993, he and a colleague received a grant to assist in the creation of a business development centre at the Academy for Economic Studies in Chisinau, Moldova.

Steven Pressman is Professor of Economics and Finance at Monmouth College, specializing in macroeconomics, poverty and public finance. He has published more than two dozen articles in professional journals on these topics, including several articles on women and poverty in the US. He is the author of *Quesnay's Tableau Économique: A Critique and Assessment* (1994). He has served on the Editorial Board of the *Review of Political Economy* since its creation in 1988, and as Associate Editor of the *Eastern Economic Journal* since 1989.

Jean Larson Pyle is Associate Professor of Economics at the University of Massachusetts at Lowell. She specializes in labour economics and economic development, with particular interest in issues of gender and inequality. She is the author of *The State and Women in the Economy: Lessons in Sex Discrimination from the Republic of Ireland* (1990). She has published articles in journals such as *The Columbia Journal of World Business* and the *Annual Review of Sociology*. She has also contributed papers to *Women Workers and Global Restructuring*, edited by K. Ward (1990) and *Women, Employment and the Family in the International Division of Labor*, edited by S. Stichter and J. Parpart (1989). Her current research includes a study of the effect of state policy on women in Singapore, and a study on the effect of changes in corporate strategy on women's employment in South-East Asia.

Hedwig Rudolph is Professor of Labour Economics at the Technical University of Berlin, and Director of the Department of Organization and Employment at the Social Science Center of Berlin. Over the past decade her research has focused on structural aspects of the education system and the labour market, and their interrelationships. Recently she has directed an action research programme on women and technology. Dr Rudolph is co-author of *Ungeschützte Arbeitsverhältnisse* (1987), *Ingenieurinnen-Frauen für die Zukunft* (1987), *Frauen gestalten Technik* (1988) and *Bridging States and Markets: International Migrations in the Early 1990s* (1993).

Gale Summerfield is Associate Professor of Economics at the Monterey Institute of International Studies. She has written extensively on the impact of economic reforms on women in China. Her recent articles appear in journals such as the *Journal of Economic Issues, Review of Social Economy, Development* and *World Development*.

Meredeth Turshen is an Associate Professor in the Department of Urban Studies and Community Health at Rutgers University. She worked for twelve years in the United Nations system with UNICEF and WHO. She is author of two books, *The Political Economy of Disease in Tanzania* (1984) and *The Politics of Public Health* (1989), and editor of *Women and Health in Africa* (1991) and *Women's Lives and Public Policy: The International Experience* (1992, with B. Holcomb). She has been on the editorial board of the *Review of African Political Economy* since its creation in 1974.

Nan Wiegersma is Professor of Economics at Fitchburg State College. She was desk officer for South-East Asia at the US Department of Agriculture's Economic Research Service from 1969 to 1972, and was part of a research project which resulted in the book *Agriculture in Vietnam's Economy*. Her book *Vietnam: Peasant Land, Peasant Revolution* was published in 1988. Her academic journal articles have appeared in the *Journal of Contemporary Asia*, and the *Review of Radical Political Economy*. Professor Wiegersma was the

United Nations representative on a World Food Programme Mission to Vietnam in 1987. She recently completed a Fulbright Scholarship, visiting the Central American Business Institute in Managua, Nicaragua.

1

WOMEN AND ECONOMIC TRANSFORMATION

Nahid Aslanbeigui, Steven Pressman and Gale Summerfield[1]

The world economy is going through tumultuous changes. Countries in Eastern and Central Europe have repudiated decades of central planning and control in favour of decision-making by individual agents and markets. Some, like Poland, have taken a shock therapy approach and rapidly introduced markets over a wide range of economic activities. Others, like Russia, have been slower to let the markets rule, and still allow planners to make wide-ranging production and distribution decisions. Regardless of the pace of change, the magnitude of these changes remains enormous.

In the less developed world, economic transformation has been associated with the attempt to generate higher rates of economic growth. The success of Hong Kong, Singapore, South Korea and Taiwan has been attributed to export-oriented industrialization. Trade has also been important for China, which in 1993 was the fastest growing economy in the world. With such role models, countries in Africa and Latin America have abandoned import-substitution strategies and have attempted to better integrate their economies into the global market-place. They have also been compelled by the International Monetary Fund and the World Bank to promote exports, in order to generate the hard currency necessary for meeting their foreign debt obligations. The restructuring that has followed usually focuses on reducing external and internal deficits, liberalizing trade and privatizing state-run industries.

Most of the existing literature has focused on how the average person gains from the current wave of economic reforms. Substantial economic transformation, however, never affects everyone in the same way. When there is great change the distribution of economic rewards will also change, thus leading to both winners and losers. The papers in this volume focus on the gender distribution of these gains and losses in different post-socialist and developing countries.[2] They ask the question: do women, who constitute almost half of the world's population, bear a disproportionate share of the costs resulting from the widespread economic transformation?

The authors find that, regardless of the country examined and regardless of

1

whether per capita income has increased, stagnated or decreased, women have been over-represented among the losers or under-represented among the winners. Women's relative losses have been manifested in different ways, but in every country examined in this volume, economic transformation has led to fewer gains or greater losses for women. The outcome of economic transformation, therefore, does not appear to be random.

The major change in the formerly socialist countries is the shift from state planning to market-based decision-making. Government-sanctioned monopolies are now under pressure to increase efficiency and workers are no longer guaranteed employment. Consequently, inefficient firms have had to close, and unneeded or unproductive workers have been laid off. The transformation process has therefore resulted in high unemployment and large losses of income throughout Central and Eastern Europe.

In Chapter 2, Hedwig Rudolph, Eileen Applebaum and Friederike Maier show that in the German reunification process women have experienced a greater increase in unemployment than men. Similarly, women have fared worse in gaining access to public-work jobs. The authors note that many of the new job openings are located in the former West Germany, involving long and difficult journeys to and from work. This puts many women at a disadvantage because they have substantially greater child-rearing responsibilities than men. In addition, many social programmes that provided benefits to East German female workers (e.g. paid maternity leaves and available, affordable childcare) do not exist in the reunified Germany. This hinders women's ability to find employment.

Bozena Leven (Chapter 3) examines the status of women as Poland struggles toward a market economy. The introduction of markets has created a significant benefit, i.e. goods and services have become more available. Consumers, therefore, do not have to spend endless hours in queues to purchase goods. Since women are primarily responsible for this task, the collapse of central planning means increased leisure time for women. However, surveys conducted by Leven in Poland reveal another important change that has taken place within the family. Husbands have reduced the amount of housework and childcare they perform, and consequently enjoy increased leisure time. As a result, women spend more time on other household chores when they spend less time shopping.

In Chapter 4, Walter Bacon Jr. and Louis Pol view history and culture as stumbling blocks to improving the well-being of women under capitalism. Communist governments afforded women equal rights to work and education. Sex segregation in employment, however, relegated women to low-paying jobs and industries. Moreover, the pro-natalist policies of the Ceauşescu government increased women's household burdens. Although the communist government espoused equality for women, it did little to change the cultural and historical beliefs regarding the role of women. When the government was overthrown, so was the ethos that men and women be treated equally. To further disadvantage Romanian women, traditional values that view women as subservient to their husbands and their fathers were strengthened.

In Chapter 5, Patrice McMahon identifies similar tensions in Russia. The Russian Communist Party was reluctant to put women into positions of political authority. Occupational sex segregation and discrimination hindered women's ability to attain positions of greater power and responsibility. McMahon conjectures that the collapse of communism will hurt women in several ways. Rebellion against the ideology of equality will likely reinforce cultural and historical views regarding the role of women. The consequence, already in evidence, is that women will bear a greater burden of the resulting unemployment and lower wages. In addition, the economic crisis will increase women's domestic burdens because family responsibilities fall more heavily on Russian women. Lacking political power, women are in no position to counter the rising economic and familial obligations placed upon them.

Restructuring in developing countries is in many ways similar to the transition taking place in Eastern and Central Europe. Under pressure from the International Monetary Fund and the World Bank, less developed countries have pursued trade liberalization, privatization, and fiscal and monetary restraint. In the short run, this has led to higher prices, higher unemployment and more poverty. Women have been disproportionately affected by these negative trends; the demands on their time have increased as they try to compensate for the loss of social services and family income.

In many African countries, the gender ramifications of structural transformation are especially daunting. In Chapter 6, Meredeth Turshen discusses the impact on women's health and health care in Sub-Saharan Africa. Structural adjustments have adversely affected women's health in two ways. Reforms have removed food subsidies and increased food prices, leading to a deterioration in food intake for women, who eat less and last. This, in turn, has increased their susceptibility to diseases. Moreover, cutbacks in public health expenditures have resulted in the privatization of state-provided services as well as in the rising role of non-governmental organizations. These trends have reduced the quantity and quality of health services more for women than for men. Yet, women have greater health needs.

Gisela Geisler and Karen Tranberg Hansen (Chapter 7) examine the impact of structural adjustment programmes on women in Zambia. In this male-dominated culture men have no obligation to contribute to the income of the household, but have control over the income of their wives. As a result, economic reforms have different implications for the well-being of women and men. In times of economic crisis, men intensify their demands on women's cash income. Cutbacks in social services, rising prices and increased male unemployment have forced women to work harder and longer, increasing their reproductive tasks and their participation in the workforce. In

3

rural areas women are unable to grow food for household consumption because they are forced to accept agricultural piecework. As a result, they and their children may eat only one meal a day. In urban areas, women have intensified their informal-sector activities, spending less time on household maintenance and childcare.

The chapters on Asia focus on the gender impact of economic transformation in the context of rapid economic growth. Gale Summerfield (Chapter 8) examines the post-Mao reforms. Trade liberalization through the promotion of export processing, the de-collectivization of agriculture and urban reforms benefit both women and men because they increase household income. Women, however, have borne a larger share of the costs associated with these policies. They have been the main targets of layoffs during retrenchment and are more likely to be identified as surplus labour. Summerfield also observes that the reforms have had two contradictory consequences for the position of women within the household. On the one hand, increased employment opportunities have strengthened the bargaining power of women; on the other hand, gender discrimination in hiring and firing has reduced the status of women in the family. Whether women actually gain will depend on economic growth, government policies and the effectiveness of women's organizations.

In Chapter 9, Jean Pyle focuses on the importance of women in Singapore's economic development. The export-oriented policies pursued since 1965 have increased female workforce participation rates and generated rapid economic growth. Despite the overall gain in employment, Pyle argues, women were denied access to higher level jobs and received lower wages than men. They also remained more susceptible to layoffs in times of economic recession. Pyle also observes that the government of Singapore enacted contradictory policies by seeking to increase female workforce participation while simultaneously encouraging women to have more children in order to increase the future labour supply. The women of Singapore, therefore, faced increased demands on their time from two different sources.

The economic success of South Korea has been well-documented, but its impact on women is controversial. Industrialization has created new opportunities for women, but it may have also reinforced traditional patterns of sex discrimination. In Chapter 10, Scott Fuess Jr. and Bun Song Lee examine the gender impact of government policies to promote growth with lower inflation in the 1980–92 period. The authors focus on the sectoral division of labour in agriculture, manufacturing and services. Fuess and Lee find that not only has the share of women's employment decreased in paid manufacturing, but also that the employment of women has acted as a buffer in the manufacturing sector. In times of economic downturn, women are more likely to be laid off than men. In addition, Fuess and Lee argue that despite their gains in paid service jobs, women are still under-represented in regular, high-status jobs.

The 1980s was a lost decade for most Latin American countries as they tried to cope with debt crises and political instability. Verónica Montecinos (Chapter 11) examines the gender impact of neo-liberal policies in Chile under the authoritarian regime of Pinochet (1973–90). She shows that poverty became more feminized because of higher female unemployment rates and lower female wages. In their attempt to compensate for the losses, women increased their workforce participation at a time when job opportunities were shrinking. As a result, they were forced to take jobs in the unstable informal sector, which fails to offer social insurance benefits. In addition, Chilean women suffered disproportionately from government cutbacks in such social services as preventive health care.

In Chapter 12, Richard Holt examines the impact of restructuring policies that the International Monetary Fund recommended to Mexico after the 1982 crisis. Following these recommendations, the government reduced its expenditures and provided incentives for foreign direct investment. It was thought that these policies would increase export production, economic growth and employment. The overall economic impact, however, has been mixed – employment of young women and men has increased in the export-processing zones, but job opportunities have not expanded elsewhere in the Mexican economy. Women's increased workforce participation, to support family income, has resulted in mostly low-paying informal jobs in rural and urban areas.

Nan Wiegersma (Chapter 13) examines trade liberalization and privatization policies in Nicaragua during the 1990s. She finds that these reforms have had their greatest impact in the garment and textile industries that have predominantly employed women. As domestic and state-owned firms in these industries were closed or privatized, the number of jobs lost exceeded those created by transnational corporations in the export-processing zones. Women over the age of 35 had the greatest difficulty of all in finding jobs. These women cannot commute to the zones due to their childcare responsibilities; and relocating is too expensive to be a feasible option.

Although the precise form and context of reforms differ in each country, several similar themes about the impact of reforms can be discerned. First, while female workforce participation trends in post-socialist and developing countries vary, these trends have the same effect on the relative well-being of women. Discrimination in hiring, limited opportunities outside low-paying sectors, and over-representation among the unemployed are common repercussions of restructuring for women.

Second, women have traditionally had little money and few assets, and are less likely than men to have accumulated capital or to have the collateral necessary for obtaining a loan. Lack of sufficient credit prevents women from taking advantage of the new opportunities created by the reforms.

Third, their meagre financial resources can be linked to the inferior position of women (and girls) within the household. Many papers in this volume recognize that the household cannot be taken as a single unit with a joint utility function. The allocation of total income within the household depends on the bargaining power of women, which tends to decrease as economic crises deepen. Thus women may be forced to work longer and harder in the workforce, but not gain any additional goods and services to make their lives easier.

Fourth, bargaining power within the household stems, in part, from cultural norms. All the countries examined in this volume have traditions of male dominance and discrimination against women. These traditions have reasserted themselves with greater force in the age of economic transformation. The most extreme example of the growing bias that accompanies structural reforms occurs in countries such as China, where female infants are murdered or abandoned, and where slave trade for wives is escalating. Less dramatic forms of bias reduce women's access to food, to education and to health care. This lowers the well-being of women both absolutely and relatively.

Finally, given biased cultural contexts, it is not surprising that women do not have a strong political voice. Women lack political representation and power in virtually every country examined in this volume. Consequently, government policies have not been enacted, or enforced, to help mitigate the greater costs that women bear in the transformation process. On the contrary, when budgets must be cut, the first programmes to go are those that tend to benefit women.

Governments have failed to prevent women from being marginalized on the assumption that reforms are gender neutral. The papers in this volume, however, have shown that economic transformation has a strong and, all too frequently, a negative impact on women. Government policy to redress the gender-bias of the reform process is thus essential for improving women's well-being. In addition, several papers in this volume point out that organizations which forcefully voice the needs of women are needed to counter cultural and familial biases against women. Such a voice would also help mitigate the losses imposed on women by the transformation process.

Significant economic changes will probably continue through the rest of this century and well into the next one. Only if women organize to voice their needs through labour unions, political office and women's organizations will they be able to become equal players in the transformed world economy of the future.

NOTES

1 The editors gratefully acknowledge the assistance of Diana Prout in typing various chapters of this book.
2 Individual papers focus on specific post-socialist (East and Central Europe) and less developed countries (Africa, Asia and Latin America). We do realize that the

distinction between developing countries and post-socialist countries is not a sharp one (China, Chile and Nicaragua are essentially both, but are usually treated as developing countries). Eastern and Central Europe have been treated as separate and more developed, but per capita income in some of the developing countries now exceeds per capita income in Eastern Europe. More general indicators of the level of economic development also give mixed results. Because they share a substantially different context, we consider the countries in Eastern and Central Europe separately.

Part I

EASTERN EUROPE

2

BEYOND SOCIALISM

The uncertain prospects for East German women in a unified Germany

Hedwig Rudolph, Eileen Appelbaum and Friederike Maier

INTRODUCTION

The political, economic and social unification of the two Germanies was initially greeted with much optimism and great expectations. However, fears about the economic future also loom large in the former German Democratic Republic (East Germany). Women comprised half the East German workforce, but their prospects are among the most uncertain outcomes of the unification process. Similarly, the future of women's life and work, and gender relations in a unified Germany, are among the most worrisome aspects of unification. None the less, the condition of women has not been a major issue in discussions concerning this process. This is all the more surprising because East Germany had a long tradition of affirmative action policies, and because the transformation process contains the risk of a serious backlash.

This chapter begins with an overview and assessment of what has been gained by East German women, taking as a reference point the situation of women in the Federal Republic of Germany (West Germany) before unification. It then discusses likely economic developments in the former East Germany over the short and medium term, and indicates why these developments may adversely impact the economic and social position of women. The chapter concludes with some reflections on why the effects of unification on German women has been a political non-issue.

WOMEN UNDER COMMUNISM

Employment

In 1949, when East Germany was founded, the female workforce participation rate was around 40 per cent. Since then female workforce participation rates have doubled, and since 1975 half of all East German workers have been female. These two figures are extremely high compared to other countries. More important, women's labour market progress has been much slower in West Germany. Female workforce participation in the former West Germany during the early 1990s barely exceeded 50 per cent, and women comprised only about 40 per cent of all gainfully employed persons.

East German women also had access to a broader array of job opportunities. They were represented in non-traditional sectors and in all levels of the occupational hierarchy to a much higher degree than women in West Germany or women in other developed countries. Their gains here have been steady over several decades.

The improving occupational status of women in East Germany is apparent from Table 2.1, which shows the distribution of women's qualifications for the years 1971 and 1985. Over this time period, semi-skilled or unskilled workers declined from 50.8 to 18.5 per cent of female employment. Conversely, women with post-secondary or college degrees increased their share of female employment from 8.1 to 22.6 per cent. Of particular interest is the prevalence of women with post-secondary schooling in the so-called non-productive sectors (services other than wholesale and retail trade and communications), where their employment share increased from 23.5 to 50.2 per cent over this period.

Table 2.2 shows that in East Germany women had greater access to areas of employment that are male-dominated in the West. Industry and craft production employed 33 per cent of East German women. In West Germany, the manufacturing and craft production sector employs 23 per cent of women, and women are concentrated in service sectors, especially social services.

One of the explicit political aims in East Germany was to support the professional advancement of women. At the end of the 1960s, East Germany started a 'training offensive' oriented towards women. Programmes were developed to train women in technical and executive administrative skills; and women only classes in technical colleges and special courses at universities and polytechnics were introduced. East German firms were also obliged to integrate females into training programmes for skilled blue collar workers.

Despite greater job and training opportunities for women in East Germany, rather traditional occupational structures tended to prevail. This is reflected in statistics on apprenticeship contracts and areas of specialization for college and university students. Public planning schemes had been used to open new fields for women until the mid-1970s. Since then, apprenticeship positions for female secondary school leavers were earmarked mainly in sectors with traditionally high participation rates of women (Nickel 1990: 12). As a consequence, women were extremely over-represented in textile and clothing, leather, chemical crafts (e.g. laboratory technicians), sales, and other services by the late 1980s. Of the ten occupations with the highest numbers of female trainees, comprising more than half of the women apprentices, six were in almost exclusively female areas, where the percentage of women apprentices

Table 2.1 Percentage of employed women in East Germany by selected economic sectors and qualifications, 1971 and 1985

Qualification level	Total economy		Industry		Transport and communications		Wholesale and retail trade		Other production and non-productive sectors (services)	
	1971	1985	1971	1985	1971	1985	1971	1985	1971	1985
College/university degree	2.4	5.8	0.4	2.8	0.3	1.8	0.3	1.5	7.8	12.9
Post-secondary degree	5.7	16.8	2.1	7.2	1.6	5.5	1.3	4.9	15.7	37.3
Supervisory grade	–	1.0	0.6	1.4	0.1	1.1	–	0.7	0.2	0.3
Skilled worker	41.1	57.9	38.7	65.7	37.9	70.5	58.8	78.6	27.3	32.0
Semi- or unskilled	50.8	18.5	58.1	22.9	60.1	21.2	39.6	14.4	49.0	17.6
All women	100.0	100.0	100.0	100.0	100.0	100.0	100.0	100.0	100.0	100.0

Source: Nickel (1988).

Table 2.2 Employment structures in the two Germanies,* 1989

	Employed men and women ('000s)		Women within the sector/industry (%)		Occupational distribution of employed women (%)	
	FRG†	GDR†	FRG	GDR	FRG	GDR
Mining/manufacturing	9,456	3,438	36	42	23	35
Crafts	–	267	–	37	–	2
Construction	1,881	560	10	17	2	2
Agriculture, forestry, fishing	1,039	924	44	37	4	8
Transport/post/telecommunications‡	1,573	639	25	35	4	6
Wholesale and retail trade	3,397	877	56	72	18	15
Banking/insurance	1,004	302	47	58	4	4
Education and health care	6,044	1,338	60	77	34	25
Public administration§	2,826	204	32	65	8	3
Non-profit organizations**	523	–	60	–	3	–
Total	27,742	8,549	39	49	100	100

Sources: FRG: Statistisches Bundesamt (1990).
GDR: Statistisches DDR (1990).

* The two countries used different definitions for industries/sectors. These are our own calculations based on the official statistics.
† Without apprentices.
‡ Including private and public sector activities.
§ Including public housing management and municipalities in the GDR.
** Excluding police/defence and other political activities in the FRG and GDR.

was over 95 per cent. On the other hand, women have increased their share in technical training – about one-third of non-college bound women completing secondary school have been channelled into skilled technical jobs each year, especially in electronics (Radtke 1990: 70).

In sum, while East Germany succeeded in raising female workforce participation, the goal of integrating women into all occupations and on all hierarchical levels was only partly achieved. Labour market and employment structures tended to remain sex-segregated, and a growing proportion of women (especially those with small children) were employed in jobs not appropriate to their qualifications. The use made of qualifications in the production process showed gender-specific differences. As a result of promotion policies, about 30 per cent of all managers were female, although most of these women were concentrated at the lower levels (Nickel 1990: 11).

Training and education

Large human capital investments in East Germany meant that the female workforce was highly qualified. Fully 87 per cent of employed women have some kind of skilled vocational certification, or a college degree. Two out of five employees with a college or university degree are female. In contrast, 65 per cent of working women in the former West Germany have completed either skilled vocational training or higher education, and only 7 per cent have college or university degrees.

Women comprised around half of the college and university student population in East Germany (Table 2.3). Their representation exceeded

Table 2.3 Female students admitted to universities and colleges, by degree in East Germany

| | Percentage female | |
Subject	1971	1985
Overall	40.4	50.8
Mathematics, natural sciences	46.3	50.4
Technical sciences	18.6	27.9
Medicine	76.5	55.3
Agricultural sciences	39.8	47.4
Economics	44.9	68.3
Philosophy, history, constitution, law	35.7	34.0
Cultural and art studies, physical education	36.9	37.0
Literature, languages	69.5	55.8
Theology	51.2	46.3
Art	41.4	43.5
Education and teacher training	64.2	73.0

Source: Nickel (1988).

two-thirds in the fields of economics and education. More surprising is the fact that women comprise more than 50 per cent of the students admitted into the study of medicine, mathematics and natural sciences – three traditionally male subject areas.

Women's share of admissions in the technical sciences (27.9 per cent) seems relatively low. However, technical sciences was the largest area of university studies in East Germany. As a result, it was the second largest field of study for female students – one out of five was admitted to engineering (only surpassed by education and teacher training, which attracted one out of three female students). The high and increasing access of women to technical fields in East Germany becomes even clearer when compared to West Germany, where the percentage of women among engineering students rarely surpassed 10 per cent. While the 'classical' hard-core engineering disciplines of mechanics and electrotechnology report the lowest shares of female participants in both parts of Germany, the rates were different in each half of Germany. The modern fields within engineering and the technical sciences offer more opportunities for women except for informatics (computer science), where women's shares of admissions are shrinking in both countries (Gruppe Frauenforschung 1990: 3ff.).

Social policies

The increase in women's paid work in East Germany cannot be attributed merely to a narrow range of labour market policies. It was due, rather, to a multi-faceted set of interlinking measures comprising political, legal, institutional and financial aspects.

The East German constitution declared that men and women not only had the right to work, but also the obligation to work. The ideological pressure on women to look for employment was considerable. This was reinforced by economic pressures. Low wages paid to men acted as a strong incentive for married women and for single women living at home to be gainfully employed. In addition, the logic of the planned economy, relying on an extensive use of resources, produced a persistent scarcity of labour. This motivated the political authorities to integrate women into the economy by mobilizing and developing the human capital of the female population.

National labour laws were specifically crafted to support these aims in two ways. First, every firm was required to have clearly defined programmes for the recruitment, training and promotion of women. Second, women, and above all mothers, had specific worker benefits. They received long maternity leaves with pay, and those with more than one child received reduced working hours without financial penalty. Obviously, the goal of supporting female labour-market participation through actively recruiting and training women conflicted with the goal of providing generous maternity and child benefits. In one case firms have greater incentives to hire women and women have greater incentives to participate in the labour market; in the other case the incentives are reversed. Political emphasis on the second goal starting in the mid-1970s helped to marginalize the first one. None the less, East German labour laws continued to spur female workforce participation.

East Germany also implemented numerous institutional provisions that gave women the opportunity to obtain formal vocational or professional qualifications. Female employees could receive paid leave (at least part-time) to attend classes. There was an enormous increase in the capacities of nursery schools and kindergartens in order to reduce the conflicts that arise from combining paid work with family responsibilities. In the 1980s facilities were available for more than 80 per cent of the children below school-age, even for those under the age of three (EAF 1990: 3). In West Germany, the situation was very different. In 1987, schooling was available for only 4 per cent of children under 3, 30 per cent of children between 3 and 4 years old, and 70 per cent of children between the ages of 4 and 5. Moreover, these averages hide large regional differences in the former West Germany (Deutscher Bundestag 1989: 62). Lack of childcare is still the main reason West German women leave the workforce for substantial periods of time.

In addition to differences in the availability of childcare facilities, there were also important differences in the quality and the cost of childcare services in the two Germanies. The nursery schools and kindergartens in East Germany were run by public authorities or by public enterprises, and they remained open from 6 a.m. to 6 p.m. Parents paid only for meals and nappies. In contrast, West German kindergartens, run by public authorities, churches or private groups (but rarely by private enterprises), could be quite expensive (although sometimes fees were means-tested). A considerable number were open only for half the day. In East Germany hot meals served in the cafeterias of enterprises and in kindergartens and schools alleviated the burden of private household work, as did publicly run laundry centres and service-houses attached to the firms (Friedrich-Ebert-Stiftung 1987: 52f.).

Finally, several other East German social policies provided financial support to women. The payment of 'Kindergeld' (child allowances) was quite important given the low average income. However, direct financial transfers had less weight in the spectrum of social welfare measures when compared to price subsidies for rent, food and social services (Stolz-Willig 1990: 285). In addition, repayment of specific credits for young couples was reduced with the birth of a child, and children claimed extra government payments. Another important advantage for women was the regulation requiring that family leave should be treated as equivalent to time spent working when calculating the eligibility and retirement income in pension schemes.

17

Household responsibilities

While education, employment and social policies all worked to improve the status of women in East Germany, family relationships worked to hold back women's ability to advance economically. East German sources confirm that, despite their involvement in paid employment, women continued to do at least three-quarters of the housework. This was especially burdensome due to the scarcity of food and consumption articles, and in particular the time required to purchase these goods. These housekeeping burdens can partially explain why 25 per cent of women worked only part-time, despite the strong political pressure against part-time employment (Enders 1986: 36).

Household responsibilities also explain the low relative female participation in worker training and retraining programmes, and why female representation in every occupation decreased drastically as the level of responsibility within an occupation increased (Friedrich-Ebert-Stiftung 1987: 17, 25). Female responsibilities for children and household chores also account for the traditional choices that East German women have made regarding vocational training. The convenient working hours of 'typically female' jobs made them attractive for mothers, inducing a number of technically trained women, to change to 'female jobs' despite their much lower wages (Zentralinstitut 1989: 23).

An additional restriction on the development of women's careers was the distance from home to the workplace. Women with more than one child were especially likely to opt for jobs not too far away from home, even if this meant employment below their qualification level (Enders 1986: 36).

None the less, staying in their field of specialization was no guarantee that women would advance to positions of greater authority and responsibility. Decision-makers have rationalized the exclusion of some women from high-status jobs by assuming that their family obligations would not allow them to be as reliable or devoted as their male peers (Burkhardt and Zierke 1990: 43). The persistent mismatch between the structure of women's skills and qualifications on the one hand, and their position in the job hierarchy on the other, was most obvious in the university system. Women accounted for more than half of the student population, 35 per cent of assistant professors and lecturers, but only 9 per cent of tenured professors (Gruppe Frauenforschung 1990: 7). These differences indicate a substantial gender gap, even though they are based on cross-sectional data.

Wage differentials

Although sex discrimination was legally banned and officially denied in East Germany, there is abundant evidence of a gender income gap. Women working full-time in 1988 had a net monthly income that was 76 per cent of male full-time pay (Ott et al. 1990: 7). Income differences between men and women were due to wage differences within the different economic branches and to the different ranks reached by men and women in the occupational hierarchy. Female–male wage differentials within a given industry were not due to different payments for equal work. They were mainly due to the greater presence of women in low wage groups and in low paying branches.

Wage rates in East Germany were set following the national central plan. Wage differentials among branches were the result of political decisions, and wages were high or increased rapidly in areas deemed 'important'. Pay in light industry, with a high proportion of female workers, was on the bottom of the scale. Social attitudes regarded women as relatively unproductive – with high rates of absenteeism, relatively high labour turnover, and with a lack of commitment to careers (Merkel 1990: 61).

Even looking at men and women with equivalent formal qualifications, the net income of female workers was on average 12 per cent less than that of their male colleagues. This was due to more favourable arrangements with foremen (Winkler 1990b: 122ff) and due to the fact that men had easier access to firm-specific extra qualifications (Radtke 1990: 75). Women's integration into the labour market of East Germany did not change the sexual division of labour at work or in society. Paid labour remained oriented towards the male full-time worker, who stood with his entire labour power at the firm's disposal.

The social ethos that assigned high values to motherhood and family and the social esteem for 'women's work' made these gender inequalities less visible and helped make the 'double burden' placed on women more accept-able. None the less, women in the former East Germany had to develop strategies that would enable them to combine full-time work, child-rearing, queuing up for food and consumption goods, and other family responsibilities. One frequently used strategy was for women to put their family first and pay the price in terms of unequal career possibilities. 'Whereas motherhood and family obligations did not prevent employment, they prevented employment according to qualifications, in more demanding jobs and professional advance-ment' (Winkler 1990a: 80).

Two indicators point out the ways that women were coping with this frustrating situation – the divorce rate of 36.2 per cent was extremely high, and about one-third of all babies had an unmarried mother (Ochs 1990: 300ff.). Men as colleagues were also confronted with the consequences of national social policies – whenever women received time off for training or family reasons, the rest of the team had to bridge the gap since no other provision for this contingency was made. Quite a number of women with families are reported to have moved out of male-dominated employment sectors so as to minimize confrontations with men who had to work longer and harder because they had a female colleague (Enders 1986: 34).

To sum up, there is considerable evidence that public policies intending to facilitate equality in employment also increased the burdens on women. They

19

contributed to the restoration, and even legitimation of traditional gender relations. By ignoring the dual burdens placed on women, they made the life of East German women more difficult, and contributed to women making more traditional career choices (Merkel 1990: 64).

WOMEN UNDER CAPITALISM

In the late 1980s, East Germany was plagued by a number of economic and political problems. Central planning hindered the flexibility of the economy and acted as a barrier to modernization. Social issues, such as environmental problems and a rotten infrastructure, became more prominent. Improved communication and greater ability to travel made East Germans aware of growing differences in living standards between the East and West. Finally, as the people of East Germany were demanding greater social respect and freedom, their government remained rigid and authoritarian. These forces all contributed to the dismantling of the Berlin Wall.

The political and economic transformation began a few weeks after the frontier to West Germany was opened on 9 November 1989 (Rothschild 1993: 260ff). Private enterprises and joint ventures were readmitted in January 1990. In March, state enterprises were formally turned into joint-stock companies, private banking was admitted, and the Treuhandanstalt was established and given the task of privatizing the combinates. The Conservative Party was the clear victor in the first free parliamentary elections in the former East Germany on 18 March 1990. In May, a state treaty between the two German governments was signed, taking effect on 1 July 1990, and combining the two countries into a single economic and social unit.

The social and economic status of women in the former East Germany will be shaped by two factors – the legal and institutional aspects of the West German 'model', and the economic growth and development of the former East Germany. On the latter question there is much uncertainty. Since the end of 1989, and especially since the monetary union of mid-1990, the economic situation in East Germany has changed dramatically for the worse. Within a few months, hundreds of thousands of people lost their jobs. By the end of 1991 only 6.5 million people were employed in the former East Germany, down from 9.8 million in September 1989. Included in this figure are 1 million people on 'short-time', who work only a few hours a week. Since most of these 'short-time' jobs should also be counted as lost, employment in the former East Germany has actually declined by around 4 million. Thus, 35–40 per cent of the workforce has already been affected by job losses (Infratest 1991; DIW 1991).

The number of men and the number of women officially counted as employed has each declined by about the same amount since September 1989. However, men and women have been affected differently by the loss of their jobs. Men have greater prospects for re-employment based on their previous work experiences. Men also face fewer obstacles in finding new jobs. They are unlikely to have significant housekeeping or child-raising responsibilities, and have greater opportunities than women to commute long distances to find work. Finally, men have benefited more than women from the public works jobs designed to help with the unemployment problem.

The economic breakdown of manufacturing industries in the former East Germany is the major source of job losses. In August 1990 industrial production was 51 per cent below the previous year; it fell another 40 per cent between August 1990 and August 1991 (DIW 1991). The process of restructuring industry encompasses nearly all sectors and occupational levels, and includes both women and men. Men had typically been employed as industrial labourers, technicians and engineers, while women constituted the majority among administrative and clerical workers and in the social departments of enterprises. Women ran childcare centres, shops, recreational facilities and repair teams. These overstaffed administrative departments have faced sharp cutbacks and layoffs. The social departments of many enterprises were closed down as state-owned firms were forced to become exclusively economic organizations. Moreover, women employed in 'male jobs' in industry (such as supervisors) had a higher risk of job-loss than their male counterparts.

Women were also over-represented in those branches that had to reduce production and employment most sharply – textiles, electronics, food processing, precision mechanics and optics. Conversely, the share of women is quite low in mechanical engineering, printing and construction. These are industries with growth potential due to the need for urban renewal and for the establishment of new industrial sites as well as public investments in the infrastructure (DIW 1990: 244).

The service sector has also undergone dramatic structural changes. Although the East German service sector was small by West German standards, it will take some time before it becomes a 'job machine'. In the course of restructuring, many segments of the service sector dismissed employees. Within two years (from the end of 1989 to the end of 1991), retail and wholesale trade laid off 50 per cent of their employees. Service industries like hotels, restaurants and catering also reduced the number of employees substantially (DIW 1991). The overwhelming majority of service sector employees had been female. The same is true for public administration and publicly run social services, where a large number of jobs had been cut. The cutbacks occurred in administrative units, hospitals, schools, universities and research institutions. Except for the latter two sectors, these all employ large numbers of women. The prospects for new jobs opening up in these areas is, unfortunately, not good.

Not all changes have been negative, however. Restructuring of the East German economy has had some positive effects on the labour market as well. New enterprises are opening and existing enterprises are being replaced by more efficient firms. But, the mismatch between jobs lost and jobs offered is substantial. This is especially true for women. Among those who have found work after a period of unemployment, only 40 per cent were women (Infas 1991: 15). One reason women have fared poorly is that job losses were concentrated in previously feminized occupations like education, social services, public administration and clerical work, while new jobs are more likely to be traditionally male jobs in manufacturing firms.

The construction industry reduced its overall employment, yet offered new jobs for (male) construction workers (skilled and unskilled). The same is true for some branches of the chemical industry and mechanical engineering (DIW 1991). Banking, insurance and real estate, consulting and other commercial services were highly feminized (about 80 per cent) under communist rule. But the new positions opening up in these industries have requirements that are substantially different from the past. Most administrative occupations, such as bookkeepers, accountants, bank cashiers and insurance administrators, required few specific skills beyond bookkeeping and did not have a high status. This makes it more difficult for women to find employment in the growing financial services sector. Consequently, it is not surprising that in November 1990, 70 per cent of all women expected that it would be difficult or impossible to get a new job (Infas 1991: 25ff).

It is clear that the labour market in the former East Germany offers only a small number of new jobs. Yet, there are alternatives for surplus labour. Migration and commuting to West Germany are two obvious options. We do not have gender-specific data on migration; we only know that more than 2 million people have left East Germany since the autumn of 1989. The number of commuters has increased steadily since 1989, amounting to nearly 6 per cent of all employed East Germans citizens in autumn 1991. Distances travelled between work and home are often considerable. Twenty-six per cent travel more than one hour each way, and more than 20 per cent do not return to their homes daily. Not surprisingly, the commuters are more likely to be young (54 per cent under 30 years), skilled industrial workers (55 per cent) and male (80 per cent). Two-thirds are employed in West Germany, one-third in West Berlin, and nearly 50 per cent are employed in only three branches – retail trade, construction and metal/electro industries (Infratest 1991: 35ff). The high percentage of male commuters is not a definitive indicator that women lack regional mobility, but it does reflect their limited ability to commute long distances due to family obligations.

The Labour Market Promotion Act of West Germany was designed to smooth the economic restructuring process through programmes such as public works, retraining and early retirement regulations. Access to these programmes, however, contains gender-specific filters. The public works programme (ABM), offering quasi-employment contracts for one or two years, had nearly 380,000 participants by the end of 1991.[1] However, the vast majority of these public works programmes have created 'male jobs' like road construction, railways, transportation and communications equipment installation. Moreover, recruitment is biased in favour of men, even in areas where women had previously been employed in large percentages. As a result, only 36 per cent of the employees in public works programmes were female. The under-representation of women in ABM and the resulting political activity led to changes in the structure and rules of the programmes during the summer of 1991. Material incentives were also offered to firms that employ women (Maier 1991a). Statistics available at the end of 1993 indicate that there has been little improvement thus far.

Training programmes that aim to improve workers' skills and qualifications also reduce the number of registered unemployed. In November 1991, 410,000 people were enrolled in retraining programmes in the former East Germany (IAB 1991). Women comprised 56 per cent of participants in these programmes, although there are considerable regional differences. However, the training and retraining offered to women are quite often in traditional female fields. The majority of women are retrained for administrative and clerical tasks with emphasis on computer-related skills and 'modern' office organization. This seems to fit both the former skills and occupations of women who have become unemployed, and the prospective demand of the developing service sector. In addition, not all training programmes are of high standard and adequate duration, so some participants do not get recognized certificates concerning the skills they have acquired. Finally, because the service sector has been shedding jobs rapidly, there is little chance for retrained women to find employment quickly. Access to training has thus become a necessary, but not a sufficient, condition for East German women to keep their jobs or to enter newly created jobs in the service sector.

In sum, the number of job vacancies in the former East Germany remains extremely low. New jobs have been created mainly in West Germany or Berlin; only a minority of positions are offered by East German firms and, temporarily, in public works programmes. Men's chances for re-employment both in new firms and in public works programmes are far better than women's. This fact is reflected in the statistical data on unemployment, which shows that female unemployment rates are rising above male unemployment rates.

Figure 2.1 shows a steady increase in registered unemployment since the summer of 1990. By the end of 1991, more than 1.1 million unemployed had been registered, implying an unemployment rate of approximately 12 per cent. Women comprised 62 per cent of the registered unemployed. One-tenth of these women had been without a job for more than a year (Infratest 1991: 27).

The age structure of those unemployed in the former East Germany reveals several interesting features. Young women, defined as those under 35 years of age, are more often unemployed than their male peers. In spring 1991, 60 per cent of all unemployed females and 50 per cent of all unemployed males had been in this age-group (Holst and Schupp 1991).

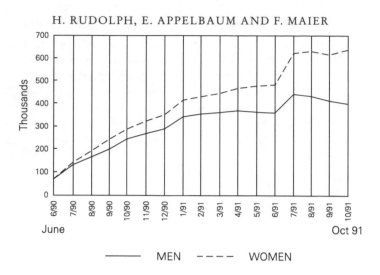

Figure 2.1 Unemployed men and women in the former GDR since June 1990 (Holst and Schupp 1991: 6)

Few young East German women (only 3 per cent) said that they would stay at home as housewives if their husbands could earn enough to support the family. They would prefer, instead, periods of parental leave or temporarily reduced working times when the children are young. The problem for these women is quite obvious. West German regulations allow young mothers to stay at home for a certain period of time (3 years since 1992), and give them the right to return to their former jobs. But despite these benefits, East German women remain quite insecure about their re-employment; integration may be quite cumbersome when one has missed work during a crucial time of rapid organizational and technological change. The reaction of young women to this insecurity is just as expected – a drastic fall in birthrates (by about 50 per cent) and a growing number of abortions and sterilizations (Holst and Schupp 1991: 12).

The problems facing young East German women are exacerbated by several institutional characteristics of West German social programmes. The high employment rate of East German women was based on a set of social policy measures favouring working mothers. These policies, especially childcare, have now been replaced by West German regulations. The Federal government and the local governments intend to reduce the capacity of day-care centres, and to financially 'persuade' mothers to stay at home with their children. This too will have a serious impact on women's employment chances. After being out of work for a substantial period of time, the opportunities for re-employment become rather limited, especially when overall unemployment is high. Abundant empirical evidence reveals that employers tend to prefer men, who are expected to be more flexible in their time schedules.

24

While the problems facing young East German women are difficult, the economic pressures on prime-aged women, those 35–49 years old, are even greater. These women are over-represented among both the employed and the registered unemployed women in East Germany. While in West Germany this age-group has a rather low workforce participation rate and is the main source of 'non-employment', prime-age women in East Germany are not withdrawing from the labour market. After their long experience in paid work these women are not willing to stay home as housewives, especially since their children are grown up by now. Moreover, without paid work, many of them face considerable financial hardship. And even those with work remain fearful of losing their job and not being able to find a new one.

CONCLUSION: SPECULATIONS ON THE FUTURE PROSPECTS FOR WOMEN

As argued above, the labour-market prospects for women in the former East Germany are much worse than the labour-market prospects for men. An economic recovery that will increase employment in the near future is unlikely. Because of historical discrimination and because of their second job as homemakers, it is only to be expected that women will have a more difficult time making the necessary adjustments to capitalism. The important question is whether they will be able to develop active coping strategies.

The institutional system of East Germany shaped women's status and gender relations in traditional ways, especially in the private sphere. Social policies, the education and training system, and employment structures all contributed to that end. Women and men, though legal equals, remained social unequals. While the institutional and political framework of communism provided little room for individual choice and freedom, the transition to a market economy opens up a whole new range of individual opportunities. However, the norms and regulations of West German society, and the problems plaguing the West German economy, do not support an easy integration of women into the labour market (Maier 1991b). A large number of East German women have already lost their main source of economic independence – paid work. Those still employed are confronted with tougher competition in the workplace as well as a devaluation of their qualifications and skills. Moreover, jobs in previously feminized domains, such as the service sector, are developing into highly esteemed 'modern' occupations with excellent career perspectives. East German women are thus finding themselves confronted with ambitious male colleagues, determined to succeed in the modern capitalist society, and who are embracing a 'survival of the fittest' ethos. These 'new men' will likely view women as competitors for good jobs rather than as colleagues, either because of a fragile masculine identity that needs to be supported by professional success, or because of their new role as the single or main breadwinner for their family (Rudolph

1990). All of this will make it more difficult for East German women during the long transformation process.

Making matters worse, West German institutions and regulations concerning the labour market, the tax system, family allowances and female employment are still based on a conservative model that views a woman's place as primarily in the home. These regulations, and the lack of institutions to support the task of combining family and paid employment, will reinforce persisting sympathies for a conservative family model in the former East Germany. They may contribute, at least partly, to an involuntary withdrawal of women from the labour market, and thus to a reduction in the overall labour supply.

The price for such a patriarchal 'solution' to the employment problem will be high – it could mean a retraditionalization of German society. Women's claims on gainful employment and economic independence are being threatened by public policies, by political action within governments, by the administration of employment and retraining programmes, and by the trade unions. The political and economic transformation taking place in Germany will be paralleled by social progress only if women receive equal access to the labour market and to the new job openings. This requires arrangements for training and working that take seriously the productive and reproductive tasks performed by women.

NOTE

1 Local communities, federal Länder, non-profit groups and private enterprises are among the institutions providing these jobs.

3

THE STATUS OF WOMEN
AND POLAND'S TRANSITION
TO A MARKET
ECONOMY

Bozena Leven

INTRODUCTION

This essay examines the economic status of women in Poland both prior to, and during, that country's transition from socialism to capitalism. The analysis is divided into two parts. The next section establishes that under socialism Polish women generally received significantly lower incomes than men, and that this cannot be explained by different educational and skill levels. The inability to justify these wage differentials using human capital theory, in conjunction with the vertical and horizontal labour-market segmentation existing in Poland, indicate that the discrimination faced by women (i.e. the different and unequal treatment) is 'intentional'.

This paper then examines the short-term economic and political effects of Poland's recent drive towards marketization on women. At present, those effects appear to be mixed. For instance, the income gap between men and women has decreased relative to the 1980s, but in the context of a dramatic decline in real income for the entire society. Similarly, economic reforms have virtually eliminated Poland's perennial long lines for consumer goods, yet many of those goods lie outside the means of ordinary Poles. And while the number of available spaces in day-care centres have improved significantly, the cost of those facilities have increased exponentially.

The effects of reforms on women's access to political power are more pronounced and have been decidedly negative. For the first time, Polish women, constituting almost 50 per cent of the workforce, can freely organize and advance an agenda; yet women's groups are numerically small and politically isolated. At the same time, women now constitute a lower percentage of government legislators than during the previous forty-five years of communism. Thus, opportunities exist for improving the condition of women through the political system, but these opportunities have not yet been realized.

HISTORICAL BACKGROUND

In the broader historic context of Poland's post-war development, women entered the workforce pursuant to a policy of rapid, labour-intensive industrialization. Polish planners sought to maximize industrial production without straining the existing infrastructure (e.g. housing, transportation networks, health care) or disrupting agricultural output. Encouraging urban women to obtain regular employment was deemed preferable to supporting an inflow of male workers from the countryside.

Towards this end, the government's approach was two-pronged. On the one hand, extensive social services were provided, including paid maternity leaves of up to 3 years, inexpensive day-care facilities and heavy subsidization of child-related products. Those services, however, were often in short supply, as resources allocated to day-care permitted only one opening per ten working mothers. In fact, the government favoured extended parental leave over large-scale investment in day-care facilities. These policies reinforced traditional sex roles and disadvantaged women in the labour market, as a disproportionate number of mothers worked nightshifts while caring for their families during the day.

On the other hand, Article 67 of the Polish Constitution guaranteed equal pay for women in 1952, and explicitly stated that all citizens were to be treated as equal 'regardless of their sex'. Further, Article 78 confirmed the equal rights of men and women in all activities, whether they be political, economic, social or cultural. Poland was also a signatory to the United Nations Convention on the Elimination of All Forms of Discrimination Against Women, ratified in 1980.

These legal guarantees were implemented through a rigid classification system that described each occupational category in detail. Wages paid by state enterprises were uniformly set according to job classification, and were determined without regard to gender. Meanwhile, government propaganda on equality and a harsh economic reality drove the majority of Polish women into the workforce. For example, in the 1950s women averaged 33 per cent of all workers. This figure increased to 36 per cent during the 1960s and 42 per cent in the 1970s. By the mid-1980s, 47 per cent of all Polish women and 72 per cent of women aged 18–60 were employed outside the home. This latter figure was one of the highest in the world.

Shared job categories and wages set by the state did not, however, imply social advancement or genuinely equal economic opportunities for women. Traditional sex roles remained static, and women had great difficulty entering desirable positions. The failed promise of socialism left women with the 'double burden' of full-time work and primary responsibility for Polish families.

GENDER BIAS IN POLAND IN THE 1980s

An empirical evaluation of income inequalities between the sexes in Poland is difficult because little of the scarce data available treat men and women separately. Nevertheless, statistics on income and employment strongly indicate that inequalities between the sexes were both widespread and institutionalized, despite government policies and pronouncements to the contrary.

Table 3.1 presents the structure of income for Polish men and women in 1987. Because that structure remained stable throughout the 1980s, we consider these data as representative of the entire decade. In Table 3.1 labour is desegregated into two categories – white-collar and blue-collar workers. The white-collar category generally refers to non-manual labour and is quite broad, ranging from clerks to professionals. Blue-collar workers consist of manual labourers and full-time farmers.

Table 3.1 Distribution of nominal income by gender in 1987 (%)

Income ('000s of zloty)	White-collar		Blue-collar	
	Men	Women	Men	Women
14 and less	1.4	8.1	3.2	16.8
14.1–18	3.6	15.6	8.1	22.4
18.1–22	8.1	21.7	17.1	25.1
22.1–26	13.3	20.8	21.7	18.2
26.1–30	16.2	15.0	18.1	9.9
30.1–34	15.3	8.6	12.5	4.1
34.1–38	12.0	5.0	8.0	2.3
38.1–44	11.7	3.0	5.5	1.0
44.1–52	7.9	1.5	2.8	0.2
52.1–64	5.0	0.6	1.8	0.0
64 and more	5.5	0.1	1.2	0.0

Source: GUS (1988: 36).

Among white-collar workers, the average income for women was 23,800 zlotys, or 68 per cent of that received by men. At the same time, the median income for women was under 26,000 zlotys, as compared to 34,000 zlotys for men. More than 81 per cent of women, yet only 42 per cent of men, received less than the national average income of 30,000 zlotys for 1987, whereas 10.5 per cent of men in the white-collar category earned more than 52,000 zlotys, versus 0.7 per cent of women.

Though significant, income inequalities were less severe among blue-collar workers. The average income for female blue-collar workers was 20,300 zlotys, or 73 per cent of the earnings for male blue-collar workers. Median income was 22,000 zlotys and 26,000 zlotys for women and men, respectively. Fully 92 per cent of female blue-collar workers received less than the national average income, as opposed to 68 per cent of male blue-collar workers. Only

3 per cent of blue-collar men earned more than 52,000 zlotys, but virtually no blue-collar women did.

These substantial income disparities are consistent with women's limited access to power, authority and social status during the same time period. For instance, available data indicate that in the 1980s only 30 per cent of middle-level managers were women. At higher management levels (i.e. vice-presidents and presidents of enterprises) the share of women was even smaller, measuring 12 and 4.5 per cent, respectively.

In the political arena, Table 3.2 shows that during the period 1952–89 women constituted between 4 and 21 per cent of Poland's Parliament, and averaged slightly over 15 per cent of all members. In general, the percentage of female parliamentarians increased until the mid-1980s. On the national level, 2 out of 26 ministers were women in the 1980s (the ministers of education, and trade and services), as were 3 of Poland's 49 governors. Locally, over 20 per cent of all regional and county councils (*wojwodzkie* and *gminne rady narodowe*) were headed by women.

Table 3.2 Women Members of Parliament, 1952–89

Years	Percentage of women in Parliament
1952–56	17
1957–61	4
1961–65	13
1965–69	13
1969–72	13
1972–76	16
1976–80	20
1980–85	21
1985–89	20

Source: *Rocznik Statystyczny Polski (Poland's Statistical Yearbook)* (1990: 65).

We see from Table 3.3 that women also constituted more than 25 per cent of the Polish Communist Party's membership in the 1980s, which was then the centre of political power. These Party membership figures are, however, somewhat overstated. Since power within the Party was highly centralized, women holding ministerial and other governmental posts typically served more as functionaries then decision-makers, though retaining some degree of discretion. All top Communist Party positions were held by men (Kuratowska 1991: 10). While women held a substantial number of 'leadership' positions in Poland's remaining two political parties, both of these parties lacked real power.

A disparity between the sexes also existed in academic ranks, which are uniformly recognized as an important indicator of social status in Poland. Table 3.4 presents the number of women in different academic ranks, as a percentage of all scholars within each listed rank. These titles lack precise

Table 3.3 Percentage of women members of political parties

	Communist (%)	Social Democratic Union (%)	Peasant Party (%)
1970	22.5	20.6	27.8
1980	26.7	31.6	29.4
1987	27.2	28.3	32.9

Source: *Rocznik Statystyczny Polski (Poland's Statistical Yearbook)* (1988: 34–5; 1987: 33–4).

Table 3.4 Percentage of women in different academic ranks

	Professor	Docent	Adiunkt	Assistant
1970	8.3	13.2	32.7	37.2
1980	11.2	17.6	33.0	30.0
1989	19.0	24.2	42.1	38.1

Source: *Rocznik Statystyczny Polski (Poland's Statistical Yearbook)* (1990: 477).

Western equivalents. However, the lowest rank, 'assistant', is roughly equal to an 'instructor' in the United States – someone with a master's degree who is actively working on a PhD. Likewise, *adiunkts* are roughly equivalent to 'assistant professors', and *docents* are comparable to 'associate professors'.

The share of women in each rank increased during the period examined. However, by 1989 only 19 per cent of professors were women (the highest rank), and this percentage improved only marginally for *docents*. Moreover, in no degree category did women constitute a majority.

Causes of income inequality between men and women in Poland

Educational differences

The mere existence of income inequalities is not proof of sex discrimination *per se*. Rather, wage differentials may correspond to disparate productivities arising from the education, experience and/or personal preferences of particular workers. The impact of these factors in Poland may be assessed relative to two theories – human capital and occupational segregation.

The human capital theory focuses on labour characteristics resulting from the investment (e.g. schooling, training) of individual workers in their own 'human capital', which improves each worker's market value.[1] This theory assumes that men and women base their investment decisions on a cost–benefit analysis. Since Polish women traditionally maintain primary responsibility for both children and the home, their investment in market skills for use in the workplace should be lower than men's, who expect to provide the bulk of family income. These differing expectations should ultimately be reflected in lower wages for women relative to men.

However, this assumption is only partially borne out by the statistical data. Tables 3.5 and 3.6 show that Polish women constituted 48 per cent of all college graduates in a country where no bachelor degrees are granted and each graduate matriculates with a master's degree or above. In fact, the number of women with college degrees was deemed too high in certain professions, leading to a government policy of 'selective affirmative action' (e.g. only 50 per cent of students admitted to Polish medical schools could be female). In 1986 and 1989, the majority of medical, economics and general university graduates were women, who constituted a minority in the remaining fields.

Table 3.5 Acquired education level of women, 1988

Educational level	% Female graduates
College education	48
Equivalent of associate degree	60
Regular high school (lyceum)	59
Technical high school	36

Source: *Rocznik Statystyczny Polski (Poland's Statistical Yearbook)* (1989: 72; 1990: 43).

Table 3.6 Percentages of female degree recipients by field, 1986 and 1989

Field	1986	1989
General university	68.8	53.2
Engineering	25.6	17.1
Agriculture	41.0	31.5
Economics	64.8	52.2
Pedagogical	65.3	45.6
Medical	65.4	66.6
Physical education	33.3	30.0
Artistic	43.8	36.4
Theological	30.1	20.0

Source: *Rocznik Statystyczny Polski (Poland's Statistical Yearbook)* (1987: 473; 1990: 473).

Generally, the income of medical and economics graduates significantly exceeds the national average. By contrast, the income of graduates from the remaining fields (with the exception of engineering) is typically below the national average. In the aggregate, these statistics suggest that the human capital investment of college-educated Polish women exceeded, or was at least roughly comparable to, that of college-educated men. To the extent that this general conclusion is inconsistent with the data set forth in Table 3.1, the human capital theory does not adequately explain the gender differentials in income that exist in Poland.

We obtain a somewhat different result, however, with respect to associate and/or high school degree recipients, the majority of whom are female. Those two educational tracks usually do not provide specialized training, and therefore generate many of Poland's lesser paid bureaucrats and service workers.

Likewise, the fact that women constitute a minority of technical high school graduates further contributes to income inequality between the sexes. These technical schools, though considered the least prestigious (and commonly reserved for the least academically capable) produce Poland's craft workers (e.g. mechanics, electricians, plumbers, etc.), who often receive higher wages than college graduates. This situation certainly results, in part, from a perception in Poland that craft occupations require 'male skills'.

Thus, the human capital investment theory does not adequately explain existing income inequalities, particularly for white-collar college graduates, though it has somewhat greater applicability for blue-collar workers holding lesser degrees. Since pay differentials between men and women are only partially attributable to human capital investment, these differentials suggest discrimination against women.[2]

Job market segregation – horizontal and vertical

The occupational segregation theory attributes wage differentials to a horizontal division of the sexes by job category, as well as segregation within a profession, which is considered vertical. As with human capital theory, the mere existence of occupational segregation need not mean that discrimination against women exists, for this segregation may be prompted by voluntary choices based on *bona fide* job requirements or personal preferences.

In particular, physical characteristics that differentiate men from women also create different occupational choices and, possibly, different earnings (Maccoby and Jacklin 1974; Papalia and Tennent 1975). For instance, women may temporarily leave the workforce to rear children. However, Polish women have long enjoyed the legal right to substantial leave periods without loss of employment. Thus, a primary potential source of wage differences was effectively neutralized.

The data in Table 3.7 show significant horizontal and vertical segregation between Polish men and women in 1988 that was apparently unrelated to job characteristics. In particular, women dominate those sectors at the lower end of the wage scale, and are under-represented in higher paid positions. Moreover, in all sectors dominated by women (except the judicial system), the average monthly salary was below the national average. In the judicial system, where average salaries exceeded the national average, the percentage of women working in each job category declined as income increased. For example, only 10 per cent of Poland's highest court judges were women, and at the regional and local levels these numbers were 27 per cent and 46 per cent, respectively (*Rocznik Statystyczny Polski* 1990: 75). Though constituting a majority of judicial system personnel, women in this sector continue to be employed primarily as clerical or legal aid workers.

Table 3.7 Job segregation and average income by economic sector, 1988

Sector	Female participation (%)	Average income ('000s of zlotys)
Finance	87	27
Medical services	81	22
Education	79	23
Trade	69	24
Culture & arts	62	25
Judicial system	55	30
Communication	57	24
Science & research	47	35
Industry	37	33
Agriculture	27	28
Transportation	23	28
Construction	18	32
Forestry	18	25

Source: *Rocznik Statystyczny Polski (Poland's Statistical Yearbook)* (1989: 70; 1988: 157).
Note: The average national income in 1988 was 30,000 zlotys.

The finance sector contains the largest percentage of women, and offers an average salary that is 10 per cent below the national average. In the next two sectors dominated by women, education and medical services, average salaries were approximately 20 and 25 per cent, respectively, below the national average and, as in the judicial sector, vertical segregation remains extensive. Polish women constitute over 52 per cent of all physicians (*Rocznik Statystyczny Polski* 1990: 476), but are concentrated in internal and paediatric medicine; women constitute only 4 per cent of surgeons, who are more highly paid. At the lower end of the income distribution chain are pharmacists and nurses, of whom 98 per cent and 99 per cent are women, respectively. Additionally, the number of nurses and nurse assistants outnumbered Polish doctors by 2.75 to 1 (*Rocznik Statystyczny Polski* 1990: 476). Uniform wages by job category therefore do not equate with equal income between genders. Instead, it is apparent that the participation of women declined as the income, the status and the authority within the medical sector increased.

The underlying question is whether the degree of job segregation described above was voluntary. Did it arise from positive job characteristics of female-dominated occupations, and were these voluntary decisions sufficient to justify existing wage differentials? For example, flex time, shorter hours, or greater benefits (e.g. on-site day-care) might have motivated women to favour one occupation over another, and those occupations favoured by women for these reasons might have paid less. Little factual support, however, can be garnered in support of this possibility. Using medical services as an example, we see that paediatricians, internists, nurses and surgeons work comparable hours. Moreover, while women were generally accorded greater child-related benefits than men, those benefits were state regulated and therefore accrued to all women regardless of their occupations. Thus wage differentials, rooted in occupational segregation, appear to be involuntary and, as such, provide further evidence of discrimination against women.

WELFARE EFFECTS OF ECONOMIC REFORMS ON WOMEN IN THE 1990s

The rapid pace of Poland's political and economic reforms since January 1990 is well known. As part of an institutional overhaul of the communist political order, the National Assembly was created to amend the Constitution, pass new legislation and revamp existing laws. The new government implemented a programme of radical economic reforms.

Many of these reforms were the direct outgrowth of a decade of unpopular and ill-conceived economic half-measures propounded by the Polish Communist Party to combat skyrocketing foreign debt, a growing budget deficit, hyperinflation and severe consumer-goods shortages in the domestic market. Facing economic collapse, Poland's democratically elected government committed itself to a 'shock therapy' programme, the vital aspects of which are economic liberalization, macroeconomic stabilization and massive privatization. Liberalization under this programme refers to a series of legal and administrative changes designed to create competitive markets for capital, labour, goods and services, as well as institutions supporting them. Macroeconomic stabilization involves restricting Poland's budget deficit to under 5 per cent of GNP, tight credit policies to reduce money supply growth, abolishing centrally set prices, stabilizing the price level, implementing progressive income taxes and establishing a realistic exchange rate that is uniform for all enterprises and private citizens, and based upon a convertible currency. Finally, privatization entails the transfer of ownership rights in thousands of enterprises from state to private hands.

A key element of Poland's reforms was their rapid implementation, reflecting a conscious political decision to use the initial euphoria of democracy to maximum economic advantage. Liberalization was introduced in the space of several weeks, from late December 1989 to early January 1990. Macroeconomic stabilization was also quickly achieved, albeit at a high cost, as prices increased over 100 per cent in January 1990, before subsiding to a mere 4 per cent increase the following month.

The most lengthy and challenging step of the reform process continues to be privatization. Unfortunately, there is no blueprint or economic precedent for this strategy, yet more than 90 per cent of Polish industry, constituting over 3,000 medium to large enterprises, needed to be transferred from the state to private citizens. Besides the sheer number of affected enterprises, such basic problems as valuing assets, in conjunction with the complex social and political issues commonly associated with industrial restructuring, have greatly impeded the transfer of large enterprises.

By contrast, small firm privatization has proceeded rapidly, and by mid-1991 40,000 small businesses had been sold or leased to private owners, including over 80 per cent of all retail stores and a majority of trucking, construction and small manufacturing firms.

The overall effects of these changes on Polish society are difficult to appraise. On the one hand, beginning in 1990, successive governments have instituted or maintained various social 'safety net' programmes, and previously unavailable goods and services may now be bought without waiting in queues. On the other hand, it must be recognized that the prices of all goods and services rose far in excess of wages, living standards have plunged, and by 1992 unemployment reached 13 per cent in a country where until the late 1980s full employment was guaranteed.

Methodology and data

Our analysis of the welfare effects of these reforms on women, which follows, is necessarily limited by the short time period involved (1990–1), and by the limited data that are consequently available. The bulk of information that is provided below originated from a recently conducted survey of 1,500 urban Poles. In it, the major topics tracked were changes in employment and nominal income, in childcare programmes, in the availability of consumer goods, in the structure of spending and in the distribution of time outside of work. Respondents were also asked to evaluate the economic and political reforms and their effects on Polish society.

The survey consisted of thirty questions related to specific indicators of economic well-being. Out of 1,500 questionnaires distributed via a network of friends and relatives, 767 responses from women and 710 from men were received, with the latter serving as a control group. The period examined was one year, from July 1989 to July 1990.

Table 3.8 illustrates the structure of the survey sample. From it, we see that the majority of men and women surveyed were between ages 26 and 45 (65 per cent women and 76 per cent men), married (75 per cent of women and 70 per cent of men) and had at least a high school education (93 per cent of women and 88 per cent of men). This structure resembles the breakdown of urban dwellers presented in official Polish statistical sources, and is therefore considered representative of the urban segment of the population (*Rocznik Statystyczny Polski* 1989: 44, 48).

Results

The first two survey indicators were changes in employment and income. In contrast to pre-reform Poland, where full employment and income were set by state regulations, the 1990 economic reforms introduced unemployment and floating wages. The survey indicates that Poland's resulting decline in

Table 3.8 The socio-demographic structure of the sample

	% Female	% Male
Age		
18–25	12	16
26–35	42	44
36–45	23	32
45+	23	8
Marital status		
Single	18	10
Married	70	75
Divorced	8	13
Widow/er	4	2
Education		
Elementary	7	12
Secondary	68	64
Higher	25	24

Source: Author's surveys.

GNP had a significant but less severe impact on employment than on production.[3] Specifically, in the face of a 30 per cent decline in production, 83 per cent of women and 84 per cent of men retained their jobs. An additional 10 per cent of women switched to higher paid positions, while only 0.9 per cent of women became and remained unemployed, compared to 4 per cent of men.

An index of job security by gender is presented in Table 3.9 on a scale of 1–5, where 5 = certainty of losing one's present job and 1 = certainty of maintaining that job. Initially, in July 1989, women had a greater sense of job security because fewer women had lost their jobs than men. The introduction of economic reforms in January 1990 left women less secure about their continued employment. By the end of the examined period, both men and women felt almost equally insecure.

Changes in average nominal income appear in Table 3.10, which shows that income inequalities persisted but the gender gap narrowed as the salaries of

Table 3.9 Average indicators of job security*

Date	Male job security index	Female job security index
July 1989	2.28	1.42
January 1990	2.29	1.91
July 1990	2.35	2.24

Source: Author's surveys.
Note: *Figures are averages based upon a 5-point scale, where 1 = certainty of maintaining one's job and 5 = certainty of losing one's job.

Table 3.10 Changes in average nominal income (in '000s of zlotys)

Date	Female		Male	
	Mean	Median	Mean	Median
July 1989	+229	+200	+447	+200
	(27)*		(41)	
January 1990	+423	+400	+698	+600
	(39)		(77)	
July 1990	+678	+600	+801	+800
	(44)		(83)	

Source: Author's surveys.
* Numbers in parentheses are standard deviations.

women rose faster than those of men. In particular, Poland's wage inequality ratio, defined as the average nominal male income divided by the average nominal female income, declined from 1.95 in July 1989 to 1.18 in July 1990.

This significant change in income distribution between men and women is partially attributable to the government's introduction of welfare pro-grammes that targeted low-income families, often headed by women. We also find a greater variability in men's income than in women's, as evidenced by a coefficient of variation. For both sexes the means exceeded medians, indicating positively skewed distributions.

Table 3.10 also reveals that the trend for median income runs counter to the trend for mean income. Specifically, in July 1989, income distribution was more centered around the mean among females than males. By July 1990, the reverse was true. At the same time the median income for males grew faster, reaching 800,000 zlotys as compared to 600,000 for women in July 1991. Thus, as the wage gap between the sexes diminished, income distribution among men became more equal.

These findings are partially confirmed by the secondary data subsequently published on Poland's income inequalities, which appear in Table 3.11.

Table 3.11 Average wage differential between men and women (in May 1990)

Occupation	Average pay ('000s of zlotys)	Women's pay as a percentage of men's pay
	Highest pay	
Experts in administration and management	1,157.0	68
Doctors	1,135.7	72
	Lowest pay	
Social workers	642.9	72
Store keepers	674.4	88
Technicians	683.6	74

Source: Kuratowska (1991: 18).

Specifically, the data presented show that in 1990 the pay gap between the sexes ranged from 68 per cent to 88 per cent across a spectrum of occupations.

A related point in our survey is the percentage of men and women on sick leave which, between July 1989 and July 1990, declined from 16 per cent to 10 per cent and from 24 per cent to 12 per cent, respectively. The average duration of each leave also declined, from 5.8 to 5 days for women and from 4 to 2.6 for men. In the past, guaranteed access to free medical services, a virtually unlimited number of permitted sick days, and relatively high wages paid to ill workers contributed to high and unwarranted levels of absenteeism.

Changes in childcare programmes constitute the third survey indicator. As mentioned above, childcare facilities were heavily subsidized by the state and therefore affordable for most families; but access to these facilities was extremely limited due to short supply. Following the market reforms and elimination of state subsidies, the average monthly day-care costs for pre-schoolers rose from 130,000 zlotys in July 1989, to 350,000 zlotys in January 1990, and then to 550,000 zlotys in July 1990. These figures constituted 58 per cent, 82 per cent and 81 per cent of the average salary for women in each designated month. Despite the extraordinarily high and rising share of childcare costs, there were no significant changes in the percentage of Polish women who worked. One reason may be that the salaries of spouses also rose during the examined period, absorbing a substantial portion of increased day-care costs. Alternative care takers (other family members, since professional childminders are rarely used in Poland) may have also been more widely employed by working mothers. At the same time, the high costs of day-care facilities undoubtedly discouraged non-working mothers from joining the workforce.

Overall, both men and women agreed that access to state-run childcare facilities (with their long waiting lists and the need for connections to gain access) had improved by the summer of 1990. Presumably, this improvement is partially attributable to the same rising costs noted above, which must have prompted non-working mothers to withdraw their children from day-care centres.[4] In addition, Poland's first private facilities were formed during this period, providing an alternative to state-run centres.

The fourth survey indicator involves changes for consumers. Both women and men noted a general improvement after January 1990. For example, 42 per cent of the women surveyed characterized consumer goods as being moderately more available, while 58 per cent of the male respondents reached the same conclusion. Correspondingly, 46 per cent of women felt the magnitude of improvement was significant, as opposed to 33 per cent of men.

In an attempt to establish the effects of rising prices on the structure of consumer purchases, survey respondents were asked to identify goods and services eliminated from their budgets for financial reasons between 1989 and 1990. Both men and women listed newspapers, sweets, citrus fruit (consider to be a luxury in Poland), higher quality brands of meat and entertainment (e.g. theatre, cinema) as goods they have done without. Women also mentioned small appliances. With respect to services, women identified pressing,[5] haircuts, and manicures. Most men reported that they had not eliminated any services from their budget.

These responses were generally consistent with the minor declines reported by households (families of two or more people) in the average share of their monthly family budget expended on clothing, entertainment and other personal goods and services (such as haircuts, manicures, etc.) For men, this share dropped from 26 per cent to 21 per cent during the period examined and, for women, from 25 per cent to 23 per cent.

The respondents were next asked to characterize their pre- and post-reform diet. Approximately 74 per cent of women considered their July 1989 diet 'very good', as compared with 63 per cent of men. For July 1990, these numbers declined to 68 per cent and 58 per cent for women and men, respectively. Conversely, 2 per cent of women and 8 per cent of men considered their diet 'poor' in July 1989. By July 1990 these numbers had increased to 14 per cent and 21 per cent, respectively.

Distribution of the respondents' time outside of work constituted the fifth survey indicator, and from answers to this question we see that phase one of the reforms made a considerable difference in the time spent shopping. In July 1989 women waited an average of 2.4 hours per day, and for men the figure was 1.9 hours. By July 1990, these numbers had declined to 0.7 and 0.66 hours for women and men, respectively. At the same time, the average daily recreational time spent with children increased slightly for women, from 2.05 to 2.28 hours between July 1989 and July 1990, but declined for men from 1.7 to 1.2 hours during the same period. Women, however, continued to exert considerably greater efforts than men on daily house chores (by approximately 2.7 hours per day).

With respect to in-house leisure activities, men increased their daily television viewing from 1.8 to 2.1 hours, while women reduced their viewing time from 2.0 to 1.7 hours. These numbers may be upwardly biased since some respondents may have considered their 'viewing time' as all time when their television set was on, regardless of whether or not they focused on the programme being broadcasted. Both men and women decreased their daily reading, from 1.9 to 1.7 hours, and from 1.2 to 0.9 hours, respectively.

More drastic changes occurred with respect to monthly cinema and theatre visits, as both the frequency and number of visits declined. For example, in July 1989, 23 per cent of women and 18 per cent of men attended the theatre at least once monthly. One year later, those numbers had declined to 12 per cent and 9 per cent, respectively. Similarly, cinema attendance dropped from 72 per cent (women) and 54 per cent (men) in July 1989 to 41 per cent (women) and 32 per cent (men) in July 1990.

Finally, the respondents were asked to evaluate Poland's present and future economic situation, and the effects of economic reform on their lives. Overall, women were more positive about Poland's general economic situation than men. Specifically, in July 1989, 48 per cent of women believed that economic life in Poland was extremely difficult, compared with 44 per cent of men. Subsequently, in July 1990, only 24 per cent of women and 36 per cent of men still maintained that view. At the same time, 28 per cent of men and 32 per cent of women reported that their own economic situation had actually improved. An additional 26 per cent of women and 28 per cent of men, whose living standards had not actually improved, nevertheless noted signs of economic recovery. Moreover, a clear majority of all men and women surveyed believed that their standard of living would improve substantially in the next five years.

The respondents' evaluation of the effects of economic reforms on men and women is summarized in Table 3.12.[6] A greater fraction of men felt that women had suffered more under the reforms. At the same time, a greater percentage of women than men thought that the negative impact of the reforms was felt more by men.

Table 3.12 Evaluation of effects of economic reforms on Polish men and women

Survey statement	Agreement by men (%)	Agreement by women (%)
Negative economic effects were felt equally by both men and women	33	21
Negative effects were felt more by women than men	38	32
Negative effects were felt more by men than women	26	30
Not sure	3	17

Source: Author's survey.

Effects of reform on women's access to political power

The effects of reform on women's access to political power is even more difficult to estimate, since the new post-communist multi-party system is still in its infancy. The available statistical data suggest, however, that Poland's changed political system may have further removed women from meaningful participation in political life.

As indicated in the previous section, under communist rule the share of women holding government and party positions was approximately 20 per cent. Since late 1989, which marked the current change in Poland's government, the percentage of women deputies to Parliament decreased from 20 to 12 per cent. More importantly, women, though very active in the early stages of the Solidarity movement, found themselves profoundly under-represented in the newly formed National Solidarity Committee, constituting only 4 of 96 members. In addition, only one woman currently holds a ministerial post (minister of culture), a mere 7 out of 100 seats in the Senate are occupied by women, and there is but one woman ambassador and no female governors.[7]

These figures are especially troubling given the absence of a women's movement in Poland. Like so many other national problems, this situation can be traced to the prior regime, in which the very existence of difficult social issues was determined by their compatibility with communist ideology. Since communism afforded women equality and guaranteed their rights, there was no need for a women's movement or feminist political agenda, and none was permitted. Thus, in today's Poland, women are not politically organized and the society is largely unaware of gender issues.

CONCLUSION

Discrimination against women continues in Poland during the 1990s. Less clear is whether institutionalized gender bias will decrease in the newly emerging Polish society. On the one hand, income disparities between the sexes appear to be diminishing, albeit in the context of a nationwide decline in standards of living. On the other, the number of women participating in government has declined and, overall, women have so far failed to develop political organizations or issues.

It is no secret that addressing this situation requires a multi-faceted approach. Certainly, women must force the issue of inequality into the political arena. Moreover, while organizing politically, women also need to organize economically. Cooperatives, lending institutions and other self-help groups oriented towards women are a logical step in this direction. Fundamental to these developments, though, is the necessity of educating Polish women not just about their problems, but also about their possibilities.

NOTES

1 For more details on human capital theory see Becker (1975) and Schultz (1963).
2 It would be helpful to examine other factors, such as seniority, when assessing the existence of discrimination. Unfortunately, data limitations preclude such analysis.
3 Admittedly, changing preferences and other factors unrelated to Poland's economic reform may well have affected the survey results. However, the effect of non-economic factors, if any, is unquantifiable.
4 It is too early to augment the analysis by state-provided data on enrolment in childcare facilities for the relevant period.
5 Pressing, *magiel*, literally refers to the pressing of linens, which is made necessary by Poland's lack of synthetic fabrics and driers.
6 The survey was completed in August 1990. In the spring of 1991, Poland's Central Office on Public Opinions conducted a series of independent surveys of people's future expectations regarding Poland's economic and political life. The results of those surveys did not desegregate responses by sex, but show a general deterioration of the public mood and more pessimistic attitudes towards the reforms than those reported here.
7 A notable exception to this trend is Hanna Suchocka, who served as Poland's first female prime minister in the years 1992–3.

4

THE ECONOMIC STATUS OF WOMEN IN ROMANIA

Walter M. Bacon, Jr. and Louis G. Pol[1]

INTRODUCTION

Images of the Romanian revolution of 1989 are indelibly etched upon the Western memory – the slaughtered demonstrators of Timişoara; the disbelieving dictator, utterly confounded by defiance from the usually fawning Bucharest crowd; the courageous freedom fighters taking cover from withering loyalist fire with frightened soldiers in bullet scarred doorways; the executed dictatorial couple; and the dishevelled and bewildered coalition of anti-Ceauşescu communists, army officers, intellectual dissidents, and aging survivors of the traditional political parties. Prominent among these conspirators were two women – the dissident poet Ana Blandiana and the Transylvanian human rights activist Doina Cornea. The presence of these two internationally known opponents of the *ancien régime* might have augured well for the role women would play in post-communist Romania; but like so many of the acclaimed initial images of the 'revolution', this proved to be an empty symbol. Aware of being exploited, Cornea and Blandiana quickly and prudently distanced themselves from the National Salvation Front, leaving the new regime with even fewer leadership females than the old one. The absence of women from the politics of post-communist Romania is symptomatic of the precarious status of women in general during the first four years of the transition.

This chapter focuses on three time periods – Romania before communism, the years under communism (1946–89), and the post-Communist era. While the major emphasis of the chapter is on the recent past, the present and the future, it is important to understand the history that led to the current situation. This also provides the context for understanding likely future developments. Romania today continues to live with vestiges of a planned system that improved the status of women overall, but never came close to realizing equal workforce opportunities for men and women. At the same time, cultural traditions, which were suppressed under the socialist regime, threaten the progress that was made after World War II. It is these vestiges, in conflict with a culture that was suppressed for over forty years, that are

43

generating conflict and uncertainty today. And, at least in the short term, some of the advances made under communism have been reversed.

ROMANIA BEFORE COMMUNISM

Contemporary Romania represents the territorial unification of a number of regions where the majority of the population is ethnically Romanian. The Principalities of Wallachia (Ţara Românească) and (western) Moldavia united under a single prince, Alexandru Ion Cuza, in 1859, forming Romania. Independence was won from the Ottoman Empire in 1877.

The 'Old Kingdom', *regatul*, as Romania prior to national unification is retrospectively called, was overwhelmingly rural; 81.1 per cent in 1899, and the vast majority of adult village dwellers (around 90 per cent) were engaged in agricultural pursuits. In this agrarian society women's subordinate social and economic status was delineated by a tradition nurtured by religion and 'biology'. Even in urban or aristocratic settings, while granted some authority in the private (household) sphere, women were denied any sort of public status other than that of their husband to whom they owed 'blind submission' (Stourdza 1911: 69–80). Under the terms of the Caragea (1815) and Calimach (1817) Statutes women had virtually no legal rights, and even the relatively enlightened Civil Code of 1865 placed them 'under the protection of men' (Buzatu 1988a: 83, 83n).

Education for Romanian women began in the early nineteenth century and was initially limited to the privileged classes and to teaching the 'social graces' that would enhance marital prospects. By mid-century, however, women were being prepared as teachers in normal schools (Iorga 1911: 138–50). In 1861–2, of 87,485 pupils registered in public and private schools, 11,000 were 'girls' (*Enciclopedia României* 1938: 462). By the end of the century, there were nineteen 'girls" professional schools, ten 'girls" high schools, and four normal schools for the preparation of female teachers. One-fifth of the students sitting for the Romanian version of the *baccalaureate* examination were women but only 490 of 5,900 university students were female (Stourdza 1911: 72). Even this modest access to education did not please traditionalists, such as the famous nationalist historian Nicolae Iorga, who regretted the absence of 'truly womanly schools of culture' through which women might learn to be 'the consoler of the man, tired from [his] struggle, the mother of children whom she is called to prepare for life, the true mistress within the four walls of her home' (Iorga 1911: 161). Preparing women, as if they were men, for careers which did not, and should not, exist for them, would depreciate their value to the nation (Iorga 1911: 162).

Under Prince Alexandru Ion Cuza (1864), Romania acknowledged the principle of free and compulsory education. In the 1890s the educational system underwent a thorough reorganization; the French model was adopted structurally and pedagogically; and vocational schools were established to provide skilled workers to burgeoning industry. A 1924 law required primary (seven years) education for both sexes and provided for secondary schools in two stages: *gimnaziu* (grades 5–8) and *liceu* (grades 9–12). The successful passing of the *baccalaureate* examination might provide admission to higher educational institutions which granted *licenţa* and *doctorat* diplomas. Tuition at all levels was free, but other associated fees discriminated against good students from poor families. Compulsory attendance was not rigorously enforced, especially in the countryside, and in 1930 the literacy rate was estimated at only 57 per cent.

As a result of the War of Independence (1877), the Second Balkan War (1913), and World War I (1916–18), Romania gained sovereignty over the Dobrogea from Bulgaria, Transylvania and the Banat from Hungary, Bukovina from Austria, and Bessarabia (eastern Moldavia) from Russia. Romania's territory and population more than doubled as a result of national unification (Rothschild 1974: 281). Unification, however, did not alter a peasant culture that resisted social modernization and maintained the patriarchal structure of the village. Women were supposed to be submissive to their husbands and fathers, and to attend to nurturing and housekeeping chores. Even as industrialization took place, gender roles, economic conditions and social structure changed little, and migration to urban areas was asymmetrically masculine (*Enciclopedia Romîniei* 1938: 139). Moreover, urbanized employment, even if carried out in a rural setting, was more disproportionally male; 70.7 per cent of the active male population was employed in agriculture and 10.7 per cent in industry versus 87.1 per cent of the active female population employed in agriculture and only 2.9 per cent in industry (*Enciclopedia Romîniei* 1938: 156). Also, women were disproportionally under-educated. In 1938 there were 1,143,000 female elementary school pupils out of a total of 2,491,000 (47 per cent of the total); and 7,000 female university students out of 31,000 (23 per cent of the total) (Kaser and Radice 1985: 96). Translated into comparative rates of literacy, according to the 1930 census rural women were 38.7 per cent literate, as opposed to 64.9 per cent of rural men; and 70.3 per cent of urban women were literate, as opposed to 84.5 per cent of urban men (*Enciclopedia Romîniei* 1938: 143).

Structurally as well as culturally, social mobility for women in precommunist Romania was truncated relative to men. While a few gained prominence through their artistic achievements or their social and familial status, women did not exercise significant political or economic power (Bacon 1981). They could not vote. In the economic sphere, women were afforded the right to work without the permission of their husbands in 1929 (Buzatu 1988a: 83). They were granted special workplace protection in 1928, limiting where and when they could work and mandating employer-provided nursing periods and places as well as maternity leaves (*Enciclopedia Romîniei* 1938: 599). Most of the 2.9 per cent of the female workforce employed in industry were unskilled labourers. There were very few female apprentices, 12.5 per cent of the total, and fewer female skilled workers and managers. In 1930 there were 11.8 skilled male workers for each skilled female worker, and there were 9.1 male managers for each female manager (*Enciclopedia României* 1939: 47, 59–60). Few women were employed in the liberal professions, although male-to-female proportions by profession suggest a significant number of women in the health and education sectors. In short, inter-war Romanian women were encumbered by a patriarchal social order, but they did make slight progress in access to education, legal equity and non-traditional economic roles.

The Church always played a central socio-cultural, as well as a religious, role in Romania. Village priests were educators, arbitrators and record keepers; and the Romanian clergy were among the most articulate spokespersons for national unification. The Romanian Orthodox Church, recognized as an independent patriarchate (in Bucharest) since 1885, claimed 72.6 per cent of the population as adherents in 1930 (*Enciclopedia României* 1938: 154). The doctrines and traditions of the Romanian religious denominations accentuated the social and economic subordination of women. Liturgically, men and women were separated. Because the communal practice of religion is a public act, men represented their families before God. Peasant understanding of the story of the Fall indicted all women for the sin of Eve (Kligman 1988: 61–4). While many women adopted the religious life as nuns (Iorga 1911: 165–73), the religious hierarchy, the ordained ministry and most theological educational establishments were exclusively male.

While industrialization and urbanization had started in the nineteenth century, inter-war Romania was still overwhelmingly (80 per cent) an agrarian society (*Enciclopedia României* 1938: 155). Families were large and patrimonial with all able family members participating in economic activity. Rural overpopulation was chronic and standards of living have been estimated as being very low. Still, the rhythms of village life were predictable and accepted. Only land hunger and crushing debts, both somewhat assuaged by inter-war legislation, tempted Romanian peasants from their political and economic parochialism. Unless sorely tried, as they had been in 1907, Romanian peasants were passive and did not challenge the established social, economic and political patrimonialism (see Roberts 1969: 6–55; Valota 1979).

Inter-war city life reflected the socio-economic tensions of a developing country. On the one hand, there were élites whose tastes and affluent lifestyles mimicked those of Western and Central European élites. Their children went to universities, in Romania and abroad, and chose careers in the liberal professions or business. They patronized the arts, cultivated a 'cafe society' imitating Paris, and participated in political life. After the economic demise of large landowners in the land reforms of the 1920s, the economic élites were the chief beneficiaries of a socio-political system that was as generous as it was corrupt.

On the other hand, there were the industrial workers, most of them newly arrived peasants, whose escape from rural poverty was urban poverty. Factory work was dangerous, poorly paid, unpredictable. While some amenities of modern life were afforded industrial workers, their upward social mobility was limited and, in their frustration, they were often attracted by radical politics.

Pre-communist Romania was in the initial stages of industrialization, lacking both the physical and human resources characteristic of the Western European or even the Soviet pre-war industrial societies. Its largely peasant population was undertrained for the tasks of industry, and was socially impeded from rapidly modernizing by village- and church-based traditions which also confined women to the private sphere. While the inter-war élites may have wished to emulate Western social norms, the vast majority of the population remained tethered to a past incompatible with either the Western or the Soviet models of development and the explicit change in economic and social status modernization brings to women. Whereas the adoption of the Western model would have gradually diminished the dominance of Romania's evolved social traditions, the imposition of Soviet-style socialism superficially obliterated them. Because that obliteration was never perceived as legitimate, when the Ceauşescu regime was overthrown in 1989, the traditions resurfaced and challenged those aspects of socialist industrialization which had changed the status of Romanian women.

ROMANIA UNDER COMMUNISM (1945–89)

World War II had significant effects on Romania's population. War-related deaths were approximately 500,000; the Holocaust claimed 420,000 Romanian Jews and an undeterminable number of Gypsies. The loss of northern Bukovina and Bessarabia to the USSR and southern Dobruja to Bulgaria resulted in a population loss of more than 3.5 million. Of these perhaps two-fifths were ethnic minorities, thus increasing the Romanian proportion of the total population to 85.7 per cent in 1948 (Jelavich 1983: 371; Schwerthoeffer 1985: 80).

Minorities were over-represented in the immediate post-war Communist Party precisely because of their alienation from the inter-war nationalist politics which had discriminated against them. A disproportionate number of the Party's leaders were Hungarians, Jews and Ukrainians (King 1980: 34–5, 82). The new regime both constitutionally and statutorily guaranteed minorities equal rights, including linguistic, cultural and educational autonomy. These guarantees gradually evaporated and assimilationist policies were pursued in the last decades of communist rule.

The first communist educational reform (1948) abolished all but state schools; established free and compulsory schooling for all Romanians; created national education plans to support the country's industrialization; proletarianized access to secondary and higher education; and initiated a campaign to eradicate illiteracy (*Romania, Facts and Figures* 1979: 54). The latter was credited for the claimed 98 per cent literacy rate during the late 1980s. Under communism the number of schools, the types of education available, and the number of teachers all increased dramatically. Compulsory education was extended from 7 to 10 years, and plans were made to require 12 years of education for all Romanians. Beginning in the 1960s, education was more closely integrated with production, and by the 1980s this trend resulted in the 'polytechnicalization' of secondary education, at the expense of the humanities and all but the propagandistically and economically 'relevant' social sciences. In the mid-1980s, only 8 per cent of the graduates of *gimnazii* were enrolled in curricularly traditional *licee*. The regime's growing anti-intellectualism, the limiting of academic opportunities, and tight education budgets in the 1980s made secondary and post-secondary institutions hotbeds of discontent and breeding grounds for the student revolutionaries of 1989–90. Participation in Party-led youth groups – the Falcons of the Fatherland, the Pioneers and the Union of Communist Youth – was virtually obligatory for all Romanian young people.

In Marxist–Leninist theory, socialist societies have eliminated antagonistic class differences although they may retain worker and peasant classes and a stratum of intellectuals. In practice, socialist Romania never achieved utopian classlessness. In the immediate post-war years the urban middle class and independent farmers were suppressed. Their places in the social hierarchy were taken by new social élites – Party and state officials, economic managers, technicians, professionals, and cultural and sports figures – the *nomenklaturist* class. Unskilled industrial and construction workers and state and collective farmers continued to occupy the lower levels of the social structure. Despite efforts to provide opportunities for upward social mobility to workers and peasants, the new ruling class became as self-perpetuating as the old.

Industrialization contributed to the urbanization of the population. However, reflecting policies emphasizing territorial dispersion of industry, smaller cities grew faster than Bucharest, and due to the density of transportation infrastructures, a significant proportion of urban workers commuted from rural homes (Chirot 1979: 475). Newly urbanized Romanians faced a chronic housing shortage or small apartments in dingy housing projects. Restrictions on the use of energy and food shortages during the 1980s made urban life even more unattractive. Still, the existing verifiable evidence suggests that the standard of living rose steadily but slowly from 1950 through the mid-1970s when consumption versus accumulation priorities were modified at the former's expense and proportional budgetary expenditures for socio-cultural activities were cut by 20 per cent (1976 versus 1971) (Tsantis and Pepper 1979: 172–82). By the mid-1980s the International Monetary Fund had estimated a 40 per cent decline in Romania's standard of living since its high point a decade earlier (Orescu 1985: 18).

Theoretically, as socialism destroys class distinctions, so too is the class-

48

based inequity of women eradicated. Women are afforded equal access with men to all levels of economic and political power not because of any special and gender-specific feminine insights needed by society, but because women are human beings entitled to the full development of their personalities (Deliman 1977). This anticipated effect of the creation of a new socialist mentality in which gender distinctions are mooted was reflected in socialist Romania's definition of purpose:

> The growth in the role of women in all aspects of life constitutes an integral part of the entire strategy for socioeconomic development; of the blossoming of the human personality corresponding to the goals of the new order [and] of the means by which the socialist sociopolitical system is activated for the realization of the principles of liberty and human dignity.
>
> (Buzatu 1988b: 45)

In a strictly legal sense, women were accorded equal rights with men as early as July 1946, a principle enshrined in all socialist Romanian constitutions (1948, 1952 and 1965) and numerous laws (Zaharia 1980: 184–215). Equality in pay was not granted as rapidly. Data from 1949 on remuneration by industry indicate that female pay was between 30 and 50 per cent less than male pay (Buzatu 1988a: 84). By the mid-1960s more than one-quarter of the industrial workforce was female, a proportion which was to rise to 42.6 per cent by 1988 (Buzatu 1988b: 46). According to a Romanian Communist Party (RCP) source, in the late 1980s, one-half of the medium-trained workforce and one-third of the highly-trained workforce were female, as was 43 per cent of the research personnel (Foreign Broadcast Information Service 1989: 69–70). However, as in many socialist countries, Romanian women tended to be employed more intensively in light industries, agriculture, health care and education (Moskoff 1978: 449). They held the lowest paying jobs and were infrequently found at managerial levels of responsibility. In addition to the feminization of the workforce in a number of industry categories, no less an authority than Nicolae Ceauşescu acknowledged that competent women were not being promoted to managerial positions, even in industries (and agricultural units) where they represented the majority of workers (Ceauşescu 1973: 602). As a result of the RCP Central Committee plenum of June 1973, the Romanian government was directed to draw up a list of some 640 work categories in which women were under-represented and to make provisions for compensatory training and placement. By 1980, the programme was alleged to have yielded some positive results (*Radio Free Europe Research* 1981: 20).

Despite some early fluctuations in membership ratios, the proportion of female members of the RCP gradually increased over time, particularly after the 1973 plenum. At the Fourteenth RCP Congress (November 1989) it was reported that 36 per cent of RCP members (1.4 million) were females (Foreign

Broadcast Information Service 1989: 19, 70). Women closely associated with Elena Ceauşescu were well represented on the RCP Political Executive Committee (Foreign Broadcast Information Service 1989: 36). The proportion of women in the RCP Central Committee, in county secretariats and in RCP mass organizations (apart from the National Council of Women) increased dramatically after 1973, although rapid promotion often led to just as rapid demotion from Party bodies (Fischer 1989: 174–5, 202; Gilberg 1990: 92). Female representation in state bodies also increased; women comprised 33 per cent of the Grand National Assembly (the socialist Romanian parliament) and more than 40 per cent of people's councils (local legislative bodies) in late 1989 (Foreign Broadcast Information Service 1989: 70). In the last pre-revolutionary cabinet, six of thirty-seven members were female, some of whom were responsible for policy areas previously understaffed by women such as finance and justice (*Radio Free Europe Research* 1989: 40–1). Although superficially impressive, the campaigns to promote women's participation in politics and at higher levels in the economy were mostly symbolic and tended to emphasize those areas identified as of special concern to women (Fischer 1985: 120–37; Nelson 1985: 152–67).

While it is true that work environments were made more accommodating to women's needs, such as a dramatic growth in childcare facilities (Moskoff 1981: 391–7), the Ceauşescu regime did not substantially alter prevailing patterns of household duties in which maternal and conjugal responsibilities subjected women to 'double' and 'triple' burdens (Buzatu 1988a: 79–88; Moskoff 1982). Indeed, beginning in 1966 when all but therapeutic abortions were banned, Ceauşescu's pro-natalist policies and their attendant emphasis on the 'socialist' family undermined women's economic equality and the homogenization of gender roles as advertised by the regime (Kligman 1992: 366–99).

Romania's economy experienced significant restructuring over the decades under communism. Table 4.1 presents this restructuring with respect to the proportion of persons employed in various branches (industries) of the national economy at the beginning of each decade from 1950. The data are produced through monthly reports from counties and enterprises that were collected and prepared by the Romanian Department of Statistics, an agency analogous to the Department of Commerce in the United States. As a note of caution, the data are subject to the same non-reporting and inaccuracy-in-reporting problems which exist in any figures of this type. While the degree of error is unknown, the error was probably small before 1990 when Romanian society was closed and reporting procedures highly standardized and routinized. Post-1989 data are likely to contain more error given the social, economic and political upheaval occurring after the fall of Ceauşescu.

Table 4.1 shows a considerable shift away from a heavy concentration in agriculture (74.1 per cent of all employees were in agricultural-related occupations in 1950) and to greater concentration in all other industries. It

Table 4.1 Distribution of employees across branches of the national economy, 1950–90 (%)

Branch	1990	1980	1970	1960	1950
Industry	37.0	35.5	23.0	15.1	12.0
Construction	6.0	8.3	7.8	4.9	2.2
Agriculture	28.2	29.4	49.1	65.4	74.1
Forestry	0.4	0.4	0.2	0.2	0.2
Transport	6.0	6.1	3.6	2.4	1.9
Communication	0.9	0.8	0.6	0.4	0.3
Trade	6.3	6.0	4.3	3.4	2.5
Municipal service housing & other non-productive services	4.9	3.8	3.1	1.5	0.7
Education/ cultural art	4.2	4.2	3.7	2.7	2.3
Science and scientific services	1.2	0.9	0.5	0.4	0.2
Health protection, social assistance and physical culture	2.8	2.7	2.3	1.6	1.1
Administration	0.6	0.6	0.7	1.2	1.7
Other	1.5	1.3	1.1	0.8	0.8

Source: *Anuarul statistic al României 1991/Romanian Statistical Yearbook 1991* (n.d.: table 3.1).

should be noted that the figures in the table for agriculture are artificially low. Agricultural workers who were salaried and worked on state farms were excluded from the data. In 1990, 2.5 million agricultural workers do not appear in the table because of this method of classification. None the less, the percentage of persons employed in industry increased from 12.0 in 1950 to 37.0 in 1990. At the same time, noticeable increases were seen in construction (2.2 to 6.0), transport (1.9 to 6.0), trade (2.5 to 6.3), and municipal services (0.7 to 4.9) over the five decades. Underlying these observations is the decline in the proportion employed in agriculture (74.1 to 28.2). Despite the decline of agricultural employment, the percentage of Romanians employed in agriculture is high by the standard of developed nations. By comparison, less than 3 per cent of the US labour force is employed in agriculture.

Along with this economic restructuring, there has been a rapid rise in the number of women who are employed and a significant shift in the branches of the national economy in which they are employed. Table 4.2 presents data on employment shifts by branch and sex from 1970 to 1990. Unlike Table 4.1, these data exclude small, single-owner/family enterprises. Unfortunately, it was not possible to obtain data that would have made the two tables directly comparable.

From 1970 to 1990 the percentage of all employees who were female

Table 4.2 Number of employees by sex in branches of the national economy, 1970–90

Branch	1990		1980		1970	
	Number ('000s)	Percentage female	Number ('000s)	Percentage female	Number ('000s)	Percentage female
Total	7,902.4	41.8	7,368.5	37.2	5,036.6	30.2
Industry	3,818.5	44.0	3,466.4	40.3	2,130.9	30.6
Construction	604.5	14.7	768.9	11.5	655.2	7.9
Agriculture	555.8	24.3	472.6	16.1	343.5	11.9
Forestry	40.4	22.5	39.5	17.2	19.7	8.1
Transport	609.4	13.3	601.0	10.3	343.9	7.8
Communication	97.2	55.2	79.9	50.7	56.4	45.2
Trade	636.0	63.7	616.2	57.6	426.6	46.5
Municipal services housing and other non-productive services	442.7	37.0	334.7	33.0	260.2	27.7
Education, culture and art	443.2	65.6	420.0	64.8	357.8	60.3
Science and scientific services	133.3	43.7	98.3	42.5	46.2	39.0
Health protection, social assistance and physical culture	303.9	75.3	281.1	74.5	224.8	69.2
Administration	64.5	45.1	61.6	36.9	67.5	31.0
Other	153.0	50.3	128.3	46.5	103.9	41.5.

Source: *Anuarul statistic al României 1991/Romanian Statistical Yearbook 1991* (n.d.: table 3.8; *Anuarul statistic al Republicii Socialiste România 1981* (n.d.: table 61); *Anuarul statistic al Republicii Socialiste România 1971* (n.d.: table 58).

increased by nearly 50 per cent. While several branches were still male- or female-dominated, marked shifts away from single-sex domination occurred. For example, industry (30.6 to 44.0), construction (7.9 to 14.7) and forestry (8.1 to 22.5) all showed considerable increases in the proportion of total employees who were female. At the same time, two branches became even more female-dominated over this time period, namely, education (60.3 to 65.6) and health (69.2 to 75.3).

While it is impossible to deny the social and economic changes wrought by Romania's communist regime, the question remains as to how lasting these structural changes may prove. Development and modernization did not save a regime which depended for its legitimacy on a cynical manipulation of nationalism and village traditions, and for its longevity on a sinister and omnipresent secret police.

Under socialism the educational and economic opportunities for Romanian women expanded rapidly, yet within the Romanian family changes in the role of women occurred at an imperceptibly slow pace. The result was that women bore double and triple burdens. The status of women may have changed superficially, as evidenced by greater female participation in the industrial and professional workforces, and by symbolic political activities; but even those who promoted social, economic and political 'homogenization' of gender roles pursued draconian pro-natalist policies which perpetuated the traditional burdens of women. In retrospect, the expansion of opportunities for women was balanced by the increased burdens forced upon them, leaving them, one might argue, little, if at all, better off than their grandmothers. When communism collapsed, the values which the despised regime had espoused, including those concerning women, were uncritically rejected and replaced by a combination of Western and traditional values that reversed some of the advances made by women under socialism.

In sum, there are several competing forces affecting the workforce status of women in Romania today. When the communist government was overthrown in 1989, a cultural vacuum was created. Ceauşescu and his predecessors had failed to obliterate many elements of traditional Romanian culture, including those which limited women's public roles. Not yet accepting Western values and rejecting communist ones, Romanians fell back on tradition even as they professed their 'Europeanness'. These rediscovered, and markedly unmodern, values emphasize the traditional female roles as wives and mothers at the expense of those public roles for which socialist education had trained them.

A SOCIETY IN TRANSITION (1989–PRESENT)

The Romanian 'revolution' of December 1989 started with a confrontation between government security forces and supporters of an ethnic Hungarian Protestant pastor, Laszlo Tökes, in the south-western city of Timişoara in the ethnically patchworked region of the Banat. Among the most vexing problems facing the post-revolutionary governments have been the long-standing ethnic, religious and social divisions of Romania.

Among the first acts of the National Salvation Front was its promise to scrupulously observe both the existing, but heretofore ignored, national guarantees of minority rights and similar provisions in the Helsinki Agreements. At first the collaboration between Hungarian and Romanian revolutionaries was close, but as Hungarian communities began to exercise their rights and as electoral politics in Romania and Hungary began to exploit nationalist and irredentist sentiments, the ethnic truce collapsed. Violence erupted in Tîrgu Mureş in mid-March 1990 between Hungarians seeking to establish separate Hungarian schools and nationalistically inspired Romanians. Less violent clashes followed in other Transylvanian locations. Hungarians demanded cultural and educational separatism while Romanians were willing to tolerate only autonomy. Politically, ethnic Hungarian priorities are well represented by the Hungarian Democratic Union of Romania which, in the two post-revolutionary parliamentary elections, has garnered about 7 per cent of the votes cast, closely reflecting the proportion of ethnic Hungarians in the Romanian population.

The revolution did not stem the tide of ethnic German emigration to a reunited Germany. Perhaps as many as 100,000 ethnic Germans, one-half of the total, left Romania in 1990 and most of the rest professed a desire to follow suit (Rady 1992: 148). The German government facilitated emigration. Since the 'revolution', a number of Jewish synagogues and cemeteries have been vandalized and anti-Semitic rhetoric has come to pervade the nationalist press. Still, in the late Chief Rabbi Moses Rosen, the small Jewish community had an articulate and internationally well-connected spokesperson. For the first time since 1954 Romanian Gypsies were allowed to organize and to publish their own newspapers and periodicals. While fragmented Gypsy party lists did not do well in the May 1990 and the September 1992 parliamentary elections, and while anti-Gypsy violence has been reported, representatives of the more than 250,000 'Romi' have access to political processes from which they had been hitherto barred.

With the fall of the Ceauşescu regime, the persecution of religions and their believers virtually ceased. The major denominations were even given access to state-run television. Under the politically supple leadership of Patriarch Teocist, the Romanian Orthodox Church has reasserted its primacy as the national church despite campaigns of proselytization by both the Roman Catholic and Protestant denominations. In their search for renewing values, Romanians often turn to the Church which, as often as not, espouses a traditionalism inimical to expanding economic and social opportunities for women.

Educational reform was among the first issues addressed by the National Salvation Front after the December 1989 revolution. The education budget was doubled. Institutions of higher education were given autonomy. Educational administrations were democratized and curricula were depoliticized. The 'depolytechnicalization' of secondary education was promised. Properties of the defunct communist youth organizations were handed over to the Ministry of Education. On 12 May 1990 the government promulgated an education law which codified many of these decisions; started a process of reinstating curricularly broad secondary education; made provisions for substantially enlarged post-secondary admissions; and modified a 1978 law pertaining to schooling in minority languages. However, as the post-revolutionary years unfolded, it became apparent that in order to meet the needs of the emerging market economy, the educational system would require extensive and expensive restructuring and reformation (World Bank 1992c: 77–102). Re-establishing curricular legitimacy, replenishing and re-invigorating depleted and demoralized faculties, rewarding genuine academic achievement, providing acceptable minority education and finding the means to pay for educational reform in post-revolutionary Romania's crippled economy remain the government's policy priorities.

Among the first legislative decisions of the National Salvation Front were the relegalization of abortions and the legalization of other contraceptive methods. While availability of birth control remains problematic, the birth rate has declined, and attention has turned to the horrible consequences of Ceauşescu's pro-natalist policies – AIDS in children, neglected handicapped orphans and a scandal-ridden adoption system (Kligman 1992: 402–18).

Clearly, there has been a great deal of change in the social and workforce status of women since 1930. Many of these changes parallel trends seen in the remainder of Europe and in the United States, though currently Romanian women comprise the majority in some professions that are male-dominated in the West (e.g., physicians). Post-1989 economic, political and cultural change has created an environment of uncertainty with regard to the status of women. Kligman (1992) has identified a movement towards what she refers to as 're-traditionalization', or the return to traditional values, family and religion, which for some will redefine the place of women as in the home (see also, United Nations 1992b: 69). On the other hand, events of the last five decades have created a momentum that will prove a serious obstacle in redefining the role of women in this way. Several trends can be identified that point both negatively and positively toward the notion that Romanian women will become 'full partners' in economic and social matters.

On the negative side, rising unemployment over the last two years has affected women far more than men. Of the more than one million persons unemployed in October 1993 (9.2 per cent of the workforce), 55 per cent (575,384) were women (*România liberă*, 19 October 1993). While it is not yet clear if and to what extent unemployment will rise in the future, women are likely to bear the brunt of its effect, being forced even more into informal sectors of the economy where their skill and educational backgrounds are not fully utilized. Even when employed, women are negatively impacted by increasing salary differentials by industry; the worst two fields, health care and education, being the most asymmetrically female (*Tineretul liber*, 30 July 1993).

Other indices of economic deterioration do not bode well for women either. The GDP for Romania *declined* by 15 per cent between August 1992 and August 1993 (Slay 1993: 54), and it is likely that women will suffer disproportionally from this decline because of their current workforce status, and because of the resurgence of more traditional views about the place of women in Romania. The privatization of state-owned businesses proceeds and the creation of new private businesses goes on. The role of women in these endeavours is not clear. While no data yet exist that provide clear indicators of the role of women in privatization, the authors have visited and worked with dozens of private businesses in Romania. In our experience we have found few that are female-owned, and few where at least one of the principals is female. Most often, when a woman is found to have a significant role in a private business, it is because she is the wife of the owner.

There are other indicators of economic distress. For the reasons stated above, we believe these forces will adversely affect women more than men in the next few years. While industrial production grew in the 1980s, albeit slowly, production declined after the fall of Ceauşescu (*Anuarul statistic al Romåniei 1991/Romanian Statistical Yearbook 1991* n.d.: table 18.14) and continues to decline. Inflation is extremely high, 220 per cent in 1992, and there is little indication that it will decline in the near future (Slay 1993: 54). A $900 million trade deficit is forecast for 1993, a substantial increase over the previous year (Foreign Broadcast Information Service 1993: 34). Together, these figures illustrate the precarious position of the Romanian economy, and women are most at risk to the effects of these economic uncertainties.

Overall, during the communist regime women held low-skill, low-wage jobs in labour-intensive industries. It has been argued that these sectors are most likely to be affected by the type of restructuring currently underway (United Nations 1992b: 7–9). Before the fall of Ceauşescu, women accounted for 80 per cent of all people earning the minimum wage and 2 per cent of those at the highest wage levels (United Nations 1992b: 12). Problems for women are exacerbated by the lack of representation at the top of decision-making organizations. In the early 1990s, all of the government's 23 ministers were male. Only one of the 59 state secretaries was female. Out of 397 deputies in Parliament, 22 were women. There were 119 senators, and one was female (United Nations 1992b: 64). The Romanian Constitution of 1991 guaranteed equal rights and duties of citizenship for all Romanians of both sexes (Article 4) and stipulated equal pay for equal work for women (Article 38) (*Constituţia Romåniei/The Constitution of Romania 1991*: 64, 76). Communist era labour legislation remains in force but the most important post-communist economic and commercial laws do not specifically guarantee women equal treatment (United Nations 1992b: 65). Women's interest groups have been organized and publications for women are part of the avalanche of post-communist print media (United Nations 1992b: 66–7). However, the women's movement, such as it is, is fragmented and thus far politically ineffective. Politicians pay lip service to women's rights and participation but, if President Ion Iliescu's opinions are representative of the post-revolutionary élites, such acknowledgements are based not on the notion of human equality but of women's special 'feminine sensibility' which adds 'an element of equilibrium' to political life (*Tineretul liber*, 15 July 1993). While such patronizing attitudes may anger feminists, they probably reflect prevailing political culture more accurately than those proposed by the communists.

On the positive side, recent trends in regard to educational training should eventually enhance the status of women. In particular, the presence of women at universities and in the professions has caused both men and women to begin to challenge the traditional views of the role of women in society. In addition to providing training and status, Romanian education has helped to redefine the role of women away from traditional subservience and towards an equal partner status. Education stands as the most significant barrier to the 're-traditionalization'.

More promising, the pro-natalist policies of the 1960s, 1970s and 1980s have been abolished. In the last years of these policies women had begun to adhere to a low-fertility norm. Birth rates have actually declined since 1989 and are projected to decline significantly between now and the turn of the century. In fact, there are few historical precedents for a country to return to higher fertility norms after having experienced low fertility for some time. Low fertility norms run counter to 'traditional' female roles and indirectly enhance the status of women in the workforce.

While economic problems may adversely affect women in the short run, there is a great deal of long-run potential for an expansion of women's opportunities. Privatization, in the form of the creation of new enterprises and the transformation of old ones, presents opportunities for women both as owners and managers. There is a general lack of business and management knowledge and experience, which does not disadvantage women any more than men. Business start-up costs and attendant risks are minimal. Therefore, opportunities for female entrepreneurs exist, particularly in small service and manufacturing businesses.

In the short run, we believe that democratization and marketization in Romania will have a negative effect on the workforce status of women. Women are simply too vulnerable to an economic restructuring that is creating negative growth and high unemployment. In fact, a substantial degree of progress made during the communist years will be lost as the economy wrenches along searching for a form that realistically matches Romania's resources, culture and national goals. Many Romanians are finding strength and comfort in the rediscovery of a culture that historically held a very narrow view of the role of women in society. Though the resurgence of some traditional values will not result in a return to the society of 1946, in many ways progress, however superficial, has been halted. In particular, there is cause for alarm as some national leaders express concern about the low current fertility rates and how these low rates negatively affect the 'vitality' of the nation. If Romania follows the lead of some Eastern and Western European nations, pro-natalist policies will re-emerge.

In the long run, the outlook is better. A system that provides nearly equal access for both sexes to higher education is producing thousands of university graduates who will be the private and public sector leaders of tomorrow. The reformation of the economic system, particularly the creation of small businesses, will provide work and ownership/management opportunities which were denied to women in the past.

NOTE

1 The authors would like to thank Dr Paul Michelson, Jackie Lynch, Alin Ceobanu and Adriana Gafency for their assistance in the preparation of this manuscript. Dr Michelson provided us with many sources that are difficult to secure outside of Romania.

5

THE EFFECT OF ECONOMIC
AND POLITICAL REFORMS ON
SOVIET/RUSSIAN WOMEN

Patrice C. McMahon

INTRODUCTION

Gorbachev's rise to power in the mid-1980s had a profound effect on Soviet society and initiated a new era for Soviet women. Economic restructuring and the need to scale back the workforce, along with rising social conservatism, have challenged women's 'dual function' as mothers and workers. Political reforms reinforced these challenges, since they have reduced the little political power held by women. This essay addresses the consequences of the multi-dimensional economic, political and social destabilization on Russia's female population.[1]

Since the origin of the current situation can be traced to the legacy of communism, the next section briefly addresses the position of women in the Soviet Union. Its purpose is to establish women's inequality despite over seventy years of propaganda which claimed that women's oppression had been resolved by the communist revolution. The second section examines the position of women in the workforce and public life in the late 1980s. It also identifies the difficulties women faced as a result of economic and political reforms. The third part of the paper lays out the threats and opportunities currently facing Russian women as their economy grapples with marketization and their country grapples with political pluralism. At present, it is extremely difficult to construct a comprehensive and reliable picture of the future facing Russia's female population. None the less, it appears to be a future with ever-increasing challenges.

WOMEN IN THE SOVIET UNION:
HISTORICAL BACKGROUND

It was Engels (1973) who developed the foundations of socialist theory regarding the liberation of women. He theorized that if women could work outside the home while domestic work and childcare were socialized, their oppression would be eliminated and communist society would bring about

59

equality between the sexes. To the disappointment of many, equality remained an elusive ideal in all socialist states. Not only did Engels overestimate the extent to which greater participation in the workforce would alter relations between individuals, but the Soviet Union, like its satellite states in Eastern Europe, proved that it lacked the commitment necessary to transform traditional stereotypes. Soviet dedication to women's liberation vacillated according to the economic needs and national objectives of the state.[2] Extensive research by Lapidus (1977, 1978) found that the failure of the Soviet experiment with egalitarianism was due to three main factors – the ambiguous legacy of Marxism, which focused on class rather than gender; the country's model of economic development; and the Soviet pattern of political authority.

Early on there were indications that politics and the mobilization of women into the workforce were, in fact, issues separate from women's liberation. Lenin himself recognized that many male communists regarded agitation and propaganda work among woman with suspicion, either because they considered specific women's sections unnecessary or because they felt that women's work had nothing to do with Party goals. The rise of Stalin and the outcome of World War II made it even more apparent that the Party saw women as potential economic and political resources to be manipulated according to changing state requirements. Women were encouraged to work outside the home and were theoretically guaranteed equality in public life; simultaneously, the government launched a campaign to strengthen the family as the 'fundamental social institution' (Lapidus 1978: 236). In fact, the government flaunted the inconsistencies inherent in its dual emphasis on larger families and women's increased obligations in the workforce by propagating the image of the socialist superwoman. According to this view, the ideal female laboured during the day in the factory, nurtured her family in the evening, and somehow managed to contribute to the goals of society by attending Party meetings and representing women's groups. Thus, the implicit meaning of women's liberation came to mean increased responsibilities on all fronts rather than deliverance from traditional toils.

Soviet women not only worked extensively in the home, which undoubtedly hampered their upward mobility in the paid sector, but they also experienced overt and subtle forms of discrimination by their colleagues and superiors. Throughout society, but especially within the Communist Party there was a reluctance to put women in positions of authority. While Khrushchev mentioned the Party's trepidation over putting women in higher positions, no real debate emerged concerning their status in society. It was not until the Brezhnev period that the state recognized the 'double burden' women experienced; but rather than focusing on ways to overcome these conditions, it sought only to ease the difficulties of everyday life by narrowing wage differentials (Lapidus 1978: 228).

The Soviet Union continuously asserted that they were reconstructing the society, but as in other aspects of the communist experience, reality was remarkably dissimilar from planned objectives. The persistence of traditional gender stereotypes, and the inability of the state to genuinely socialize domestic work and childcare, prevented women from significantly improving their status. By the late 1980s, almost 80 per cent of women in the Soviet Union were active participants in the workforce, a figure higher than any other country in Western Europe or North America, except Sweden. None the less, despite its loyalty to equal rights and its ability to increase the number of women in higher education and in scientific and technical fields, Soviet women were not any more successful than women in the West in reaching positions of power (Rendel 1981; Janova 1992).

Comparative studies of socialist and non-socialist countries have found that women's representation in decision-making positions in industry remained minimal. In the 1970s approximately 4 per cent of working women in the United States workforce were managers, officials or proprietors; and in the United Kingdom female managers never exceeded 1 per cent of all managers in the country. Yet in the Soviet Union, as throughout the socialist bloc, women were less successful in achieving leading positions in the economy. While representing over 50 per cent of the workforce, only 0.5 per cent of managers or directors were women (Wolchik 1981).

Politically, women's representation in the Soviet Union is often over-estimated. The relatively high percentage of women in parliament since the 1950s should not be taken as a sign of real political power. While comprising approximately 30 per cent of parliament throughout the 1980s (see Table 5.1), women were poorly represented in leading positions of the Communist Party, the real source of political power. During the post-war era women never achieved more than 4 per cent of the seats in the Central Committee of the Communist Party and few women have been included in Soviet governments. In 1986, women made up 4 per cent of the Central Committee, a number similar to women's decision-making authority in the United States and the United Kingdom (Browning 1987: 21). However, these women were often awarded a place in the Central Committee merely because they represented the 'ideal communist female' and not because of their commitment or experience in politics.

THE GORBACHEV ERA

In 1985 Mikhail Gorbachev announced an economic reform policy to modify the socialist economic system. *Perestroika*, or reconstruction, was a recognition on the part of the Soviet leadership that it was necessary to reverse the economic crisis plaguing the country since the mid-1970s. Gorbachev's analysis of the ills facing the Soviet economy was radical, especially in light of previous reform efforts. He argued that the root problem facing the Soviet Union was its particular form of socialism, a socialism which neglected the human dimension of organizing production. His ill-defined agenda focused

Table 5.1 Women in parliament (Lower House): an East–West comparison

Country	1980(%)	1985(%)	1990(%)
Austria	9.8	10.9	10.9
Belgium	7.5	7.5	8.5
Denmark	23.4	26.2	30.7
Finland	26.0	30.5	31.5
France	3.6	5.7	5.7
Germany*	9.8	9.8	20.5
Greece	3.3	4.3	4.3
Iceland	5.0	15.0	20.6
Ireland	4.0	7.8	7.8
Italy	8.4	7.3	12.8
Luxembourg	13.5	14.6	13.3
Netherlands	13.3	16.6	25.3
Norway	23.8	34.4	35.8
Portugal	6.8	6.4	7.6
Spain	6.8	6.3	13.4
Sweden	26.4	30.9	38.1
Switzerland	10.5	11.0	14.0
United Kingdom	2.9	4.3	6.3
USSR	32.9	32.9	20.3

Source: (Janova 1992: 117).
* After reunification.

on two main areas – democratizing economic institutions and introducing market elements into the economy. To achieve these goals, Gorbachev embraced the notions of openness and democratization.

These policies were designed to accelerate socio-economic development through greater efficiency. The reforms were gender-neutral, and simply sought to link wages to productivity and eliminate unprofitable industries. In fact, the plans for the Party, as outlined in the 'Fundamental Direction of Economic and Social Development of the USSR for 1986–90 and up to the Year 2000', envisaged better working conditions for all workers as well as the improvement and systematization of worker training and retraining, especially for women (Gruzdeva and Chertikhina 1987–8). The new economic plan also included various strategies for improving the condition of working women by increasing the wages of workers in public education and initiating programmes that would decrease domestic burdens. These latter programmes attempted to decrease children's illnesses, increase childcare facilities, and locate childcare services closer to the places where women worked.

Like most segments of society, women greeted Gorbachev's vision of change and new thinking with enthusiasm. To a great extent openness and democratization provided women with small, but nevertheless important, benefits as well as a sense of hope. For the first time since the 1930s debates were allowed on rape, contraception and prostitution. The new environment also facilitated objective research on women's issues and the development of independent women-only groups. Yet, like other segments of the population, women quickly became disappointed with the outcome of reform.

Imperceptibly, economic alterations became a full-blown systemic transition; lacking, however, was an overall conception of the final outcome. In 1985 the Soviet GNP grew by less than 1 per cent; and while it increased 4.1 per cent in 1986, by 1990 growth turned negative, with output declining by 3.7 per cent (Kotz 1992). Deterioration of the economy intensified, rather than relieved, women of everyday responsibilities; longer lines, food shortages and price hikes left women with little time to enjoy their new-found freedoms.[3] Appropriately summarized, the Gorbachev period 'revealed, condemned and deplored, but it had not delivered' (Buckley 1992: 7).

As the economy worsened, and as social problems became more acute, conservative forces made the tenuous position of women in a changing environment even more precarious. Frequently male politicians, looking for an easy solution to cutting back the workforce, heralded a new era of women's liberation – one that would free them from their jobs and return them to the home with their children. At the same time, the Gorbachev government betrayed its unwillingness to protect women from the backlash of conservatism and uphold women's rights. In his book, *Perestroika – New Thinking for Our Country and the World* (Gorbachev 1987), the Soviet leader suggested that the way to deal with the social problems stemming from a weakening of the family was to return women to their 'purely womanly' mission.

Women in the workforce

Since the 1940s women have comprised approximately half of the Soviet population and workforce. This does not mean, however, that no gender differences existed with regard to wages and employment. On the contrary, throughout Soviet history women have occupied a relatively narrow band of positions and have remained in lower and mid-level positions. These horizontal and vertical divisions within the Soviet workforce have greatly influenced women's salaries and decision-making potential. Compared with Western countries, Soviet women had made great strides in penetrating traditionally male-dominated sectors of the economy; the majority, none the less, remained in a narrow band of sectors such as light industry, education, commerce and the health fields. As indicated in Table 5.2, female workers dominated in white-collar positions. Yet, the strong emphasis placed on heavy industry and military strength meant that these 'feminized' sectors were less renumerative than the preferred sectors, which coincidentally were dominated by men. Occupational differences between women and men greatly influenced earning potential, and women's average salaries were approximately one-third lower than men's (Rimachevskaya 1991: 31).

Table 5.2 Female percentage of all workers

Sectors	Female % of all workers	% of total female workers
Industry	48	30.0
Agriculture	40	6.0
Forestry	18	0.1
Construction	26	6.1
Transport	25	4.0
Communications	71	2.0
Commerce	80	13.0
Information/computing	82	0.4
Other material product	47	1.0
Public utilities	52	5.0
Health/social protection	83	10.0
Education	79	13.0
Arts	55	0.4
Culture	75	2.0
Science	53	4.0
Banking/insurance	90	1.0
Administration	67	2.0
Total	52	100.0

Source: Fong (1993).

Table 5.3 examines the Soviet economy by sector or branch, and by wage level and gender composition. It confirms that the higher the percentage of women in a sector, the lower the average salary in that sector. These horizontal divisions within the workforce point to an important structural reason for lower salaries among women – women are highly concentrated in low-paying, non-productive spheres of the economy.

Further insight into women's status can be gained by examining the vertical structure of the Soviet workforce, which left female workers at lower and mid-level positions. As a result, substantial differences between men's and

Table 5.3 Average monthly wages in 1989 by economic sector

Branches	Monthly wages (rubles)
National economy	240.4
Industry	263.7
Agriculture	233.5
Construction	316.9
Transport	287.7
Trade and non-production services*	187.1
Health and social protection*	163.3
Education*	175.5
Culture*	136.2

Source: Rimachevskaya (1991: 32).
* More than 50 per cent of the employees in this sector are female.

women's salaries exist even within sectors. For example, in heavy industry female salaries are 63 per cent of men's salaries, in light industry 70 per cent, in education 64 per cent, and in health and medicine 67 per cent (Fong 1993: 15–16). In 1990 women represented over half of all engineers, economists, accountants and medical workers, yet they represented just 7 per cent of the top administrators. Even in the most 'feminized' sectors of the economy, such as education, where women represented close to 75 per cent of those employed, the directors were often male. Studies conducted in 1990 and 1991 confirm that there were levels at which women were entrusted as supervisors, but once a certain plateau was reached few women rose to the top. A good example of the career ceiling imposed on women is found in education. More than 83 per cent of primary school directors were women; yet, the percentage of female directors drops by almost a half in elementary schools, and falls to 39 per cent in middle schools, although the gender composition of teachers at these levels does not change significantly (Fong 1993: 13).

In all sectors of the economy, women in the Soviet Union experienced the 'glass ceiling' syndrome and were under-represented in positions of power relative to their share of the workforce. The inability of women to become high-level decision-makers was clearly not due to inferior education. In fact, among individuals in the workforce, women were more educated than men. Table 5.4 confirms that in 1989 a higher percentage of female workers had completed higher and secondary education. Yet, in 1991, of men with higher education or specialized secondary studies, 48 per cent were engaged in managerial duties compared with 7 per cent of women with similar skills. In this respect, women have been adversely affected by economic and political reforms; while the proportion of women among heads of enterprises in the Soviet Union peaked at 11 per cent in 1985, it has been on the decline ever since (Mirovitskaya 1993a: 45).

Table 5.4 Education level of Soviet workers in 1989 (%)

Level of education	Male workers	Female workers
Higher and secondary	91	93
Only higher	14	16
Specialized secondary	19	30
General secondary	37	30
Incomplete primary	20	16

Source: Fong (1993: 13).

There are three interrelated reasons for the bottom-heavy pyramid structure of the female workforce, all of which relate to the nature of Russian society itself. The first and most obvious explanation for the inability of women to reach high-paying positions is outright discrimination. Despite decades of communist egalitarianism, Russian society has, in fact, remained a bastion of patriarchy. Research by Malysheva (1992) explains the failure of Soviet egalitarian philosophy by pointing to an incongruence between Soviet progressive legislation, inspired by intellectuals at the time of the revolution, and the traditional patriarchal Russian society. According to this perspective, throughout the Soviet period the dichotomy between these two forces remained largely ignored. Consequently, relationships between men and women were characterized by the latter's strict subordination and obedience to men rather than by equality and partnership. Instead of altering people's perceptions of gender roles, the imposition of alien concepts only served to preserve traditional Russian values. Unlike the West, the Soviet Union's drive for modernization was not accompanied by the natural evolution of women's consciousness. As a result, men and women both became confused by government-imposed dictates and legislation, and they continued to embrace traditional roles in the home.

In the workplace, historical and cultural traditions translated into institutional bias against female workers. Since the 1930s Soviet law incorporated gender distinctions into labour legislation. In doing so, it reinforced women's femininity and made their position in the workplace fragile. The 'Lists of Jobs Banned for Women' was meant to prevent women from engaging in physically demanding or hazardous duties. In reality it appears that such legislation prevented women from obtaining positions which often included training in technical equipment and which usually came with higher pay. It often did not protect or prevent women from working in dangerous conditions; approximately one-third of Soviet women who were employed in industry worked under conditions deemed hazardous, and more than four million Soviet women worked in conditions that did not meet national safety standards (Mirovitskaya 1993a: 45).

Discrimination in the workplace can help to explain why women have been relegated to lower positions, but social factors come into play as well. If Malysheva's research is correct, and the basic relationship between men and women did not change during the reign of communism, women's careers (whether willingly or unwillingly) had to be negatively affected by the conscious choices they have made in order to assume domestic responsibilities. The 'double burden' of working in the paid sectors as well as taking care of the home and children led many women to prefer work that was closer to home, less physical and included fewer responsibilities.

The economic crises in the late 1980s expanded the scope of women's domestic burdens; not the least of which involved waiting in lines and obtaining affordable foodstuffs. In 1990 the average Russian woman spent approximately 35 hours per week on housework and childcare and 38 hours in paid employment; throughout the week, women spent nearly 48 hours more than men on housework and childcare each week (Fong 1993: 19). In rural areas, where homes often lack modern conveniences, such as sewer systems or electricity, women are believed to work approximately 8 hours a day on domestic chores in addition to 7 hours at the state farm compared with men who work 2 hours at home and 7½ hours outside the home (Mirovitskaya 1993b: 27–30).

Finally, women's inability to reach high-level positions was also due to the fact that in the former Soviet Union career advancement was often linked to skills rather than education. Up to age 24 wage differences between men and women were approximately 15 per cent; in later years the gap increases substantially, by almost 50 per cent (Mirovitskaya 1993a: 36). Thus, as women marry, few are likely to improve their skills and advance professionally. While no comprehensive research has been done as to why fewer women participate in training programmes, investigations conducted throughout the 1980s confirm that approximately two-thirds of married women did not improve their professional skills, suggesting that women's other duties prevented them from taking advantage of career advancement opportunities (Fong 1993: 14).

In the last phase of communist rule, the marginalization of women in the workforce and their return to the home became the unofficial answer to the resolution of both economic and social problems. From 1985 to 1987 more than 80 per cent of all labour cutbacks were made at the expense of female workers; and in 1989 and 1990, women comprised approximately 60 per cent of those who had lost their jobs (Mirovitskaya 1993a: 45). In most cases the state sought to discourage women from working by extending maternity leave for new mothers or by replacing full-time work with part-time positions with flexible hours. In many instances, women were attracted by the notion of extra time off to spend with their families and to forage for affordable products. However, the failure of the economy to provide adequately for its citizens has meant that women's labour is an economic necessity for most families.

Women and politics

As the first country to constitutionally guarantee equal rights for men and women, the Soviet Union placed a great deal of emphasis on women's position in public life. However, the significant presence of women in society did not translate into important decision-making positions. Since the 1950s, the percentage of women in the Supreme Soviet of the USSR has fluctuated between 23 and 32 per cent. At lower levels, such as territorial, regional and village soviets, women comprised approximately one-half of all deputies. Yet, despite women's seemingly impressive contributions to public life, their political functions were limited to traditional female interests, and they were largely absent from the higher echelons of decision-making bodies. As in other socialist countries, 'the law of increasing disproportion', which characterizes the representation of minorities in organizational structures, follows for women in politics. As the importance of the office increases, the proportion of women declines. Thus, women in the Soviet Union were better represented in local bodies than in national ones and were more often found in the deliberative organs than in the executive organs of the élite. In socialist countries this has meant that women were better represented in symbolic positions than in more effective positions.

The political reforms initiated by Gorbachev had two immediate consequences for women's political activity – an overall drop in the number of women in official political organs, and the emergence of less institutional forms of political participation, such as social initiatives and women's groups. The 1988 electoral law, which introduced the partial elimination of quotas, brought a substantial decrease in the number of women elected to national and local offices in the 1989 elections. Women deputies to the Supreme Soviet were reduced by almost half, from 33 to 16 per cent, and women accounted for only 3–7 per cent of the representatives to republican and local soviets. This outcome suggests that not only were women less likely to stand as candidates for public office, but they were not seen as attractive candidates because of their gender. In fact, many voters expressed the opinion that women were the 'least desirable' candidates (Buckley 1992: 60–1).

Women's low profile in government must partly be attributed to their relative position within the Communist Party. In 1989 women comprised 53 per cent of the Soviet population, but accounted for just 29 per cent of Party members. In response to questions about the ability of the political system to incorporate women, Soviet citizens tend to blame women themselves for not getting more involved; survey respondents considered them either uninterested in politics or too passive in Party organizations. Yet, a study of women's political functions in the Party reveals that women were most often recruited for positions involving either indoctrination or 'consumer welfare services', but were virtually denied access to positions relating to national security or foreign relations (Moses 1977: 349).

CHALLENGES AND OPPORTUNITIES FACING RUSSIAN WOMEN IN THE 1990s

The August 1991 coup in the Soviet Union forced President Gorbachev to relinquish power. It also led to the break-up of the Soviet Union and the emergence of an independent Russian state. Upon assuming office, President Yeltsin, along with his coterie of young advisors, pressed for the intensification of Russia's transition to an open and free market economy. Initially unfettered by political opposition, the newly elected president undertook a programme based on four interrelated pillars: (i) the macro stabilization of monetary, finance, and fiscal conditions to curb inflation; (ii) the liberalization of prices; (iii) the privatization of state-owned industries; and (iv) the reform of the country's legal system, political bodies and banking system.

In any state undergoing a radical transformation, women and men both confront enormous risks and uncertainty. In light of their experience in the late 1980s, women are undoubtedly one of the most vulnerable groups (along with the elderly). The three most serious problems for Russian women will be unemployment, decreases in social welfare entitlements, and a resurgence of social conservatism that is bent on fully restoring Russian patriarchy.

In theory, ongoing structural changes in the economy could prove beneficial to women as the emphasis on heavy industry is replaced by the development of a service sector. Females in these 'non-productive' sectors would have a great deal to gain from the increased need and the greater prestige of white-collar positions. On the other hand, they may be forced out of positions in previously feminized sectors such as banking, economics, and finance, which are considered attractive and lucrative in capitalist systems. Moreover, the future of the Russian economy relies on a strong and expanding private sector, and women are far more reluctant to participate in this high-risk sphere. As a leading businesswoman confirmed, Russia's legal system does not prevent women from starting their own businesses, but women are more fearful of getting involved with what was not so long ago considered the 'black market'. In addition, they lack business connections and have little access to the start-up capital that is necessary to move independently into the private sector.[4]

Research conducted in St Petersburg in 1992 suggests that women are indeed more pessimistic and fearful about the marketization of the economy. In a study of 4,500 individuals aged 20–50, between 11 per cent and 20 per cent of women found the transition to the market economy 'unacceptable' compared with between 4 per cent and 6 per cent of men in the same age-group (Lehmann, forthcoming). As expected, older and less educated women (as well as men) were more attracted to the state sector and found the transition to the market economy unsatisfactory.

The unemployment picture in Russia during the last three years has justified women's fears for their future in a capitalist economy. Unemployment, virtually absent prior to the economic and political reforms, began to rise in early 1992. Of the 1.1 million unemployed workers seeking jobs during the first six months of 1992, 39.5 per cent were men and 60.5 per cent were women. Of those obtaining positions during this period, 36 per cent were men and 23 per cent were women (Fong 1993: 18–19). By the end of 1991 female workers comprised approximately 70 per cent of the registered unemployed. By the spring of 1993 women made up close to 80 per cent of those counted as out of work. Of these women, 25 per cent have degrees in higher education and 33 per cent completed technical school; 9 per cent of these women are single mothers.[5] According to all reports, a 'typical' unemployed Russian citizen is a middle-aged, professional woman with some higher education or at least secondary education (Gendler and Gildingersh 1992: 57–8).

Middle-aged, educated women will have a difficult time finding suitable employment, especially in an environment where foreign and domestic firms alike have begun advertising job openings according to gender and age. Newspapers in Russia are filled with job advertisements seeking 'young and pretty girls' to become secretaries and personal assistants, and on occasion sexual relations with the boss are implied (Pankova 1992: 6). In one newspaper a female reader remarked that in the new Russia a job for women essentially means that she is also a woman of easy virtue (Shlapentokh and Marchenko 1992: 45f). Without the threat of party reprisal, and with the virtual elimination of any policies to promote female employment, women have little recourse against such abuse.

During the Soviet period, women's obligations in the paid sector were made more bearable by a generous system of paid maternity leave, extended leave for mothers with young children, and other benefits. However, legislation from 1990 to 1992 transferred the responsibility for financing such benefits from the Social Insurance Fund, or the government, to local enterprises. For a profit-oriented company that is forced to finance the costs of maternity leave and other benefits for female employees, the incentives are obvious – don't hire women or don't provide the mandatory benefits. Moreover, changes within the social welfare structure will be exacerbated by society's desire to throw off the vestiges of communist thinking in all spheres. As a state no longer dedicated to egalitarian goals, women's rights will likely be shelved behind other pursuits.

Despite the dismal prospects for women in the 1990s, social awareness of problems specific to women continues to grow. The advent of political and social change in the Soviet Union in the 1980s inspired a nationwide programme to further the advancement of women. To a great extent, the institutions currently representing Russian women have not changed since the Soviet Union's collapse, but they have received assistance from numerous women's groups. The activities of some 300 women's organizations throughout Russia are not limited to Moscow and St Petersburg, as some might expect; in small towns around Moscow, Siberia and along the Volga River, women are reacting to the challenges of the market economy and political liberalization through various social organizations.

Based on interviews and observations in Moscow and St Petersburg, five types of Russian women's organizations can be identified: conservative, independent, professional, self-help and feminist (though the distinctions are not always clear). Of these groups, the two that hold the most potential for affecting women's advancement within the government and masses are independent and conservative groups. Among independent women's groups, the Moscow Centre for Gender Studies within the Russian Academy of Sciences maintains an unchallenged position. Inspired by its current director, Anastasia Podsadskaya, the Centre has assumed a number of responsibilities and interests since 1990. With approximately thirty researchers and activists, its projects include consciousness-raising and grassroots networking, political training, consulting and academic research. The Centre is known in Russia and abroad for its successful efforts in 1991 and 1992 to organize the Independent Women's Forums held outside Moscow (in Dubna) under the slogan 'Democracy Without Women is no Democracy'. Over 500 participants at the conference adopted a platform entitled 'Nezhdi' (Don't wait) which articulated four broad goals for women's advancement in Russia – economic independence for women, social and political empowerment, a women's information bureau, and research on women's position in society. The Second Independent Women's Forum, entitled 'From Problem to Strategy', was organized to provide women with more concrete information on politics, women in business and women's organizations.

The members' ability to articulate the most urgent needs in society and generate grassroots support has made the Centre for Gender Studies the organization of choice for international and foreign bodies interested in assisting Russian women. But as expected, women at the Centre feel over-burdened and, at times, frustrated with their growing responsibilities. As Director Podsadskaya admits, the Centre has essentially outgrown its initial function as a purely research unit and it must begin the process of dividing its functions and clarifying its status.[6] Legally, it is a government-sponsored research centre which cannot accept outside funding for social projects carried out by its research associates. Therefore, in the near future the Centre will be divided into three smaller groups with more narrowly defined interests, although it is likely that they will work closely with each other.

Conservative women's organizations are those with close ties to government organs, either because of their position during the Soviet period or because of their current affiliation with government organizations. Undoubtedly, the most influential member of this group is the legal successor to the Soviet Women's Committee – the Union of Russian Women (UWR). Although the Union is no longer accepted as the sole repository of conservative interests and is continually challenged by independent groups, its well-developed infrastructure throughout the country and its close contacts with foreign governments makes it (possibly) the most powerful group currently representing Russian women. UWR has undergone a radical evolution from a communist-inspired and -controlled institution to an autonomous coalition of members. Despite these changes, many women's organizations are still sceptical of UWR's intentions and are unwilling to work closely with its members. Its ties to the former Soviet structure as well as its unwillingness to see itself on the same level as newer women's groups continues to make it an unappealing base for a future women's movement.

Undoubtedly, programmes to help women adapt to the new economic environment are urgently needed. And small groups are surfacing almost weekly throughout the country in response to this need. Radio Hope, which claims to be 'Russia's only all-women's radio station', runs weekly programmes for women and advertises job opportunities throughout the former Soviet Union. In 1994 Russia may be home to three Women's World Bank affiliates (in Moscow, Siberia and St Petersburg), which will seek to develop financial support and training programmes for women entrepreneurs.

CONCLUSION

If the Central European experience with post-communist development is any indication of what Russian women will face, their future will probably be a mixture of short-term obstacles but long-term benefits.

On the one hand, further moves towards a market economy mean that women will not only be the first targets of unemployment, but will also suffer from a lower re-employment rate than men. According to reports from the United Nation's Commission on the Status of Women and the Committee on the Elimination of Discrimination against Women, the economic reform processes in the former Soviet bloc are eliminating the advantages that women gained under the communists and further damaging their current status. Moreover, the Central European trend of an absolute decline in the number of women in national politics[7] foreshadows the likely social impediments Russian women will face as the government renounces its quota system, which reserved a certain percentage of parliamentary seats for female politicians.

On the other hand, the transition from communism to democratic pluralism has not been entirely negative for women in Central Europe. The emergence of strong, articulate female leaders as well as budding women's movements in these countries suggests that with the pluralization of society and genuine competition in the political arena, women could gain in the long term.[8] In this regard, the situation in Poland is highly relevant. Although the number of female politicians has declined in absolute numbers in the post-communist period, their presence in public life has increased significantly. In addition to electing Poland's first female prime minister, two out of the three speakers in parliament were women. The creation of a Women's Parliamentary Caucus in 1991 is also an important sign that a women's consciousness is emerging in post-communist Poland.[9]

In light of the communist legacy and the post-communist precedent in neighbouring countries, Russia's female population is gradually mobilizing its resources to challenge the suggestion that a return to pre-communist, traditional society is possible. While no unified women's movement has emerged, the presence of research institutes, economic networks and consciousness-raising/feminist groups provides some hope that women will be able to combat the negative consequences of Russia's transformation.[10]

NOTES

1 Technically, 'Russian women' refers to women in Russia after the 1991 coup and break-up of the Soviet Union, while 'Soviet women' refers to women before the

break-up. However, since Russia makes up such a large part of the former Soviet Union, the two terms are at times used interchangeably in this paper.

2   An analysis of the composition of the Soviet workforce since 1920 confirms women's increased participation at economically crucial periods, while during stages of economic reform and relative growth their involvement decreased. Since 1919, the share of women in the Soviet workforce has been generally over 40 per cent – 1919: 40.9; 1924: 27.7; 1940: 38.9; 1945: 56; 1960: 47.2; 1970: 50.8; 1980: 51.2; 1985: 50.9; 1989: 48 (Rimachevskaya 1991: 14).

3   Since Russians spend approximately two-thirds of their total income on food, women have been entrusted with the task of enlarging the family garden and producing canned food items for sale in the open markets. In addition, women have had to rediscover talents, such as making clothes and handiwork, to supplement the family's income (Shlapentokh and Marchenko 1992: 6).

4   Author's interview with Olga Romashko in June 1993 in Moscow.

5   'The Position of Women in Russia', *Kommsomolskaya Pravda*, 26 May 1993: 2.

6   Interview with Anastasia Podsadskaya, June 1993.

7   In the first democratic elections women's participation decreased in all Central European countries – in Bulgaria from 21 per cent to 3.5 per cent; Hungary from 21 to 7; Czechoslovakia from 29 to 3.6; Poland from 20 to 13; Romania from 34 to 4 ('Norma Spodnic w Parliamentach', *Gazeta Wyborcza*, 16 July 1992: 1).

8   For information on the emergence of the women's movement throughout Central and Eastern Europe see Funk and Mueller (1993).

9   There are several examples throughout Central Europe of women being elected or nominated to prominent positions of leadership – in Bulgaria, Emilia Maslarova, Minister of Labour and Social Affairs; in Czechoslovakia, Havel's government appointed Olga Klimova as Ambassador to the US, Dagmar Buresove as Minister of Justice for Czech regions, and Vera Caslavstra as adviser on social affairs.

10   During the summer of 1993, the author interviewed more than forty leaders of Russian women's organizations, female politicians or academics in Moscow and St Petersburg. This research was supported by the American Council of Teachers of Russian (ACTR).

Part II

LESS DEVELOPED COUNTRIES

6

THE IMPACT OF ECONOMIC REFORMS ON WOMEN'S HEALTH AND HEALTH CARE IN SUB-SAHARAN AFRICA

Meredeth Turshen[1]

INTRODUCTION

Despite decades of international assistance, poverty is on the rise in Africa. The United Nations Development Programme (UNDP) estimates that Africa's share of the world's poor will rise from 30 per cent to 40 per cent, and that more than half the continent's population will live below the poverty line by the year 2000. Increasingly, poor women outnumber poor men in Africa. In addition, African women fare worse than African men in important areas. The Human Development Index for women is only half that for men in Kenya, the only African country for which data are available (UNDP 1991: 23, 17).[2]

Over the past decade, the International Monetary Fund has prompted and pressured countries in Sub-Saharan Africa to institute economic reforms. These reforms have reduced the public provision of health, education and other social services. For a number of reasons, the cutbacks have affected women more adversely than men. First, African women were poorer than men when the reforms were enacted (World Bank 1990:31), and the poor rely more heavily on public services than those living above the poverty line. Second, poor women are more vulnerable to the inflation, social conflict and uncertainty which structural adjustment policies tend to increase (Bienefeld, cited in Elson 1992:32). Finally, more poor women than poor men live outside the cash nexus, mainly in rural areas, which excludes them from fee-for-service arrangements. Consequently, the loss of services provided by the government will mean the total loss of these benefits.

The economic reforms themselves are also gender-biased because they ignore the unpaid labour of women in the maintenance and reproduction of the workforce (Elson 1992:34) and they contain economic distortions (Palmer 1991:3). For example, structural adjustment policies assume that land is the scarcest resource in Sub-Saharan Africa. In reality, labour is more scarce than land in agriculture and women provide most of the farm labour. Critical moments in the agricultural cycle are planting and harvesting; but above all labour is needed for weeding, which is exclusively women's work. Lacking mechanical equipment, needing assistance and unable to hire labour, women use the labour of their children. The costs to maternal and child health are tremendous,[3] yet adjustment policies ignore the unpaid labour of women and encourage the misuse of this resource (ibid.: 135–7, 156).

The economic reforms in Sub-Saharan Africa have hurt women more because they rely more on social services. This can be traced to the biology of reproduction and to social arrangements that give women more responsibility for care of the young, the elderly and the ill. The loss of public services means that women are forced to spend more time providing such services for their family. They carry water farther, nurse sicker kin (ibid.: 144), search for informal credit arrangements, and stand in long queues to obtain 'exemptions' (Brand et al. 1993: 298).

This chapter focuses on the adverse impact of economic reforms on women's health and access to health care in Sub-Saharan Africa. An overview of the reforms in social services is followed by a detailed examination of privatization efforts, the role of non-governmental organizations, and the new World Bank model. The argument is that reductions in public spending for social services and poverty alleviation programmes impact women and men differently, both quantitatively and qualitatively. Reduced public spending affects greater numbers of women than men and has a more adverse impact on women than on men.

REFORMS IN SOCIAL PUBLIC SERVICES: AN OVERVIEW

African governments generally allocate a smaller share of their total spending to health care than European governments. In the 1980s, however, many Sub-Saharan countries accepted austerity measures, reducing public expenditures on social services in general and on health in particular (see Table 6.1).[4] Some governments virtually abandoned their historic role in the health sector. In Senegal, budget reductions led to shortages in hospitals and public health centres, the introduction of payment for consultations and medical care even for the destitute, and a freeze on the recruitment of doctors (Bathily 1989: 131–2). Other governments accepted various forms of international aid to help balance state health budgets. In some countries, these external sources of funds amounted to 80–90 per cent of total investments in the health sector (Waty 1993: 35).

In evaluating the impact of health reforms, two sets of indicators are commonly used – process indicators, which measure such changes as declining health service attendance after the introduction of fees, and outcome indicators, which follow long-term changes such as rising rates of illness and death.

Table 6.1 Central government expenditures for selected African and industrial countries, 1972 and 1990

Country*	Population mid-1990 (millions)	GNP 1990 ($ per capita)	Health spending 1990 ($ per capita)	Percentage of total expenditure							
				Health		Housing, social security, welfare		Education		Defence	
				1972	1990	1972	1990	1972	1990	1972	1990
Tanzania	24.5	110	4	7.2		2.1		17.3		11.9	
Malawi	8.5	200	11	5.5	7.4	5.8	3.2	15.8	8.8	3.1	5.4
Nigeria	115.5	29	9	3.6		0.8		3.6		40.2	
Burkina Faso	9.0	330	24	8.2		6.6		20.6		11.5	
Ghana	14.9	390	14	6.3	9.0	4.1	11.9	20.1	25.7	7.9	3.2
Central African Republic	3.0	390	18	5.1+		6.3+		17.6+		9.7+	
Zambia	8.1	420	14	7.4	7.4	1.3	2.0	19.0	8.6	0.0	0.0
Zimbabwe	9.8	640	42	5.5+	7.6	7.8+	3.9	15.5+	23.4	25.0+	16.5
Senegal	7.4	710	29	4.7+		9.5+		23.0+		16.8+	
Côte d'Ivoire	11.9	750	28	3.9+		4.3+		16.3+		3.9+	
United Kingdom	57.4	16,100	1,039	12.2	14.6	26.5	34.8	2.6	3.2	16.7	12.2
Italy	57.7	16,830	1,426	13.5	11.3	44.8	38.6	16.1	8.3	6.3	3.6
Australia	17.1	17,000	1,331	7.0	12.8	20.3	29.7	4.2	6.8	14.2	8.5
Netherlands	14.9	17,320	1,500	12.1	11.7	38.1	42.3	15.2	10.8	6.8	5.0
Austria	7.7	19,060	1,711	10.1	12.9	53.8	48.2	10.2	9.2	3.3	2.5
Canada	26.5	20,470	1,945	7.6	5.5	35.3	37.0	3.5	2.9	7.6	7.3
United States	250.0	21,790	2,763	8.6	13.5	35.3	28.2	3.2	1.7	32.2	22.6

Source: World Bank (1992b: 218–19, 238–9).
* Ranked in ascending order of GNP per capita.
+ Data for 1980 (World Bank 1993b: 258).

Structural adjustment policies do not affect these indicators directly because other, often pre-existing, factors intervene. Health, for example, can deteriorate through unbalanced or insufficient diet, which reduces resistance to disease. The World Bank's structural adjustment policies and the International Monetary Fund's stabilization programmes increased food prices. Several countries in southern Africa (e.g. Zambia and Mozambique) removed food subsidies, causing a real increase in food prices. In Mozambique, food prices rose 400–600 per cent; in January 1989, 1 kg of tomatoes or onions cost 5 per cent of an office worker's monthly wage (Loewenson 1993: 722). The increase in food prices caused a 'widespread deterioration in the nutritional status of children and pregnant and lactating mothers in both rural and urban areas. . . . Mothers are unable to buy enough food of the right type to feed the whole family, and in many cases priority in feeding is given to adult males' (Elson 1989: 68).

Zambia offers a case study of the complexities of evaluating health trends. A study of Zambian women and children reports reduced food consumption, especially of expensive foods like milk, meat and poultry – foods high in proteins critical to good nutrition (Muntemba 1989: 121–2). Some families reduced the number of meals per day from two to one. Increases in mortality and morbidity in both urban and rural areas were associated with a marked rise in malnutrition, which underlies deaths attributed to acute respiratory diseases, measles and other infections. The study concluded that many factors, including such structural reforms as de-controlling of prices, created a severe health problem in Zambia (see Chapter 7).

Health reforms have resulted in two major trends. Government policies have shifted provision and financing to the private sector, thereby privatizing health care delivery. They have also increased the use of non-governmental and private voluntary organizations to deliver health care.

PRIVATIZATION

In 1987, the World Bank attributed the general deterioration of financial resources in developing countries to a slowdown in economic activity and, in some areas, to drought. The World Bank also observed that the decreased ability of governments to finance health care was affected by rapid population growth. To improve the situation, privatization was recommended in the following forms: (i) introduction of user charges in state health facilities, especially for consumers of drugs and curative care. It was argued that by making the 'rich' pay for curative care, governments would have more money to spend on community services and public health care for the poor;[5] (ii) promotion of third-party insurance schemes such as sickness funds and social security systems; (iii) promotion of private facilities, and donors' investment in upgrading private hospitals and clinics; and (iv) decentralization of planning, budgeting and purchasing for government health services. It was also suggested that governments use market incentives to motivate staff and to allocate resources (World Bank 1987: 1–15).

Many privatization schemes assume that the health sector can be treated in the same way as urban transport or telecommunications. Market conditions are, however, not the same as problems of imperfect information and are more pervasive in the health sector. The unique relationship between physician and patient offers scope for supplier-induced demand. Problems of cost inflation arise through the combination of a strong profit motive and opportunities for providers to determine the level of services supplied (as in the provision of unnecessary care, the overuse of surgery and the excessive provision of drugs).

The recommendation to privatize health care delivery in Sub-Saharan Africa is surprising because the government accounts for less spending on health care in this region than in Europe.[6] In Sweden and Norway, the public sector accounts for 90 and 95 per cent of health expenditures. In Zimbabwe and South Africa, however, government outlays account for 52 and 57 per cent of health spending, respectively (World Bank 1993a: 210–1).[7] African households already bear a substantial share of national expenditures on health (Cornia and deJong 1992: 268).

The World Bank's recommendations were universal – that is, they were applied regardless of a country's specific historic, social, political, or economic situation (including variations in the leading causes of death and availability of health services), and without reference to sex, age and race or ethnic composition of national populations. The World Bank made the same recommendations in Sub-Saharan Africa where, it acknowledges, health resources (especially personnel and skilled facilities) are meagre and levels of ill-health and poverty higher than elsewhere in the Third World (UNDP 1993; World Bank 1993b).

Even within the same country, the World Bank's recommendations will have different impacts depending on such factors as geography and gender. Between 50 and 90 per cent of the rural populations of Benin, Botswana, Burundi, Chad, Kenya, Lesotho, Malawi, Sierra Leone, Somalia, Sudan, Swaziland, Tanzania, Zaire and Zambia lived in absolute poverty during the 1977–89 period (UNDP 1993: 170). Poverty in Africa is increasingly feminized because of the rising number of female-headed households – 45 per cent of households in Botswana are headed by women, 29 per cent in Malawi, 22 per cent in Sudan and 28 per cent in Zambia (United Nations 1991b: 14). Female-headed households have less labour available; women have less access to credit for hiring labour or labour-saving devices, plant fewer acres, produce less, consume a higher proportion of their harvest, and have less left over for sale. As a result, their incomes are lower. Health reforms affect women and rural populations more adversely relative to men and urban residents.

Cost recovery through user charges

Studies find that charges for the use of health services deter patients who are at the greatest risk of disabling and fatal illnesses, the very patients for whom cost-effective interventions – both preventive and curative – are available (Creese 1990: 15). Women and children, the greatest consumers of health care, are particularly vulnerable to price barriers, especially where the rates of maternal mortality are already high. In Mali, where the maternal mortality rate is 2,000 per 100,000 live births and the under-five mortality rate is 225 per 1,000 live births, only 32 per cent of births are attended by trained health personnel. In Somalia, where the maternal mortality rate is 1,100 per 100,000 live births and the under-five mortality is 211 per 1,000 live births, only 2 per cent of births are attended by trained health personnel (UNICEF 1993: 80).[8]

In Zaire, where women and children make up 90 per cent of the health centre clientele (Schoepf and Engundu 1991: 158), a rapid increase in the price of health care sharply decreased the demand for curative services, prenatal visits and clinics for children under 5 years of age. In Ghana, use of all government health facilities dropped significantly after major increases in fees were instituted in 1985, and lower attendance rates continued in rural areas. In Swaziland, a 1984 policy decision to raise charges at government health units by 300–400 per cent led to an overall drop of 17.4 per cent in use. In Lesotho, following a 1988 increase in fees, attendance at all government facilities dropped appreciably at hospitals and health centres, and in mountainous areas the change appeared to be permanent (Creese 1990: 13–15). In Nigeria, 'with the introduction of hospital fees and increasing economic hardship at the household level, there has been a striking and sustained decline in attendance for antenatal care and for hospital delivery at the Wesley Guild Hospital' (Owa et al. 1992).

The negative impact on women can also be measured through the declining fraction of births in public maternities. Ogbu and Gallagher (1992) report that the number of births taking place in public maternities between 1975 and 1985 dropped in Botswana, Cameroon and Senegal. More births taking place at home has also contributed to increased sickness among infants. Women who give birth at home bring their sick newborns to hospitals for treatment of jaundice and infections of the umbilical cord.

Touré et al. (1992) justify user fees in Guinea (Conakry) on the grounds that very few drugs were available in health care facilities when health care was free of charge. Since fees were introduced, the availability of essential drugs has improved considerably. Elsewhere in Africa, however, fee systems yield on average only 5 per cent of operating costs; receipts are even smaller if collection costs are included (Creese 1990: 5; UNDP 1991: 67). Some studies show that the costs of fee collection are higher than the yield from user charges (Creese 1990: 5).

Cost recovery arrangements have also been plagued with administrative problems. Attempts to protect the most vulnerable populations – the poorest women and children – by waiving fees proved impractical. The Kenyan government, for example, was not able to easily identify those people who could not pay, and was thus unable to implement a system of exemptions. As a result, it abandoned the exemptions only eight months after instituting them in 1989 (Huber 1993). Zimbabwe has provided free health care since September 1980 to people earning less than ZWD 150 per month; that cut-off point did not change even though the minimum industrial wage rose from ZWD 85 to ZWD 202 by 1990, leaving fewer people eligible for the exemption (Chinemana and Sanders 1993: 321). Many eligible women are unable to comply with the requirement that their earnings be verified because they do not keep accurate records. This is true of the majority of women who work in the informal sector, many of whom are illiterate (Brand *et al.* 1993: 297).[9]

Small, hard-to-administer fees – as opposed to large, easy-to-administer taxes, such as higher taxes on alcohol and tobacco (Green 1991: 33) – can result in mismanagement and disappearance of the sums actually collected. Foster (1991: 1203) studied essential drug supplies in Africa and found that health service personnel pocketed surcharges for drugs in Cameroon. Where trained medical personnel are in short supply, a climate of profit-making in the health sector leads to the practice of patients paying government health service staff privately for services that are supposed to be free of charge (Brunet-Jailly 1991: 11; UNDP 1991: 65). Van der Heijden (1992) noted this practice in Uganda, where government health workers developed a range of economic survival strategies to supplement their token and often delayed salaries; the most common was informally charging patients for nominally free services.

Health reforms have resulted in community financing schemes, such as those used in the Bamako Initiative;[10] individuals, families or community groups make contributions to support part of the costs of health care. These schemes have exacerbated existing inequalities within communities (Abel-Smith 1988, cited in Creese 1990: 10), undermining claims for the redistributive effects of cost recovery through user charges.[11] Moreover, a community-based approach to the delivery of social services really means mobilizing the unpaid labour of women as volunteers in the provision of health care and social infrastructure (Elson 1992: 41).

In some countries such as Côte d'Ivoire, hospitals defray expenses by requiring patients to bring their own drugs, cotton, alcohol, surgical gloves and bandages (Guillaume 1991: 181). Given the chronic shortage of supplies in government stores, patients are making their purchases on the 'free' – that is to say, most likely, the 'black' – market at costs far above what the Ministry of Health would have paid if it bought in bulk through international tender. This practice is highly inefficient.

The promotion of user charges to recover costs generally assumes that the costs of health care are fixed. The little available research suggests, however, that it is possible to reduce costs by trimming the extensive wastage in staffing and pharmaceuticals. The government of Mali, for example, could save up to 40 per cent of its expenditures on drugs (Brunet-Jailly 1991); Mozambique saved 25 per cent of its pharmaceuticals budget by substituting generic drugs for brand-name medicines for the ten most widely used products (Cornia and deJong 1992: 261). Malawi's principal hospital could save 44 per cent of its recurrent (non-salary) budget by a series of simple management improvements (Creese 1990: 7).

Insurance schemes

Sub-Saharan governments are promoting a variety of insurance schemes, sickness funds and social security systems that would enable users to pay for health services. These policies include: (i) the promotion of supplementary private health insurance by encouraging better-off people to take out extra private insurance in addition to coverage by the public system; (ii) the promotion of voluntary health insurance, either public or private; (iii) financial arrangements to reduce risk such as reinsurance or stop loss provisions that would encourage the establishment of new private insurance companies; (iv) the provision of tax relief to all who opt for private health insurance; (v) permitting firms to opt out of compulsory social insurance if they provide a satisfactory alternative insurance scheme; and (vi) legislating compulsory health insurance for all firms with a minimum number of employees (WHO 1991: 9).

There is little experience with insurance in Africa. In South Africa, perhaps the most highly developed country in the region in this respect, only 8 per cent of the black population hold private health insurance as opposed to 85 per cent of the white population. Given the high unemployment rates and the predominance of the informal sector, it is unlikely that many more South African blacks can afford health insurance. The problems with insurance are well-known – insurance schemes generally raise the cost of health care, a counter-productive measure in countries with little money to spend on health. The World Bank admits that 'insurance programs in industrialized countries and in Latin America have undoubtedly contributed to rising health care costs' (1987: 5).

In countries with a small number of wage-earning jobs, sickness insurance benefits a tiny fraction of the population, usually a relatively privileged socio-economic group (Roemer 1987: 118; Brunet-Jailly 1991: 11). In Mali, for example, only 6 per cent of the population could benefit (employees and members of their families), mainly people in the capital city, whereas 80 per cent of the population is rural (Brunet-Jailly 1991: 13). Moreover, women account for only 16 per cent of the workforce in Mali (UNDP 1993: 151), so the number of women eligible in their own right is extremely small.

Insurance funds typically cover personal health services, whereas the majority of Africans are better served by public health interventions. The needs of so many suffering from communicable diseases are better addressed on a community-wide basis. The special problems and needs of women with tropical diseases have long been ignored in research and service programmes;[12] for example, the World Health Organization first addressed these issues in 1989. The choice of individual care over collective measures for the community involves high costs. In 1980, Burundi's population was under five million; yet health care and drug expenditures for 45,000 employed workers exceeded the regular budget of the Ministry of Health (Nkanagu 1985). A related reason for emphasizing public health in Sub-Saharan Africa is the high proportion of the population (49 per cent) under the age of 15 (World Bank 1993a: 289). Combined with high birth rates and high dependency ratios, these figures indicate the need for expanded maternal and child health care, which is normally part of the public health service.

Many social security systems compete with the government for personnel. Where resources are scarce, these independent and autonomous systems are wasteful and duplicative (Roemer 1987: 118).

Private drug sales, practitioners and facilities

The promotion of commercial drug sales, private professional services and non-governmental facilities dramatically affects the price of health care and therefore women's access to services.

Pharmaceutical supplies

Several agencies of the United Nations (UNCTAD, UNCTC, UNICEF, UNIDO and WHO) have devoted a great deal of effort to controlling the costs and quality of pharmaceuticals, in part because drugs can account for 40 per cent of a developing country's annual health budget. Over strenuous objections from the pharmaceutical industry, the World Health Organization recommends that: (i) governments centralize drug purchases at the national level or, in the case of countries with very small populations, at the regional level; (ii) governments order only essential drugs (about 200 in all), which facilitates bulk purchases of generic items and makes the government a more important buyer; and (iii) national governments take advantage of competition on the international market (WHO 1988; Dumoulin et al. 1991: 67). These policy changes represent an important advance over the former situation. Previously, pharmaceutical companies flooded the market with thousands of different brands of drugs, and hired sales people to visit each hospital and physician to take orders for brand-name drugs. The multi-national pharmaceutical industry has opposed every United Nations reform. It constantly introduces new ways to maintain its control over the market (Muller 1982; Chetley 1990; Kanji et al. 1992).

It is difficult to control private sector prices, and high prices deter the poor, especially poor women. In Burkina Faso and Mali, the price of French brand-name drugs in private pharmacies was set at 150–200 per cent of the retail price in France (ibid.). Extravagant prescription practices and the sale of expensive and unnecessary drugs were considerable problems in Nigeria, among other countries, before the adoption of essential drug lists (WHO 1991: 29).

The sale of drugs through private pharmacies and pharmacists also raises problems of urban bias in distribution. Foster notes that of a total of 542 pharmacies in nine French-speaking West African countries, 301 (56 per cent) were located in the capital city (1991: 1202). Because 70 per cent of the people of Sub-Saharan Africa still live in rural areas and because African cities still have greater numbers of men than women (a colonial legacy), the urban bias in drug distribution disproportionately affects women.

None of the private sector or cost recovery schemes deals with the fundamental problem faced by countries that do not produce their own drugs, namely the need for foreign exchange to import supplies (Creese 1990: 10). The shortage of foreign exchange is a consequence of the International Monetary Fund's fiscal reforms; it has caused a shortage of pharmaceuticals in most eastern and southern African countries. Women suffer from shortages of all drugs, including contraceptive supplies. They crowd distant hospital emergency wards because they know their local dispensaries have no drugs (Due 1991: 115–16).

Professional services

The introduction of user fees in the public sector makes private services more competitive with free public services. Governments are also supporting private practitioners through offers of training courses and drug supplies. African governments already subsidize the education of health personnel; a few recover some costs by requiring mandatory service of graduates. African medical graduates, however, can no longer count on government employment. As a result, there are many unemployed doctors in countries that have desperately high ratios of population per physician. These doctors may demand high fees to perform certain operations like abortions and clitoridectomies privately (N. Tubia, personal communication, 17 January 1994).

If more professionals open private practices, geographic inequities will increase because private practitioners tend to congregate in well-off urban areas, leaving poor and rural (largely female) populations without access to trained personnel. In Zambia for example, 100 per cent of the urban and 50 per cent of the rural population have access to health services; in Somalia, the percentages are 50 and 15, respectively (UNDP 1993: 155).

The maldistribution of doctors and nurses is well documented world-wide. In Senegal, virtually all dentists, 70 per cent of physicians and pharmacists, 60 per cent of midwives and over 40 per cent of nurses are concentrated in the Dakar–Cap Vert region, where less than 30 per cent of the population lives (World Bank 1987: 22–3). Only the government has the authority to redistribute personnel by restricting medical practice in well-served areas, for example, or by posting personnel to under-served areas; the private sector is driven by profit and services are not distributed on the basis of need.

Decentralization

The World Bank recommends that government health systems be decentralized to local units to improve efficiency. Under this plan, responsibility would shift from the centre to the periphery for planning and budgeting, for collecting user fees, and for determining how funds will be spent (World Bank 1987: 44). Control over education, training and investment in new facilities would remain with the central authority. The purpose of decentralization is to give managers incentives to generate fee revenue.

This scheme resembles the British colonial practice of district self-sufficiency in which local treasuries financed local services. Critics found it to be the basis of inequities and uneven regional development because districts with the poorest people could provide only the poorest services (Turshen 1984: 33–5).

Choosing the local district to manage health systems in Sub-Saharan Africa is also unfortunate. The World Bank sees poor management as a government weakness and maintains that the private sector has greater managerial expertise, a reason for switching to it. But the district level is notably lacking in managerial capacity and is less skilled at these tasks than the national government (Turshen 1989: 256–9; WHO 1990: 37–9).

NON-GOVERNMENTAL ORGANIZATIONS/ MISSION FACILITIES[13]

Non-governmental organizations (NGOs) and private voluntary organizations (the term NGOs as used here covers both types) are proliferating in Africa.[14] Their numbers recently doubled in Kenya and Tanzania, and there are fifty-nine operating in Swaziland, where the total population is 800,000. NGOs provide a significant proportion of health services in Sub-Saharan Africa. In Zimbabwe NGOs supply 94 per cent of services for the elderly (WHO 1991: 16); and in Lesotho they are responsible for 50 per cent of the country's hospitals and 60 per cent of its clinics. In Uganda and Malawi NGOs provide 40 per cent of all health services; and in Ghana they supply over 25 per cent of hospital care. In Cameroon church missions are responsible for 40 per cent of facilities; in Zambia missions offer health care to 35 per cent of the total population (DeJong 1991: 14).

The trend is to funnel more and more resources to and through NGOs. In 1986, an estimated $1 billion reached Africa in this way (ibid.: 3).[15] The trend to shift service delivery to NGOs is particularly important to women. Many relief agencies in the health field reinforce sex stereotypes by viewing women only in their domestic roles, as dependants with children or as pregnant or lactating mothers. Some NGOs reinforce patriarchal norms because they wish to appear sensitive to the local culture or because their ability to work successfully at the community level depends on it. 'They do not want to be accused of cultural imperialism by tampering with sex roles, roles that are enforced by family and community and thus are the most resistant to change' (Yudelman 1987: 181).

NGOs are said to be more flexible than state bureaucracies, but flexibility may be a euphemism for highly individual, even maverick or eccentric, approaches to health care. When governments are attempting to standardize treatment so as to maximize resources, flexibility amounts to anarchy, as Gloyd (1992) discovered in Mozambique. Flexibility is also a code word for operating from one project to the next, which leaves no room for institution-building.

NGOs are community-based, reaching into peripheral areas, but they do not always locate where they are most needed and they may duplicate government services (Cornia and deJong 1992: 270). The foreign staff of NGOs rarely speak the local language and may have little contact with the population. Female patients who cannot communicate with male doctors cannot participate meaningfully in their own treatment, let alone in the management of what ought to be a community facility. A preponderance of expatriate staff leaves NGO services dependent on donors. For example, only 30 per cent of the senior staff of church facilities linked through the Private Health Association of Malawi are Malawi nationals (deJong 1991: 11).

Intersectoral NGO programmes that are not specialized offer certain advantages over inter-agency rivalries and awkward mechanisms of inter-agency coordination that frequently fail.[16] The trade-off is that non-specialists are doing the work of specialists with little or no training. For example, after the famine in Sudan attracted a large number of NGOs, many relief officers chose to stay and work in the health sector, whether or not they had the appropriate health skills (ibid.: 12). NGOs' lack of expertise extends to poor documentation of projects, no evaluation of results and no contribution to needs assessments.

Finally, there is the issue of accountability, which is rarely strong where democracy is weak. The accountability of international NGOs is compromised by their tenuous relations with host governments. Foreign NGOs are accountable to international donors, not to the local populations they service. Few are held accountable by the national governments of the countries in which they operate.

THE NEW WORLD BANK MODEL

The 1993 World Development Report features the health sector and indicates that in some respect the World Bank has changed its policies. Taking account of criticisms about the inapplicability of a universal model, the World Bank distinguishes the needs of low-income countries from those of middle-income and formerly socialist economies. Stepping back from the recommendation to privatize all health care, the World Bank now advises governments to provide some health services for the poor. It suggests that those unable to afford this expansion turn to foreign aid, which will probably increase dependence on donors and give donors more control over the internal affairs of client states.

For low-income countries, the World Bank recommends a clinical package consisting of perinatal and delivery care, family planning services, management of the sick child, treatment of tuberculosis and case management of sexually transmitted diseases. 'Clinical' in this context means services provided by nurses and midwives, not physicians.

This package limits women's health care to services during childbirth, showing once again that women are valued only for their reproductive role. Governments will subsidize family planning services but, because little money is intended for clinical services, women will be given contraceptives without medical supervision, which is potentially dangerous. Sick children are the main beneficiaries of this package in keeping with the assumption that families will limit the number of births only after child mortality falls. The package includes the treatment of tuberculosis because the World Bank presumes that the recent rise in cases is related to the spread of AIDS (rather than to the spread of poverty or the breakdown of basic health services). AIDS also motivates the inclusion of clinics for the treatment of sexually transmitted diseases that are thought to accelerate the spread of HIV.

Although the differentiation of health reform packages on the basis of GNP addresses the fallacy of universal prescriptions, other faulty aspects of the 1987 recommendations have not been corrected. The World Bank still does not examine the interface between public and private sectors, the impact of privatization on the quality of public care, or the geographic distribution of services. The World Bank's policy amounts to a two-tiered system; good clinical care and environmental services for the rich, and second-rate care for the poor. Women will inevitably lose ground.

The 1993 World Bank report does acknowledge, for the first time, violence against women as a health issue. Domestic violence, rape, sexual abuse and genital mutilation are problems implicated in maternal deaths, miscarriage, low birth weight and sexually transmitted diseases (including AIDS), as well as in higher rates of mental illness, alcoholism, drug addiction, depression and suicide.[17]

The World Bank, however, stops at domestic violence. It does not consider the tremendous health impact of political violence on African women and children, who make up the bulk of civilians caught up in war, civil unrest and torture with their attendant deaths, disabilities, psychological stress and the destruction of health services (Zwi and Ugalde 1989). Indirect effects of violence also take their toll in decreasing food production and distribution, destroying families and displacing people. Refugees, 75 per cent of whom are women and girls, are especially vulnerable to violence, a major issue in Sub-Saharan Africa where the number of refugees is high.

CONCLUSION

The World Bank's policy to privatize public services increased poverty and made life harder for those whose access to health, education and other social services was reduced (Gibbon 1993). The policy was enforced in Sub-Saharan Africa despite the knowledge that 'the free play of market forces can generate levels of poverty that are socially unacceptable' (Cornia and deJong 1992: 258). The cumulative evidence presented in this chapter shows that the privatization of health care delivery has not improved the quality or quantity of health services in Sub-Saharan Africa. Rather, health care service has deteriorated and become less available. Because women have greater health care needs, especially during and after pregnancy, they have suffered most from the attempt to limit public provision of health care.

Women's ability to influence the health-sector reforms in their favour is hampered by several concomitant trends – the lack of political voice in government, the weakened state, and the new role of the Bretton Woods organizations in setting national policies at the international level.

The lack of women in government is not peculiar to Sub-Saharan Africa and, given their low levels of literacy, it is not surprising. Women are excluded from all decision-making jobs at the four highest levels of government in twenty-one African countries (United Nations 1991b: 31). In the mid-1980s, African women represented only 6 per cent of members in national legis-latures and only 2 per cent of cabinet members (Parpart and Staudt 1989: 8). The World Bank's education policies, which are similar to its health policies, reduce girls' chances for education and will perpetuate this situation for at least another generation (Jespersen 1992: 32–6). Although African women join organizations in large numbers, their impact on state policies has been minimal; nor has the creation of women's bureaux, women's ministries and women's wings of national parties wrested significant resources for women from the state (Parpart and Staudt 1991: 8–11).

This is not to suggest that women are only victims, as some studies devoted to the impact of economic reforms suggest. Poverty-stricken women struggle every day against the effects that austerity measures and structural adjustment programmes have on their lives (Daines and Seddon 1993). They have directed their protests at the state and in times of crisis they have succeeded in bringing about change. Nowhere in the literature, however, is there any suggestion that women have succeeded – individually or as members of movements – in influencing the provision of social services by the private sector. Women's illiteracy and lack of education reduce their ability to apply consumer pressure on private health providers to deliver better quality care at more affordable prices.

The World Bank's motivation for lending in the health sector is of special concern to women. In 1980 it expanded its role in health, stating that its presence in the health sector would help it to pressure governments to control population growth (World Bank 1980: 8). One reading of the World Bank's 1993 health policy document is that its purpose is to lower the population growth rate in Africa. To the World Bank, population control is the crux of sustainable development. Yet, African women have consistently found that their personal needs for family planning are not well served by national or international programmes to curtail population growth (Turshen 1991). Many women's groups have organized to articulate an alternative to Bank policies and present them to the decennial International Conference on Population and Development, to be held in Cairo in September 1994 (Women's Global Network for Reproductive Rights 1993).

The role of the state in economies reformed by the World Bank and the International Monetary Fund has changed. At a recent World Health Organization meeting (1991: 11), ministers of health and senior decision-makers from twelve countries concluded that changes in public/private responsibilities require a strengthened and expanded role for government, even if the share of the ministry of health in total health service provision is reduced. Yet the anti-statist tendencies in the World Bank and International Monetary Fund augur ill for the prospects of stronger government. The private sector exerts greater pressure on the government in a mixed system, making it harder for governments to implement national health policies (WHO 1992). The ability of governments to regulate private producers to behave in the interests of national health goals is not likely to be enhanced by cutbacks in public budgets. Decentralization further undercuts the ability of central governments to manage large units, such as hospitals, which already absorb a disproportionate share of national health budgets. Privatization curtails government access to the information needed for both regulatory and policy-making roles. The coordination of non-governmental organizations is a difficult undertaking for weakened health ministries.

The Bretton Woods organizations are now setting national policies at the international level, bypassing weakened states and lessening their importance. The mechanism used by the World Bank and the IMF is conditionality, the practice by which powerful institutions impose their agenda on weak governments as the price of international financial aid. Conditionality trans-forms policies once considered internal matters, such as subsidies on basic foods or funding policies for health and education, into international con-cerns, subject to outside influence if not outright control (Stoneman 1993: 87). The World Bank's influence in the health sector extends far beyond its own loan programme, which totalled $3.4 billion for loans to population, health and nutrition projects by June 1993 (World Bank 1993b: 168). The

World Bank's policies inform much of the current practice of many other donors, and its economic reforms have brought about a shift of health care provision from the state to non-governmental organizations – directly, by encouraging donor financial support for NGOs, and indirectly, by squeezing state resources and obliging consumers to patronize the private sector (Gibbon 1993: 16).

Will African women have greater success in influencing international policy than they have had in making national health policies more responsive to their needs? The World Bank's record on women's issues is not promising as judged by their latest annual report in which women are accorded only two pages under the heading of human resource development (1933b: 44–5). The World Bank's undemocratic structure, which is under attack by developing nations that want to change it to the 'one nation–one vote' system of the United Nations General Assembly, renders it especially resistant to outside pressure. Women's best hope is to make their voices heard in large international forums such as the Fourth World Conference on Women to be held in Beijing in September 1995.

NOTES

1 The author gratefully acknowledges a grant from the Rutgers University Research Council to collect the data for this paper. She thanks Pascale Brudon-Jakobowicz, Andrew Creese, Robert Emory and Joseph Scarpaci for generously sharing their resources, Mike Greenberg for his comments on an early draft, and Bea Vidacs for invaluable research assistance. An earlier version of this paper was presented at the Conference on Sustainable Development with Equity in the 1990s held in Madison, Wisconsin in May 1993.

2 The Human Development Index, developed by the UNDP, is based on estimates of life expectancy, adult literacy, mean years of schooling and wage rates.

3 Loss of weight during pregnancy and shortened spaces between births take their toll on maternal body stores. The health costs to children can be measured through low birth weights, prematurely reduced or terminated breast-feeding, and reduced washing and feeding of infants as well as other children.

4 In Madagascar, expenditures fell 24 per cent between 1977 and 1985; they fell 14 per cent in the Central African Republic in the 1982–91 period, and by 13 per cent in Zaire between 1980 and 1987 (Waty 1993: 34). Sahn maintains that 'spending in the three years before and after donor-financed adjustment programs began reveals no pattern of increase or decrease in real levels of total and social sector expenditures' (1992: 673). He also argues that population growth accounts for the fall in per capita expenditures. Jespersen's analysis (1992: 37) suggests that Sahn's choice of indicators is too insensitive and his time-frame too short to evaluate the trend.

5 This reasoning is faulty on a number of grounds. Personal health services are needed by the rich and the poor alike; if anything, the poor are ill more often and need more services. Further, because free preventive measures or routine screening for the early detection of disease are rarely available, poor people tend to demand treatment later in the course of an illness and require more intensive care. The dichotomy between preventive and curative is specious in dealing with diseases

such as tuberculosis, which require both treatment to reduce pools of infection and immunization to protect infants and children. In general, the health conditions common in poverty require this combined approach.

6 Consider the context in which the Bank proposes its agenda for reform of health service financing. In 1990, high-income countries accounted for 80 per cent of total global public and private expenditures on health services – about $1,900 per person. The United States consumed 42 per cent of the global total. Developing countries spent nearly 50 times less than the industrial countries, an average of $41 per person. In Africa, the median was $14 (World Bank 1993a).

7 The World Bank figures for the public sector include external aid in the government's share of total spending on health, which inflates the real numbers for Sub-Saharan Africa. For example, in 1991 the Mozambican government's share of public expenditure on health was 5 per cent; the donor community financed 95 per cent of the budget (Kazilimani 1993: 3).

8 Maternal mortality rates in the more developed countries are typically 12 per 100,000 live births and 98 per cent of births are attended by trained personnel; the under-five mortality rate averages 11 per 1,000 live births.

9 In Africa, the female literacy rate is only 34 per cent, compared with 56 per cent for males (UNDP 1991: 436).

10 The Bamako Initiative was adopted in 1987 by twenty Sub-Saharan countries with guidelines from WHO and UNICEF. The purpose is to provide decentralized, self-sustained primary health care in African villages. Communities share in the financing of local services by buying drugs above the wholesale purchase price; the proceeds are used to maintain supplies (UNICEF 1989b: 50).

11 It is argued that user charges could be a redistributive vehicle through taxing the rich and further subsidizing access to care for the indigent. The catch, according to Creese (1990: 16), is that fee income must be channelled into improvement in the quality and accessibility of services and priority given in the use of these resources by needy populations.

12 According to WHO (1990: 140), the tropical diseases are malaria, leprosy, schistosomiasis (sometimes called bilharzia or snail fever), filariasis (including elephantiasis and onchocerciasis or river blindness), African trypanosomiasis (sleeping sickness) and the American form called Chagas' disease, and leishmaniasis (including kala-azar which destroys visceral tissues).

13 This critique recognizes that the practices of NGOs range from those of Oxfam to World Vision and that the countries in which NGOs operate range from Tanzania to South Africa. The critique is not about individuals or particular organizations, it is about the NGO project in the context of economic reforms. This project is analogous to the role of missionaries in the colonial conquest of Africa.

14 According to Green (quoted in Gilson and Sen 1993: 5), six types of NGO operate in the health sector – religious organizations, international social-welfare groups, locally based welfare groups, unions and professional associations, non-profit specialist groups (concerned with occupational health for example), and non-profit prepaid health care plans like HMOs. This chapter's discussion concerns the first two groups: church missions and non-governmental international aid agencies like CARE.

15 Many governments subsidize NGOs, including parochial organizations; for some, this represents an extension of colonial practice. Subsidies take the form of relief from import duties, taxes and other financial obligations (DeJong 1991: 6).

16 Rivalry among NGOs is no better. The lack of coordination among NGOs and between NGOs and the ministries of health makes national health planning impossible.

17 Stewart (1992) reports that domestic violence and rape are serious social problems in Zimbabwe. Armstrong (1987), who studied the rape cases prosecuted in Swazi courts, concluded that the incidence of sexual assault is high, and that girls under 16 account for the majority of cases tried, but that conviction rates are very low. Rates of rape in South Africa appear to outstrip even those in the United States and have increased dramatically in recent years – the figures for 1988 are 34 rapes per 1,000 adult women in South Africa compared to 18 per 1,000 for the United States (Heise 1993: 177).

7

STRUCTURAL ADJUSTMENT, THE RURAL–URBAN INTERFACE AND GENDER RELATIONS IN ZAMBIA

Gisela Geisler and Karen Tranberg Hansen

INTRODUCTION

A number of stark images highlight the complex gender and class issues existing in Zambia. On the one hand, maize meal or used clothes are exchanged for rural women's labour and maize-meal coupons given to low-income urban residents; on the other hand, grain bags sit on living room floors and maize meal fills the freezers of well-off urban households (Geisler 1992: 121, 124, 129). These images call into question the IMF/World Bank structural adjustment programmes (SAPs) that were supposed to promote growth and turn around the declining economies of Africa during the last two decades. There is increasing evidence that, at least in Africa, the adjustment process is neither quick nor linear, and that market reforms have their limitations (Gibbon *et al.* 1993).

At a more theoretical level, two major criticisms have been directed at adjustment programmes advocated by international institutions, principally the IMF and the World Bank. First, exporting an economic model from the developed world to developing countries disregards local specificities and ignores important issues of income distribution. Secondly, directing macro-economic reforms principally on the agricultural sector assumes a sharp distinction between rural and urban areas that bear little resemblance to African realities. Given their Western orientation, it is not surprising that the IMF/World Bank have experienced difficulty in comprehending the social effects of SAPs, especially their gender ramifications.

Feminist critics of SAPs have argued that these policies contain built-in biases in favour of men (Elson 1991; Palmer 1991). Seeking to understand local responses to SAPs, they have called for analyses of how access to productive resources is obtained and how social institutions are structured, especially in gender terms (Moore 1988: 54–64; Whitehead 1990). It is necessary, they argue, to examine the extent to which women and men can place claims on resources within and beyond the household. As we illustrate

95

for the Zambian case, as long as men control productive resources (e.g. land, labour, tools, credit, housing, etc.), women's prospects are likely to differ from men's, the more so under conditions of economic pressure.

Finally, there is the issue of SAPs' spatial dimension. Urbanization has not been a major matter of discussion. When alluded to, the city is looked at as a disproportionate user of revenue, the seat of a bloated and corrupt civil service, and the home of a small élite bent on conspicuous consumption. Most SAPs target the rural areas where the majority of Africans live. But while Africa is the least urbanized continent, it has the fastest growing urbanization rate (Harris 1989: 176). Significant rural–urban interactions may thus cause SAPs to have substantially negative 'urban impacts' (Stren et al. 1992: 37).

In this chapter, we attempt to identify the economic effects of SAPs on women in Zambia. However, we recognize the importance of factors outside the realm of economics. Cultural norms, and assumptions of male authority and superiority, shape the social domain and cause work to have widely different gender implications regardless of whether descent is patrilineal or matrilineal. Across class, and in both rural and urban settings, a woman's access to productive resources is mediated through a man – her father, husband, brother or uncle. In marriage, men's attentions are uncertain as customary law does not obligate them to support wives and children. Support depends on the quality of the interpersonal relationship, especially on the husband's goodwill, since his income is not considered a common purse to which a wife has equal access. But while wives have no claim to husbands' earnings, husbands make culturally legitimated claims on their wives' time, work and in some cases income. In short, unequal power relations within households, and insecurities regarding men's support, affect the nature and scope of women's economic activities.

Focusing on Zambia, our discussion contributes to the ongoing debate about the effects of SAPs in two ways.[1] Demonstrating how SAPs impact gender dynamics in rural and urban production, we draw attention to specific social and cultural practices in Zambia that hinder their effectiveness. In addition, focusing on the historical links between town and countryside which current SAPs accentuate, we point out another problem area. Our chief concern is with married women rather than female heads of households whose vulnerable position has been well documented in the literature (Safilios-Rothchild 1985). Married women, we argue, experience additional problems because of the demands their culturally constructed relation to husbands place on their labour and output.

We begin with a brief overview of Zambia and its troublesome relationship with the IMF/World Bank. Drawing on observations from the Northern and Eastern Provinces and on urban case studies, we then discuss the rural and urban effects of SAPs, highlighting some of their interconnections. In conclusion, we argue for a more inclusive approach to development intervention, one that transcends the ways in which culturally defined notions of power turn women and men into unequal partners.

ZAMBIA – AN OVERVIEW

Zambia has one of the highest urbanization rates in Africa. Of a total population of nearly eight million, 42 per cent or more are urban. The capital, Lusaka, has doubled in size every decade since independence in 1964, and had an estimated population of one million in 1993. A long history of rural–urban migration helps to account for this, as does an annual population growth rate of 3.2 per cent over the 1980–90 decade (Republic of Zambia 1990: 6). There is some evidence of recent reverse migration from urban to rural areas mainly from the Copperbelt, where a declining mining industry has caused widespread unemployment (Republic of Zambia 1985: 10, 12, 17–9, 33). By the end of the century, more people are projected to live in Zambia's towns than in the countryside (UNDP 1993: 155).

Zambia's rural–urban migration was set into motion by British colonial policy. Until the post-World War II years, African migration to the growing mining towns on the Copperbelt and white commercial farms was restricted to male workers, who were forced to return to the rural areas upon completing work contracts. While colonial policy gave white farmers preferential access to land, extension services and attractive producer prices, it discouraged the development of African commercial agriculture until the 1940s. The economic policies of the post-colonial government have largely replicated this pattern of unequal access. Over 90 per cent of the country's export income is derived from mining. Agricultural policies favour a small group of commercial farmers (some of whom are white) at the expense of peasants who make up some 90 per cent of the rural population. The low priority given to the agricultural sector and to peasant production in particular, is exemplified by extremely small government budget allocations (4–8 per cent) to agriculture during the 1980s (Andersson 1990: 31).

Zambia's rural–urban disparities have narrowed in the wake of overall economic deterioration in the mid-1970s, created by the declining worldwide price of minerals as well as the oil crisis. Developments during the 1980s did not bring about recovery. The foreign trade deficit grew, the debt burden increased, and foreign exchange shortages constrained local production. The availability of basic services in towns declined, the infrastructure was not maintained, consumer goods were scarce and, when available, beyond the means of many town dwellers. Between 1980 and 1991, formal-sector employment declined from 23 per cent to 9 per cent of the total workforce (EIU 1992: 18). These figures hide large gender and class discrepancies. A 1986 workforce survey showed 4 per cent of all women and 25 per cent of all men in formal-sector employment, two-thirds of them in urban areas (CSO 1991: 27). And in 1990, the average formal-sector wage in real terms was only 40 per cent of its 1983 levels (EIU 1992: 19).

During this economic decline, the informal sector grew in significance as a provider of work, shelter and a variety of services. These activities involve several socio-economic strata and forms of work that are part of the overall Zambian economy.[2] They have no exclusive territorial basis, are conducted in public and private, in cities and in the countryside. They include a hetero-geneous set of activities, among them small-scale trade, repair work, artisanry, transport, building and services. Their chief commonality is that they are not legally established and thus not subject to state regulation (Sanyal 1991: 41).

According to a 1986 survey, more women than men worked in the informal sector: 42 per cent of all women compared to 40 per cent of all men in the rural areas, and 9 per cent of all women compared to 6 per cent of all men in the urban areas (CSO 1991: 27). These figures undoubtedly have increased during recent years, but the direction in which gender dynamics in the informal sector might have changed is not clear.

As family heads, men exercise much authority over the distribution of income within most Zambian households, regardless of class or geography. They choose which assets are to be allocated to household consumption, to the market, and to their personal needs. Although on average, rural Zambian women perform 75 per cent of all agricultural labour, and virtually all of the daily reproductive tasks (GRZ 1981: 29), men are in a position to determine what constitutes food and/or cash crop. A strict and distinctly unequal division of labour, in which women do the more arduous tasks such as planting, weeding, harvesting and processing of crops, makes their labour indispensable to market and subsistence production alike. When men's contributions to household consumption are insufficient, women seek to make up for the shortfall – rural women by performing agricultural piece-work, and rural and urban women by conducting informal-sector activities such as beer brewing or small-scale trade. Yet even the small earnings that women make from such work are subject to their husbands' control.

In many of Zambia's rural and urban households, food security is pre-carious even in the best of times. A combination of drought, increasing prices for food and agricultural inputs and shrinking employment opportunities have made the situation threatening in recent years. Few women have direct access to the formal market, many command only limited resources, and most have little control over their earnings. Meeting both household consumption needs and the demands of husbands is difficult, and in times of crisis, virtually impossible. In the struggle for access to scarce resources, women – and by implication other dependent household members – almost always lose out. The SAPs in Zambia, which we describe next, have had precisely that effect in many poor rural and urban households.

ZAMBIA'S ON-AND-OFF RELATIONSHIP WITH THE IMF/WORLD BANK

SAPs represent the latest in a series of economic and political interventions that have directly affected the material and social conditions of rural and urban lives in Zambia. After more than a decade of unsuccessful economic adjustment programmes under the government of Kenneth Kaunda, Zambia recently returned to the IMF/World Bank fold. The new and democratically elected government (1991) has been so faithful in implementing the IMF/ World Bank's measures that it has received positive responses from international finance organizations which describe Zambia as a 'model' and reward it with extensive financial support (*The Economist* 1993a: 48; Howe 1993: 31). The major elements of this ongoing effort towards stabilization and economic growth include the restoration of balance of payment, exchange rate devaluation, a reduction of inflation, liberalization of markets, the abolition of price and import controls, and privatization of state enterprises. The government is to reduce its budget deficits through retrenchment of public sector employment, wage freezes, the elimination of subsidies and the introduction of user fees. Sectoral rehabilitation is encouraged through agricultural diversification, especially by developing non-traditional export crops.

One of the more contentious issues in previous adjustments was the withdrawal of maize subsidies, which accounted for 17 per cent of budget expenditures in 1988 and an estimated daily cost of $500,000 by 1991 (*The Economist* 1991: 58). In fact, in 1987 the government abandoned a major adjustment programme scheduled with the IMF in 1983 after urban populations rioted against the withdrawal of maize-meal subsidies. A home-made adjustment programme was, however, put into effect which reinstated subsidies and price controls. This was abandoned in 1989 when the policies outlined above had been worked out with the IMF/World Bank. Like previous interventions, the new SAPs targeted a stagnant and inefficient agricultural sector that since independence had contributed only 13–15 per cent to GDP on an annual basis (Gibbon *et al.* 1993).

During 1989, price controls on all crops, except maize, had been lifted. Marketing of all agricultural products was liberalized, and subsidies on maize and fertilizers were greatly reduced. This led to substantial increases in the producer prices of some crops. Although the state-controlled producer price of maize was adjusted upward, it remained sub-economical and failed to keep up with the rising costs of agricultural inputs. Both producers and consumers were adversely affected by increased transportation costs, due mainly to price hikes for fuel and spare parts. Many peasants were forced to purchase their inputs at high costs and sell their crops at deflated prices. On the consumer side, the official price of maize meal doubled several times while its unofficial price in remote areas grew astronomically. Prices of other less vital goods, which were no longer state controlled, rose even more sharply.

In short, the supposed beneficiary of SAPs, the agricultural sector, suffered. The liberalization of markets was far from smooth. Cooperative Unions, which until then had been heavily subsidized as the sole marketing agents, were now starved for funds, and incapable of delivering inputs or collecting produce in remote areas. Private marketing agencies either did not emerge or failed to pay peasants the high prices they expected. Sharply rising interest rates further affected production and marketing. Much of the small amount of maize that was produced remained uncollected and rotted.

The vast majority of peasants were unable to obtain agricultural inputs, and found it difficult to grow enough for their own needs, let alone the market. As a direct consequence, maize production declined dramatically, falling in 1991 to 3.6 million 90 kg bags, substantially less than half of the country's own maize requirements. A serious maize shortage that year pushed consumer prices to such levels that increasingly larger sections of the urban population could not afford to buy sufficient amounts of food.[3] The situation for urban consumers was further aggravated by shrinking employment and wage freezes. As if this were not enough, the costs of essential services in both rural and urban areas were getting too high for many who now had to pay user fees in schools and clinics.

The 1989 structural adjustment package included a Social Action Program designed to cushion 'vulnerable' groups against the shocks of adjustment. One of its chief elements was a maize meal subsidization scheme in which coupons were distributed to low-income families. The scheme was of doubtful effect, partly because it targeted urban populations, and partly because eligibility criteria were so ill-defined, control mechanisms so rudimentary and corruption so widespread (Pearce 1989; Geisler 1992: 125). Last, but not least, attempting to identify some exceptional groups as 'vulnerable' ignored Zambian realities.

Poverty is deep-seated and widespread in Zambia. It affects the majority of households both in urban and rural areas. A large proportion of households relying on the informal sector in 1990 had incomes in the range of K400–700, much below the poverty line of K3,500 per month for a family of six (Prices and Income Commission 1990).[4] That year, a security guard in Lusaka earned K300–400 a month, and a nanny received as little as K120 per month (Banda 1991: 60).[5] In the rural areas, where 80 per cent of households were estimated to live below a basic needs level in 1980 (ILO 1981: xxi), the incidence of poverty has not lessened during the intervening decade. In the Northern Province, for example, where cash crop fields are small, peasants complained that a pair of shoes cost as much as their earnings from the sale of one 90 kg bag of maize; and transport to the provincial capital 80 km away where they could buy shoes cost even more. Many peasants lost half of the value of their crop on loan repayment (Geisler and Narrowe 1990: 30). It is no wonder that chronic child malnutrition is increasing: in the North-Western Province more than half of all children under 5 years old were classified as such in 1990 (Chipulu 1990).

The confidence that Zambians held in their new government wanes as they experience the effects of a 'slavishly' implemented reform programme that has not improved their living standards (Mupanga 1993: 37). Real GDP growth, which had been negative since 1989, declined 5 per cent between

1991 and 1992. Consumer prices in 1992 rose 160 per cent compared to 92.6 per cent the previous year. And Zambia's external debt increased to 262 per cent of GNP in 1990, up from 159 per cent in 1989 (World Bank 1992b: 264; EIU 1993: 3). No doubt the severe drought in the southern Africa region in 1992 contributed to the economy's poor performance. Since food takes up over half of household expenditures, reduction of maize subsidies and food price liberalization affects consumer prices, contributing to the growing rate of inflation.

Rural and urban populations have much to grumble about. In 1993, the price of maize meal had increased six times in just over one year, pushing it to levels where an average monthly wage could barely buy more than the monthly food requirement (*Africa South & East* 1993: 22). Peasants and commercial farmers consider the 1993 producer price of maize to be too low to make up for the sevenfold price increase of fertilizer the previous year. They have threatened to sell their maize crop locally rather than to urban areas or even to smuggle the much needed grain at higher profits across Zambia's borders (*National Mirror* 1993a, b).

With an estimated 18 million 90 kg bags, maize production in 1993 was a 'bumper harvest'. Yet it might not have reached the towns. Shortly before the onset of the rainy season a marketing disaster was predicted as only 2 million bags had been brought to storage (*Weekly Post* 1993). Three years after the liberalization of agricultural marketing, the private maize markets that are so central to SAPs were nowhere in sight. Having few profitable options to market their crop, peasants bartered maize by the tin in return for a used T-shirt or a cup of coarse salt, at values amounting only to a fraction of the producer price.

In terms of policy, the latest wave of SAPs may have shifted the emphasis from subsidization of urban consumption to agricultural production to some degree. Yet, their effects are not spatially discrete. As we demonstrate next, a number of parallel processes simultaneously increase the pressures to expand economic activities in both villages and towns, This, in turn, accentuates the already existing rural–urban interconnections (see below).

SAPS, GENDER AND CLASS IN ZAMBIA'S RURAL AREAS

Zambia's Fourth National Development Plan of 1989, operating in tandem with the latest SAPs, clearly identifies its goals: 'to turn the small scale and peasant sector into the main producers of staple food crops' (GRZ 1989: 90). Unfortunately, these goals have not been achieved; food production has further declined and the living standards of the majority of Zambian peasants have deteriorated. Perhaps less visible are the effects of these deteriorations within households – on the division of labour and more specifically on the erosion of women's small but exceedingly important areas of control, rights and their ability to feed and maintain their family.

Observations from the Northern and Eastern Provinces show that peasants' reactions to SAPs depended on the local farming systems and cultural practices. Regardless of such differences, however, poor peasants can no longer afford costly agricultural inputs, particularly fertilizer, causing maize production to decline. In areas where maize remained exclusively a cash crop that did not affect local dietary habits, the shift from maize to low input, high value crops was relatively smooth. But changes were more complex and more critical for peasants who both market and eat maize. And everywhere, women are suffering the greatest losses.[6]

During the 1980s, maize production had increased by 850 per cent in the Northern Province (Geisler 1992). The boom had little impact on the cultivation of staples, millet and cassava but may have eased the local adaptation to SAPs. One year after the liberalization of markets, entire villages had abandoned maize in favour of soya beans, which do not require fertilizer and were no longer subject to state-controlled marketing. The change, which amounted to substituting one cash crop for another, caused little controversy. Men were the undisputed 'owners' of both fields and crops. What did create conflicts was the fact that men also began claiming their wives' crops.

Mixed beans have long been an integral part of crop rotation in this region, and beans are both eaten and sold on a small scale to urban traders. The incomes were considered to be women's, for they were the 'owners' of that crop. Husbands might claim a part, but never all the money, and women used it mainly for household expenditures. Thus, the sale of beans constituted an important means for women to meet household needs. With the new economic liberalization the importance of beans grew. Their cultivation required no expensive inputs, was not particularly labour-intensive, and informal marketing channels were already in place. In 1989 bean production in the Northern Province increased 289 per cent compared to the previous year's 65 per cent (Geisler and Narrowe 1990: 129). If the trade in beans had been of limited importance previously, it now became a major source of cash, and therefore a domain that men felt entitled to.

Women realized that they were losing control over their assured source of income. The rising cost of essential consumer goods and services meant that they, rather than men, had to secure more money to keep the household together. Their chances of deflecting male claims on the source of their income would have been limited if the underdeveloped market had not played into their hands. Because of the growing volume of beans on the market, traders were strapped for cash and conducted their trade in kind. Salt, low-quality used clothing and occasionally school exercise books took the place of cash. That benefited the traders, who could exploit both the lack of established barter equivalents and the increasing value their barter goods attained in rural areas. It also served the interests of women, as

T-shirts and salt are less easy for men to divert from household consumption than cash.

Such small gains did not offset losses due to the rising cost of living and persistent male claims on women's earnings. Cash was still needed for what could not be bartered, such as clinic and school fees as well as for paraffin and soap. Beer brewing, one of village women's chief sources of income, turned less profitable. The market for home-brewed beer is restricted in general, and at a time of economic adversity the major customers, men, were less willing and able to pay for their beer.

As a last resort, women performed agricultural piecework for those who could still afford to hire workers. Wages for this work, previously performed for the most part by female heads of households who were unable to maintain their fields, have always been extremely low. Women receive only one-third of male wages and, unlike men, they typically choose to be paid in kind (Geisler et al. 1985: 17). With single and married women's growing dependence on piecework, wages fell even further. Consequently, women's ability to satisfy the needs of their children and, when married, to comply with the demands of their husbands, also declined.

While women in the Northern Province could rely on the food crops they grew to meet housekeeping needs, at least for a while, many women in the Eastern Province could not even maintain that small margin of security. Once hailed as the grain basket of Zambia, this province relied on maize both as a cash crop and a staple food. Here, the drastic decline of maize production was not a result of choice or of substituting a new crop. The overall decline of agriculture had direct bearings on household food security and consumption patterns.

While the number of maize growers in the Eastern Province fell by only 8 per cent between 1989 and 1990, both production and sale of maize on average halved, and no other crops showed marked increases (Geisler and Narrowe 1989: 36). Like beans in the Northern Province, groundnuts might have presented an alternative since this crop has a place in the farming system and is both consumed and marketed locally. The value of groundnuts rose sharply with the liberalization of the market and the crop was in high demand from private traders. Still, production declined by over 30 per cent in the first year of SAPs. This seemingly irrational response is explicable only in terms of a severe food and labour crisis that restricted household strategies. Groundnut cultivation and processing are among the most labour-intensive tasks and, significantly, they are women's work. Women had neither the money to buy groundnut seeds nor the time for cultivation and, last but not least, they had few hopes of retaining income from groundnut sales for household expenditures.

Peasant production of both local and hybrid maize for subsistence and markets relied heavily on the application of fertilizer. When the subsidy on fertilizer was removed, many households could no longer afford to purchase sufficient quantities to maintain previous production levels. Some households managed to grow hybrid maize for sale at the expense of food crops, while others avoided the costly input altogether, ending up without cash crops and greatly reduced quantities of food crops. In this way, the majority of households not only experienced a rapid decline of incomes from cash cropping, but their food production dropped below subsistence level. Yet much more cash was now needed to secure basic survival. The cultivation of food had become so expensive that it could no longer support a family throughout the year, and the larger quantity of purchased foods now needed had increased in price. Barely able to purchase enough food and fertilizer, many rural dwellers could no longer afford to buy other consumer goods that were not vital for survival. And parents could no longer afford the fees and uniforms their children required for school.

Women with child-rearing responsibilities were most severely affected. As more resources were needed, and husbands earned less or nothing, women could rely even less on male contributions to the household and had to find even more income in the limited informal sector that exists in rural areas. The acquisition of food for cash was crucial. Many women resorted to agricultural piecework, which does not ensure subsistence because it is casual and highly seasonal. Women's pay for piecework has long been much lower than men's (Geisler et al. 1985: 17). The greater supply of women offering to do piecework combined with the growing value of the goods women received as payment in kind caused a further decline in pay. The work required for one basket of unshelled maize grew from one to four days within one year. To make matters worse, some women had to accept a much lower remuneration in maize meal, either because they were too overworked to pound their hard earned maize themselves, or because their employers were short on maize (Banda 1991: 28; Geisler 1992). In 1990, earnings were so low in the Lundazi district in the Eastern Province as to leave the average household with only one meal per day.

To stretch their resources, some women accepted salt as pay, exchanging tiny quantities of this commodity for maize with households that still had some food reserves but could only afford salt by the pinch. Men were less affected by their wives' struggle. Many declined to perform 'women's work' on the fields which, in turn, were neglected because of women's piecework. Men did occasionally perform piecework even though the cash pay for male labour in this sector has not changed since 1987.[7] Even during acute food crises, wives complained of their husbands' continued demand for spending money.

These two regional examples show rural women's responses to the far-ranging problems caused by economic adjustment. This should not come as a surprise since adjustment policies are based on the premise that economic actors are able to shift resources from less to more productive areas without problems. The majority of Zambian peasants have never been able to accumulate productive resources and have precious little to fall back on. With new incentives, adverse reactions may be limited if households possess a resource base that remains relatively unaffected by the upheavals of SAPs. But if the subsistence base is adversely affected by agricultural adjustment policies, then the tenuously balanced household economy is likely to collapse.

Poor peasants, less able to feed themselves from their own fields, are becoming more dependent on agricultural wage labour and other informal off-farm activities. Those who can draw on the growing pool of impoverished peasants benefit from this process. Apart from large commercial farmers, the upper strata of what development reports call 'emergent farmers' are the most likely to gain. And as they get ahead, the lower strata become increasingly worse off. In 1990 it was clear that only those peasants who had off-farm incomes were able to maintain their positions. They included civil servants and small businessmen, such as headmasters of village schools.

SAPs not only contributed to rural class differentiation, they also increased gender inequality. This is most pronounced among poor peasants. Even in the best of times, low-income married women are denied access to formal markets precisely because male-dominated market production depends so crucially on their labour. The opportunities for women are better in middle- and high-income rural households that have shifted from the exclusive use of family labour to hired workers. Women in more affluent households enter the labour market on a more equal basis and have more control over their own incomes (Chilivumbo and Kanyangwa 1984).

In Zambia's impoverished rural areas only a few peasant households have been able to respond to new agricultural incentives, either because they are too poor or too remote. If such incentives reach the household, they only get to women indirectly. Women may be called upon to perform the labour needed to respond to new incentives, but the benefits that women actually receive depend on their husbands' share of additional resources (Palmer 1991: 118). Rewards are less probable among the poorer households where such sharing would be most important. The gender and class inequities revealed in these processes have not, so far, been a central focus of the design or implementation of SAPs.

SAPS, GENDER AND CLASS IN LUSAKA

Stagnation of wage employment since the mid-1970s, recent public sector retrenchments, removal of subsidies on maize meal, wage freezes and rapid inflation have also turned making of a living into an uphill battle for all urban residents. Here, the effects of SAPs on gender and class manifest themselves as well. Although maize meal today is readily available, economic stringencies are forcing poor urban households to cut down on protein sources, reduce the number of meals per day, or even eat the staple food *nshima* (maize porridge) without relish. This has had dire consequences for the nutritional status of those who have always eaten least and last – women and children

(Muntemba 1987: 24–6). Their experiences differ from those of well-off households who, fearing maize meal shortages in 1990, stored grain in their living rooms and filled their freezers with maize meal (Geisler 1992: 121).

Skyrocketing prices for essential commodities and men's difficulty in holding on to, or finding, wage-labour jobs have increased the pressures on poor women to contribute to household income. The proportion of female small-scale traders in Lusaka's markets and streets has grown steadily since independence, to the point where they presently dominate the daily-provisions trade (especially fruit, vegetables and dried fish). In this situation, women's culturally defined duty to the household meets head on with the demands of SAPs, forcing them to work harder and longer. Yet, the entrance of more women into small-scale trade means reduced profits. In trades where both sexes work, men earn more. They dominate the more lucrative activities and control the upper echelons of trade. Although women's involvement in market trade has greatly expanded with SAPs, societal norms and expectations continue to hedge in the scope of their enterprises. For women depend on start-up capital from husbands, relatives or friends, and rely in the main on downtown markets and retailers to purchase their goods. Above all, because women are expected to feed and take care of children, their income from small-scale trade is subordinated to daily provision. In short, the implementation of SAPs depends on women's activities in order to relieve the resulting pressures on low-income urban households.

Case studies from Lusaka show a variety of informal-sector activities that mobilize material and social resources in different ways.[8] The sale of used imported clothes is among the most recent and noticeable. Liberalization of import and foreign exchange regulations has helped this trade expand so dramatically over the last five years that the used-clothes section today is many times larger than the food section in local markets in both Lusaka and the provincial towns.

A 34-year-old female believed that holding a job was 'a waste of time; there [was] no money in it'. She explained how she began by taking unpaid leaves from work to buy used clothing and other goods from Tanzania for resale in Zambia. Eventually, she had quit her position in the ministry after 13 years to trade on a full-time basis. Other people chose sideline activities – professional and technical staff from the University of Zambia and the University Teaching Hospital hired young relatives or wage labourers to sell used clothing in market stalls.

For people with capital and connections, peri-urban farming for a growing urban market is another popular sideline activity. So is transport – in the form of trucks, or more frequently mini-buses and private (illegal) taxis, that make up for the shortage of public transportation. Interviews in the homes of wage-employed Zambian women in high-income areas revealed additional examples of such diversification – tailoring, beauty care such as hair dressing, cosmetology, and retail trade (for instance, operating a shop in a nearby market). By owning or buying a sewing machine, some women would arrange to produce clothing either in their home or at a rented location.

Female or male public sector workers, especially civil servants who launch informal sideline activities, keep their options open by diversifying. They draw on broader resource bases, including skills and contacts. This enables women and men from more advantageous class positions to establish more lucrative enterprises. Increasing urban income differentials have thus become a noticeable result of SAPs.

Reactions to recent public sector retrenchments illustrate how retirement decisions differ both in class and gender terms. In general, this pruning began at the bottom of the public sector involving, for instance, the janitorial staff and messengers. Although a laid-off worker's wife/or wives might continue to contribute to household income, the accelerating urban costs of living are difficult to meet without a regular wage. Retirement raises the question of reverse migration to the rural areas. The return involves long-term planning, securing rights to land, perhaps building a house, and above all plans for some economic activity – in many cases *not* farming.

The two cases described below, involving wives who are supportive of their husbands' retirement decisions, contrast the meticulous advance planning for retirement of a bottom level public sector worker to the *ad hoc* decisions of an upper level civil servant taken by surprise by SAP retrenchment. The first, a retired airport porter had carefully prepared to return to the village. While still living and working in Lusaka, he extended his house with rented quarters. One wife worked a stall in the market while the second took charge of things at home. He owned a sewing machine and made some money on the side by sewing for sale. The rural return he envisaged was not a life of cultivation. A daughter had bought him a welding machine. On his return, he planned to hire someone to operate it and the sewing machine in a small provincial town near his village. In 1992, he had in fact moved to the Eastern Province with his two wives. Like many others, this man did not sell his house when leaving the city. Considering the house as his 'bank', he put a relative in charge of collecting rent. Because urban low-income housing is in short supply and rents are increasing, absentee ownership is a hedge against inflation. Retaining the house in town also provides those who move to the village a place of return if rural life proves unbearable.

Public sector workers who are suddenly retrenched by SAPs are unlikely to have spent years of advance planning for retirement. This was the case of a high-ranking civil servant in the Works and Supply Ministry who lost his government house in a high-income area upon retirement. As he had not constructed a house of his own while working, he bought one in a low-income area. Before his retirement, his wife had a tailor shop in one of Lusaka's downtown markets. The chief burden of securing household income now fell on her, and she set herself up as a trader in used clothes in the township's market. Dividing her time between attending to the needs of her husband and her market stall, she was assisted by two young male relatives who had come to town from the rural area after completing secondary school. In addition, children in good jobs in Lusaka and other towns in part supported this household.

Not all wives are as supportive of husbands' decisions regarding retirement. The move to the countryside is generally a difficult one for most long-term urban residents. In spite of the hardships SAPs impose, some women clearly prefer town over country, refusing to accompany retiring husbands to villages. To explain this, they refer to the customary expectation that once a man returns to the village, rural elders will encourage him to take a second wife. Having spent most of their adult lives in town, they claim to know nothing about cultivation, and want no part in polygynous marriage. Instead, they choose to remain in town as single heads of households, supporting themselves from trade and occasional contributions from children. Some widows are also reluctant to move to the country. Not wanting to be inherited by a relative of the husband, they remain in town as single heads of households.[9] They also fear that a move to the village might strip away the autonomy they have established in the economic sphere and in relation to men. Finally, single heads of households with few resources, such as never-married women, often lack the means to leave the city.

Regardless of whether people remain in or leave the city, the implementation of SAP retrenchment policies depends on continued involvement in informal work by either the retiree, his spouse/s, paid or unpaid workers, and contributions from children. Kinship and a variety of exchanges link rural and urban areas, constituting resources and networks that make up for the inadequacy of state-provided services at either end. The different responses to SAPs discussed so far are influenced by how gender shapes access to resources, and how socio-cultural norms and practices inform resource use. Thus, women's unease over decisions to return to rural areas encompass not only their economic responses to SAPs but also their personal gender struggle.

URBAN–RURAL INTERCONNECTIONS

In the wake of SAPs, the expansion of informal economic activities testifies to complex interactions between urban and rural areas in an ongoing circulation of people, goods and ideas. In the process, gender and class distinctions have become more pronounced. Specifically, the informal sector has increased its importance as a source of income in both urban and rural areas. It has expanded as well as an avenue for exchanging goods and services for the growing number of rural and urban poor who constitute the chief consumers of daily provisions sold in small bulk and for used clothing. In this expansion, women crowd the least profitable activities, and the poor constitute the chief source of labour.

Urban informal-sector traders have found captive markets in rural areas for commodities that are in short supply such as used clothing and a variety of basic consumer goods. As noted previously, at times, some of these commodities function as means of exchange in rural areas. Some urban traders of used clothes undertake regular country visits, during which they sell the garments urban customers consider unfashionable or poor quality. Yet, the expansion potential of both urban and rural markets for such items is limited by the overall decline of incomes in Zambia, especially for the poor.

Our discussion of informal-sector activities reveals rural–urban interconnections of a larger scale. Urban residents with capital who set up farms in peri-urban areas or their home villages, and those involved in the transport business, depend on the cheap labour of the rural and urban poor. They particularly rely on those laid off or unable to find paid work in the city, and on rural dwellers who are unable to grow sufficient food. Most of the larger enterprises linking town and country are operated by men. Throughout Zambia's urban areas, there is widespread recruitment of rural young adults who perform poorly paid work in urban households and assist in trading. Female and male, many of them school drop-outs, they perform the tedious tasks of tending market stalls and running errands. Young relatives are also drawn on in this way, for instance, in the sideline business of driving private taxis for long hours while their 'uncle' is in the office. These young workers subsidize the undercapitalized work of many informal activities.

Central to SAPs is the notion of markets that favour people who already own capital at the expense of those who do not. This is significantly biased in favour of men. The proliferation of informal activities by women (and young adults) should not be mistaken for a solution to Zambia's economic problems. Because society privileges men's claims over women's, rural and urban women's informal-sector work reinforces their subordination to men and perpetuates their impoverished status. The centrality of gender in such processes is evident, for implementing SAPs depends on women's work to tide households over.

The government frequently scapegoats female street traders of daily provisions as the cause of Zambia's economic ills and has blamed used-clothes traders as a health hazard in recent instances of cholera (*Times of Zambia* 1992: 1). Traders interpret such campaigns for what they are, namely temporary deflections away from the inadequacies of state-provided public services effected by SAPs. As scholars and observers of Zambia, we must explain the expansion of women's work without losing sight of the gender and class inequalities that constitute both the cause and the outcome of these processes.

The economic dependence of the village on towns is giving way to a growing rift between classes in rural and urban areas alike. Gender inequality is becoming more pronounced. The disenchantment of rural and urban populations with their new government is rooted in the hardships inflicted by SAPs. In this perspective, spatial distinctions become subordinated to class and to the particular realization that SAPs affect women adversely regardless of whether they live in rural or urban areas.

CONCLUSION

Although the World Bank has acknowledged that SAPs have adverse effects on the poor, the extent and nature of these impacts remain hidden behind the suggestion that they are temporary and mainly affect 'vulnerable' groups (World Bank 1990: 3). Zambia's Social Action Program identifies as vulnerable 'women and children (especially in households with no male earners), the young (school drop outs), the disabled, agricultural small holders, and the chronically unemployed' (GRZ 1990: 1). This list puts the vast majority of rural and urban populations alongside the handicapped, and most strikingly suggests that women are only 'vulnerable' when they lack husbands.

We have presented a different scenario. Far from being exceptional, weak, or passive, the affected poor have undertaken unprecedented levels of economic activity. Our analysis shows that women bear the brunt of adjustment, since they are affected both as income earners and as dependent members of households. We argue that poor married women experience the pressures of adjustment with particular force.

Regardless of their marital status, women are adversely affected by SAPs because cultural practices influence their ability to perform gainful work and entrepreneurship. It is the women who bear the burdens of household work and other reproductive tasks, have greater difficulties in obtaining loans and credit, receive lower wages, and are relegated to the most insecure of informal activities. In short, SAPs exacerbate women's unequal access as well as their burdens. Reproductive tasks are increasing in the face of diminished state-provided services. Men's declining employment reduces their financial contributions to the family, while the accelerating cost of living forces women to work harder and longer in order to tide household budgets over.

In both rural and urban areas, wives have had to make up for their husbands' decreased earnings and diminished contributions to household expenditures. Like female heads of households, many married women are in effect the chief income earners. Yet according to cultural norms, they remain dependent on husbands who can make legitimate claims on their labour and incomes. The evidence we have presented indicates that men's demands on household food and cash incomes grow in times of economic pressure. This process is pronounced in poor peasant households where husbands take over crops, marketing channels and incomes that once were the fragile prerogative of wives and constituted the basis for household food security. The process also affects urban wives whose husbands make claims on their hard earned gains from small-scale trade, or who view their spouses' earnings as an excuse for not contributing to household expenditures.

The least recognized but most disturbing effect of SAPs is the aggravation of gender conflicts they set into motion. The IMF/World Bank policies have not confronted the bedrock of gender inequality within households. Despite much evidence to the contrary, economic theory and policy largely treat households as units characterized by a joint utility function. They ignore the inequitable burdens of adjustment on women and men and their divergent interests in household matters. It is sadly ironic that development policies should concentrate so much on female heads of households whose labour and incomes are not subject to the demands of husbands. There is no doubt that many female heads are poor, yet they retain control over what little they earn or grow (Kennedy and Peters 1992: 1083).

In spite of massive external financial intervention over the past fifteen years, poor households have not benefited much from SAPs. Living standards have fallen, and food self-sufficiency has not improved. Health has declined, nutritional levels in both rural and urban areas have deteriorated, and morbidity and mortality levels have risen (Freund 1986: 884–6). The ramifications are daunting, particularly for women who are the first to experience economic loss and the last to gain.

Feminist critics believe that the adverse effects of SAPs on women threaten the success of these policies. They argue that SAPs ignore women's contribution to the maintenance and reproduction of human resources by wrongly assuming that they will continue to perform their function, regardless of how resources are allocated (Elson 1989: 57). In the sexual division of labour, by task and by time, women's and men's priorities rarely coincide. Under pressure to perform additional labour, women's ability to carry out their reproductive tasks might erode. The same argument can be made for women's ability to continue food production, expend additional labour on cash cropping, and other male-dominated activities. Our observations from different rural and urban regions confirm this general point – urban women who carry out several lines of work have little energy for household maintenance and childcare; and rural women who perform agricultural piecework are unable to grow both food crops and adequately process the maize for which their labour is remunerated.

The Zambian government and the SAPs share the goal of turning the peasant sector into the main producer of stable food crops. But this requires more than market reforms. Above all, efforts must be directed to reduce the discord between women and men on the household front, and to confront the cultural norms and assumptions about male dominance and female subordination. Judging from the Zambian case, this remains an uphill battle.

NOTES

1 This paper is a product of cooperation. During their individual research in Zambia, Geisler and Hansen overlapped several times. Geisler conducted her research in

several rural areas of Zambia, including the Southern, Northern, North-Western and Eastern Provinces as well as in Lusaka in 1981–8, 1990, 1991–2, with the assistance of the Deutscher Akademischer Austauschdienst (DAAD), and commissioned and financed by the governments of Germany, Norway and Sweden. Hansen carried out research in Lusaka in 1971–2, 1981, 1983–4, 1985, 1988, 1989 and 1992 with support from the National Science Foundation, the Social Science Research Council, the University of Minnesota and Northwestern University. Geisler wrote the sections on the IMF/World Bank, the rural context and the conclusion; Hansen wrote the introduction and the sections on the urban context and rural–urban interconnections. We thank Paul Freund for advice and suggestions.

2 Space prevents us from entering the extensive discussion about the informal sector. For a stimulating recent contribution, see Mingione (1991). For the urban informal sector in Zambia before SAPs, see Hansen (1980).

3 The Zambian Trade Unions, once closely allied with the MMD, have in the interest of their urban constituencies demonstrated their unwillingness to heed new government calls for restraint in wage demands if prices continue to rise (*National Mirror* 1993c).

4 One US dollar cost 28 Kwacha (K) in 1990. Subsequent devaluations changed the dollar exchange rate against the Kwacha as follows: K61 in 1991, K125 in February 1992, and K195 in September 1992, and K535 in September 1993.

5 Banda suggests that an urban household of five in 1990 required a minimum of between K5,400 and K9,700 for basic food, transport and fuel needs. This excluded housing costs (1991: 50).

6 The research on which these observations are based was commissioned and financed by the Gender Unit of the Swedish International Development Authority (SIDA) in the latter half of 1990. SIDA's original plan to continue this research as an ongoing monitoring exercise has since been abandoned.

7 Cash payment for agricultural piecework rose from K4 per day in 1986 to K10 per day in 1990 in Chipata of the Eastern Province, representing roughly the same amount of maize meal (Banda 1991: 28).

8 These examples are drawn from research in Lusaka on women's and men's involvement both in wage labour and informal-sector work. The discussion of the low-income population is based on follow-up studies conducted between 1971 and 1989. Insights on the rapidly growing trade in used clothing are drawn from a study of markets in Lusaka during 1992. Both research settings comprise a range of occupational groups that in addition to self-employed and semi-skilled workers include teachers, clerks and nurses. Observations on the civil service and the professional ranks derive from interviews with Zambian employers of domestic servants in high-income residential areas in Lusaka, undertaken in 1983–4 and 1985. For general findings from these studies, see Hansen (1980, 1989a, b, 1994).

9 The inheritance of widows is a customary practice whereby a widow is taken over by a male relative of the deceased husband. Although many widows object to it, it does occasionally take place today.

8

CHINESE WOMEN AND THE POST-MAO ECONOMIC REFORMS

Gale Summerfield

INTRODUCTION

With the birth of the People's Republic of China in 1949, the Communist Party stated its intention of assuring equality for women. Paid employment was viewed as the means of achieving this goal and most policies regarding women sought to increase their employment. During the next few years, women entered the workforce rapidly, their number increasing from approximately 600,000 in 1949 to over 8 million by 1959 (Davin 1976). By 1982, the workforce participation rate of women was 70 per cent, one of the highest in the world (Foreign Broadcast Information Service 1988c: 34–5).

Rural women received a share of land during the land reform of 1950; and when agriculture was organized into collectives and communes, women, like men, worked in the fields and shared in the returns based on work points. Rural–urban migration was strictly controlled for planning reasons. As a result, women in the cities found work more easily than if they had faced competition from rural migrants.

In the social sphere, the communist government outlawed foot binding and took steps to give women more choice in marriage and divorce with the Marriage Law of 1950. To facilitate women's workforce participation, the government set up childcare centres and canteens, especially in the cities. Gains in health care and education were particularly impressive. Although incomes grew slowly under communism, China achieved life expectancy and literacy rates comparable to the more developed economies of the West. Life expectancy increased from 34 years in 1950 to 62 years in 1970; infant mortality fell from 236 per thousand in 1950 to 69 in 1970; and adult illiteracy decreased from 80 per cent in 1950 to 31 in 1988 (World Bank 1993b, 1992).

Despite this progress, discrimination against women was not obliterated under Mao by any means. Few women, for example, could earn the maximum number of work points per day; a woman typically could earn a maximum of 8 points for a day's work while a man could earn as many as 10 (Wolf 1985). Moreover, most urban women worked either in predominantly 'female' factories run by the state or in collectives at lower pay and with fewer benefits relative to men. The communist rule of gender equality, however, suppressed gender biases to some degree.[1]

In the political power struggle that followed Mao's death in 1976, his rivals, mainly Deng Xiaoping and his associates, surfaced as victors. This group had long held views that were strongly opposed to Mao's Cultural Revolution style policies. Economic problems such as slow growth in agriculture that barely kept pace with population growth, the need for ever increasing rates of investment to elicit output from state-run industries, and a pressing surplus labour problem, called for drastic measures.

The post-Mao policies (1976–present) promoted international trade through the establishment of four Special Economic Zones, privatized agriculture by returning farms to the family, and put greater emphasis on efficiency and markets. In addition, in order to control population growth, the state attempted to limit each family to one child. Except for the one-child policy, the reforms have not been directed specifically at women; they have, nevertheless, had strong, sometimes unexpected and negative, gender effects.

This chapter examines the impact of post-Mao economic reforms on women, emphasizing three sets of policies – the focus on international trade through the opening of the Special Economic Zones, the reorganization of agriculture, and the attempt to improve efficiency through urban reforms. The gender impact of each is examined through changes in employment and income, intrahousehold allocation, and indicators of human development.[2] Because the available data on Chinese women are fragmented and at times misleading, official sources are supplemented by such sources as Foreign Broadcast Information Service (FBIS) reports, the *Beijing Review*, personal interviews and anecdotal evidence.

ECONOMIC REFORMS IN POST-MAO CHINA

International trade and Special Economic Zones

International trade has played a substantial role in China's rapid economic growth during the reform period. The trade share of GNP increased from approximately 10 per cent in 1978 to more than 36 per cent of the much larger GNP in 1991 (Gottschang 1992: 269). Initial steps to promote trade focused on setting up export-processing zones, called Special Economic Zones, patterned after the zones existing in other developing countries.

Special Economic Zones were established in 1979 not only to generate employment and earn foreign exchange, but also to demonstrate the benefits of integrating capitalist institutions into a socialist setting. The zones were set up in coastal areas to facilitate connections with Hong Kong, Macao and Taiwan. Of the four initial zones, three (Shenzhen, Zhuhai and Shantou) were located in the Guangdong Province, adjacent to Hong Kong; the fourth (Xiamen) was in Fujian, directly across from Taiwan. Despite being near ports, the zones were situated in regions lacking the modern infrastructure required by transnational corporations. A substantial commitment to investment was needed to bring them up to the desired level; and the planners expected foreign businesses to supply most of the required funds.

Despite short-term problems,[3] the zones have been quite successful economically. They increased the value of their exports from $9 million dollars in 1979 to $1.8 billion in 1988; and the number of contracts with foreign businesses doubled between 1987 and 1988 (*Beijing Review* 1989b: 12). The demonstration effect of the zones' success was evident as trade spread beyond their boundaries.[4] In 1984, fourteen coastal cities were given more freedom to process exports and manage trade; Hainan Island became an export-processing zone in 1988. In addition, rural industries began to partake in export-processing activities; about 20 per cent of China's exports came from rural industries in 1990 (Endean 1991: 753). In 1993, export-processing led the growth in exports with a value of $44.25 billion (Reuters 1994).

Rural reforms and the household responsibility system

Reform of domestic production began in the late 1970s with the reorganization of agriculture from communal to family-based farming. Through the Household Responsibility System, the state provided seeds and other inputs to families that agreed to supply a certain amount of grain to the state. The price for state-purchased grain was also raised 15–20 per cent, and bonuses for exceeding the family quota were increased from 30 to 50 per cent (Sicular 1991: 347). Excess grain could be sold on the re-appearing free markets. The family decided how to use the land – now allocated to them under long-term contract of 15–30 years – for production of cash earning crops (e.g. vegetables) and sideline activities (e.g. animal husbandry). Families could also engage in production of handicrafts and other small businesses.

The new decision-making abilities and incentives released a torrent of entrepreneurial talent, and production soared. Agriculture generated discretionary incomes that could now be used for investment. In the mid-1980s, privately owned industries flourished under the new freedom to open community, collective and private factories. By 1987, rural non-state industries had become 'the most dynamic sector in the Chinese economy' (Byrd and Lin 1990: 107). Many of these industries were located near coastal cities, and firms frequently processed exports, especially near Hong Kong. By 1993, the new firms employed approximately 100 million people; a sample survey of Nanhai and Shangrao showed that women comprised 51.2 per cent of the workers in non-state rural firms (ibid.: 101, 406).

Urban reforms and the emphasis on efficiency

Urban reforms did not get underway until the mid-1980s, after the rural reforms had achieved notable success. In the cities, the focus was on improving efficiency by reducing costs and by eliciting greater work effort from employees through incentives such as piece rates, bonuses and retention of profits by enterprises. The need to eliminate redundant workers in state enterprises has been frequently discussed but relatively little action has been taken at present, except for hiring more workers on contract. The increasing share of contractual jobs is illustrated in Table 8.1. Contract workers accounted for 12.1 per cent of total staff and workers, up from less than 1 per cent in 1983.

Until the post-Mao reforms, workers in China had been assigned to lifetime jobs with little opportunity for upward mobility, and small chances of transferring to a different firm or a new line of work. The beginnings of a labour market permit people to choose jobs more in accord with their own tastes, with the trade-off that they do not have assurance of finding a position. While managers may still be reluctant to fire or layoff workers, the use of the contract system makes these decisions much easier – managers simply do not renew worker contracts.

Table 8.1 Proportion of staff and workers on contractual jobs (%)

	1983	1990
State-owned units	0.6	13.3
Urban collectives	0.3	8.1
Other	–	26.3
Total	0.6	12.1

Source: *Statistical Yearbook of China* (1991: 96).

Price reform, which relies on markets rather than administrative fiat to set prices, has been more extensive in the goods market than in the labour market. In November 1993, 90 per cent of prices in the goods market were set by supply and demand. Planners have announced their intent to expand the role of market forces in labour, real estate and financial markets (*The Economist* 1993c: 35).

THE POST-MAO REFORMS AND WOMEN

Although there have been bouts of inflation and retrenchment, the success of these reforms is evident. At present, China has the fastest growing economy in the world. Between 1980 and 1991 the annual rate of growth of GDP (Gross Domestic Product) in China averaged 9.4 per cent, and during 1993 the economy grew an impressive 13 per cent (World Bank 1993b: 240; *The Economist* 1993c: 35). Table 8.2 shows that annual net per capita income

Table 8.2 Income changes during the post-Mao reforms, in yuan

	1981	1990
GNP per capita	480	1,558
Annual net income, per capita		
Rural, nominal	223	630
Rural, real	202	319
Urban, nominal	463	1,387
Urban, real	446	685

Sources: *Statistical Yearbook of China* (1991); World Bank (1992a: 4).

increased from 480 yuan in 1981 to 1,558 in 1990. Moreover, the gains have been widely distributed in both rural and urban areas. The number of people living in poverty declined from 270 million in 1978 to 97 million in 1985, but no further reductions were achieved between 1985 and 1990 (World Bank 1992a: 1–5).[5]

In conjunction with these gains in per capita income, the economic reforms have created many new employment opportunities for women. Well-being, however, depends upon more than the number of jobs created and the growth of per capita income. This chapter uses Sen's concepts of capabilities and well-being to evaluate the impact of post-Mao reforms on women. According to Sen (1990: 126), capabilities comprise the actual choices of what a person is able to do or be; for example, 'the ability to be well nourished, to avoid escapable morbidity or mortality, to read and write and communicate, to take part in the life of the community, to appear in public without shame.' Greater well-being implies that the expansion of capabilities is not only based on higher incomes but also on the type of job one holds, the source of one's income and on changes that affect education, health and intrahousehold decision-making. The following sections examine the impact of reforms on variables that affect Chinese women's capabilities and well-being.

Women's employment opportunities in Special Economic Zones

The opening to international trade has stimulated the economy and provided many opportunities for Chinese women. In the Special Economic Zones, as in most export-processing zones, young women (18–23 years old) hold an average of 70–80 per cent of the newly created production jobs (Foreign Broadcast Information Service 1988d: 41–2; Andors 1988: 28).

While employment creation is positive, the hiring pattern reflects the global tradition of female predominance in the assembly work of light industries rather than an overt decision to employ women (Grunwald and Flamm 1985: 168). The positions are at the lowest level, in monotonous, assembly-line work with little if any chance of promotion. As in export-processing zones of other developing nations, the traditional hierarchy of male managers overseeing unskilled female employees is maintained (Andors 1988: 30; Ward 1990: 12–13). These factors (along with the relatively small number of workers employed in the zones) limit the ability of export-processing positions to improve women's position relative to men.

Still, wages in the Special Economic Zones are more than double the average wage paid outside the zones, and the jobs created in the zones help to offset the trends of increasing employment discrimination against women elsewhere in the country (see below). Official estimates place the wages paid in the zones at 20–30 per cent above other areas; other reports estimate the wage gap to be even higher (*Beijing Review* 1989a: 19; Croll 1983: 55). The average annual wage in state-run industries in 1985 is recorded by *China Urban Statistics* (State Statistical Bureau of the People's Republic of China 1985: 672, 676) as being 1,103 yuan, but for Shenzhen it is put at 2,342. The sample of plants taken by Andors (1988: 28, 32) finds the average wage for a production worker to be 150 yuan per month (compared to an average of 50 elsewhere). Chu (1987: 81) also reports wages within economic zones to be approximately three times the average paid outside the zones. Benefits paid to zone workers are probably less than the average for a worker in an urban, state-run factory, although there are no hard data to support this. Factories in the zones, however, do subsidize expenses for room and board, and most workers do receive a package of benefits (Andors 1988: 35–6).

The employment opportunities provided to women have had a positive impact on the well-being of women. The zones provide paid employment to young women who are looking for their first jobs and who have the hardest time finding employment in China today. The zones also impact women who live elsewhere. The number of Chinese women employed in the Special Economic Zones may be low[6] compared to the amount of surplus labour in the country as a whole, but the new demand for female labour does relieve the problem to some extent. The zones have also demonstrated the prosperity of export-processing activities which has rapidly led to demands by other areas to participate more in international trade. This means additional job opportunities for women.

Employment impact on rural women

The growth of non-state rural industry engaged in export processing can, in part, be attributed to the demonstration effect of the Special Economic Zones. Employing approximately 100 million people, these rural industries can provide opportunities for a much greater percentage of Chinese women than the zones. Recent reports from the Ministry of Agriculture state that, in 1990, rural industry provided 34 per cent of China's coal, 63 per cent of its nylon, 60 per cent of its garments, 80 per cent of its farm machinery and equipment, and more than 90 per cent of its bricks (World Bank 1992a: 61).

The survey of rural industries conducted jointly by the World Bank and the Chinese Academy of Social Sciences in the late 1980s revealed that non-state rural industries usually offer wages greater than those run by the state (about 20 per cent greater in Shangrao and Nanhai) (Byrd and Lin 1990: 406). Gelb's regression analysis of the wage data collected, however, indicated that women earned approximately 14 per cent less than men in the non-state rural firms (1990: 297).

Most Chinese women remain in agricultural work, which is now centred on family farming. As men migrate to the city for more profitable work or find jobs in industries nearby, the share of women in the agricultural workforce has grown. Although the arrangements increase total family income, they also augment men's traditional patriarchal control over the household. The enthusiasm for the household responsibility system's impressive income gains has waned with the awareness that women are being pushed back into traditional family settings for earning activities. The absence of an explicit wage blurs women's contribution to total family income, reducing their intrahousehold bargaining power (Aslanbeigui and Summerfield 1989).

Employment impact on urban women

Women in the cities have also found new employment opportunities under the reforms, especially in foreign-funded enterprises and through self-employment. Table 8.3 shows that the employment share of women increased somewhat from 35.41 per cent in 1980 to 37.66 per cent in 1990. The employment share of women grew in every sector except construction and real estate management. Although the data are not broken down by gender, Table 8.4 presents official statistics on wages in 1985 and 1988. By comparing these wage data with the employment figures of Table 8.3, we can examine how sectors that employ more women have fared over time compared to other sectors. Since wage data for 1990 are not available, the comparisons will be made for the 1988 employment figures.

Table 8.3 shows that women are over-represented in four sectors and under-represented in another four. According to Table 8.4, the four sectors with relatively high percentages of women – industry, commerce, real estate management and health care – pay wages less than or close to the national average. Three of the four sectors with relatively low percentages of female workers – geological survey, construction, transport and government – pay wages that are significantly higher than the national average.

Table 8.3 also reveals that between 1980 and 1988, female employment gains (measured in percentage change in employment share) were greatest in geological survey, commerce, health care, banking and government. According to Table 8.4, in three of these five sectors relative wages fell between 1985 and 1988 as relatively more women entered the sector.

Table 8.3 Employment share of women by sector

	Female staff and workers					
	1980		1988		1990	
	Total (millions)	(%)	Total (millions)	(%)	Total (millions)	(%)
Total staff and workers	36.98	35.41	50.36	37.01	52.94	37.66
Farming, forestry, animal husbandry, fishery & water conservancy	2.96	34.95	3.05	35.97	3.04	36.17
Industry	18.73	39.33	25.30	41.08	26.43	41.44
Geological survey & prospecting	0.20	20.00	0.25	23.36	0.24	23.88
Construction	1.76	23.82	2.03	20.46	1.99	20.47
Transport, postal & telecommunication services	1.53	21.98	1.86	23.60	1.92	24.08
Commerce, food service, material supply, marketing, storage	4.96	39.46	7.56	43.72	8.07	44.53
Real estate management, public, residential & consultancy services	1.18	46.27	1.65	45.71	1.80	46.23
Health care, sports & social welfare	1.41	49.13	1.98	52.80	2.10	53.57
Education, culture, art, radio & TV broadcasting	2.84	34.76	3.91	35.84	4.22	36.94
Scientific research & comprehensive technical services	0.36	34.29	0.50	34.72	0.52	34.48
Banking & insurance	0.26	29.21	0.61	35.26	0.79	35.89
Government, parties & social organizations	0.79	16.12	1.66	19.71	1.91	20.52

Source: *Statistical Yearbook of China* (1991: 83, 95).

Table 8.4 Annual wages by sector as a percentage of national wages

	1985	1988
Total staff and workers	100.00	100.00
Farming, forestry, animal husbandry, fishery & water conservancy	77.77	75.04
Industry	100.82	102.00
Geological survey & prospecting	140.56	131.54
Construction	120.42	112.59
Transport, postal & telecommunication services	113.16	114.94
Commerce, food service, material supply, marketing, storage	87.48	89.52
Real estate management, public, residential & consultancy services	97.73	98.80
Health care, sports & social welfare	97.91	100.29
Education, culture, art, radio & TV broadcasting	101.63	100.00
Scientific research and comprehensive technical services	110.62	110.53
Banking & insurance	100.91	99.54
Government, parties & social organizations	98.28	97.71

Sources: *Zhongguo Shehui Tonji Ziliao* (1991: 80, 1987: 68).

A total of 38.35 million women, or 76.15 per cent of female staff and workers, worked in sectors where wages increased relative to the national average – industry, transport, commerce, real estate and health care. Although there is no indication that women actually received these higher wages, these statistics are positive for showing *potential* improvements in the well-being of working women.

Table 8.5 illustrates the increasing importance of bonuses, piece-rate wages and above-quota payments for worker salaries. Under the reforms, tying work to effort is key to more efficient production. Women, however, may be at a disadvantage under a payment system that relies on bonuses because they have the burden of housework and childcare on top of their paid job. Therefore, it is often more difficult for women to stay after work hours or put in extra time. As long as bonuses are determined by objective criteria, the disadvantage for women should not be too great; it is comparable to not being able to work overtime.

Table 8.5 Average wages of staff and workers, in yuan

	1980	1990	1990 as a percentage of 1980
Average annual wage	762	2,140	280.8
State-owned units	803	2,284	284.4
Urban collectives	623	1,681	269.8
Other ownerships	–	2,987	–
Bonuses, piece-rate wages & above-quota payment	69	390	565.2
State-owned units	78	436	559.0
Urban collectives	41	245	597.6
Other ownerships	–	626	–
Subsidies	–	444	–
State-owned units	115	497	432.2
Urban collectives	–	288	–
Other ownerships	–	457	–

Source: *Statistical Yearbook of China* (1991: 102).

Employment statistics hide labour-market fluctuation during the period. In the late 1980s, some women were being sent home at reduced wages. These actions were taken by firms in response to a growing awareness of the cost of redundant workers; surplus labour estimates place the numbers at about one-third of the national workforce. Surplus labour is a particular threat to the employment of urban women. Increasing migration from rural areas forces urban women to compete with rural, as well as urban, men for scarce jobs.

Table 8.6 also demonstrates that employers typically choose to remove women from the payroll rather than men when cuts are necessary. Although it is not consistent with economic theory to identify an individual worker as surplus, such identification appears common in Chinese industry where

Table 8.6 Surplus labour, 1988

Industry	% Female, of those targeted for dismissal as surplus is reduced
Commerce and service trades	82
Machine-building, metallurgy, petrochemicals, electronics, textiles, transport & communications	60
Electricity, power, post & telecommunications	35
All industries	64

Source: *Beijing Review* (1988: 19–20).

workers targeted for layoffs are labelled 'surplus'. Media reports consistently state that more than 60 per cent of these surplus workers are female. (It should be noted that these percentages are greater than the female employment share in these industries.)

In the cities, women entering the workforce also find an increasingly biased market. According to many job advertisements, attractive young women have a higher likelihood of finding jobs. The markets, however, are in general unfavourable because of gender discrimination as well as higher costs associated with female maternity leaves and health care. The benefits that Chinese women receive place extra costs on factories, making managers reluctant to hire them when efficiency and profits are their objectives. These incremental costs for two areas are shown in Table 8.7.[7] Even female university graduates frequently find that employers prefer to hire men.

Professional women who are already employed face less discrimination than less-skilled workers. Recent changes in retirement policies reflect these differences. For professional women, the retirement age was raised from 55 years to 60 years to make it the same as that for men; for factory workers, however, women are now often compelled to retire at age 42 (interviews).

Intrahousehold decision-making

Many of the post-Mao reforms manifest their indirect or unanticipated effects within the household. A good example of this is the household responsibility

Table 8.7 Relative costs of employing women, 1988

	Costs in yuan
Beijing General Automobile Replacement Plant Annual loss of profit per pregnant and nursing woman	6,600
Nanning Annual loss of profit per woman	1,898

Sources: Foreign Broadcast Information Service (1988e: 42–3); *Beijing Review* (1988: 18).

system in agriculture. The household can be viewed as a group of individuals with some interests in common and with some interests that clash: a cooperative conflict (Sen 1985). At times the household may act to maximize a joint utility function, but a bargaining-power game is likely to emerge. How much power a woman has in this situation is influenced by employment opportunities and other factors such as education and property rights (see Sen 1990). It is also likely to be influenced by where and how the woman is employed.

Women in the Special Economic Zones

The young woman working in an export-processing plant is probably the daughter rather than the wife in the Chinese household. Typically she would have very little power and would turn over to her family most of the income she earns (see Wolf 1985: 193; Lim 1990b: 110). In the zones, she is probably living away from home for the first time. It is unlikely that she will be required to turn over all of her salary since she has living expenses (not directly observed by family members), but strong cultural traditions pressure her to remit some. In times of crisis, she may well pool her income with that of other family members as Wolf (1985) observed for Java.

At work, however, she is expected to dress well and will probably spend most of her earnings on clothes, hair care and possibly even entertainment such as audio cassettes (Andors 1988: 37). Clearly some independent decision-making occurs. If she returns home after her contract is fulfilled, she may be able to retain some of her new power through habit, saved earnings or opportunities based on acquired skills. Most likely she will soon marry.

The employment opportunities provided by the zones and trade-related enterprises throughout the country have a positive impact on intrahousehold decision-making as well as status in society. Because there is little opportunity to advance in most of the firms doing this work, the effect on status is moderate.

Rural women

The gains from income expansion in the countryside have been widespread and contribute positively to the well-being of rural women. Even if the wife does not personally receive the higher earnings, she benefits through purchases made by the family, such as having a better house, a sewing machine and other appliances.

The most disturbing, reform-related phenomenon for rural women has been the change in the source of income effected by the household responsibility system. As the patriarchal household becomes the centre of production for many, an individual's contribution is blurred when compared to earning wages. This can easily lead to undervaluing a woman's contribution in a setting that traditionally discriminates against her. A reduction of the woman's power in making decisions and in bargaining can be expected. Offsetting the focus on the household is the growth of rural non-state industry. Some are family-run, but there are many alternatives. These industries provide options for rural women that can increase bargaining power.

The daughters within the household are in a somewhat different position from the wife. They gain from the positive changes, but some have been pulled out of school as the implicit opportunity cost and out-of-pocket costs of education rise. The traditional arrangements – a girl relocates to her husband's village upon marriage and makes contributions to his family but not to her own – promote discrimination against the education of female children.[8] In 1990, 4.8 million school-age children dropped out; 80 per cent of them were girls (World Bank 1992a: 84). Most of the drop-outs occur in rural areas.

Urban women

The post-Mao reforms have resulted in contradictory changes within urban households. On the one hand, women have frequently been direct bene-ficiaries of the rise in income as a result of economic growth and planners' reluctance to lay off surplus workers. This expands women's choices and opportunities. On the other hand, difficulties in finding or keeping a job can reduce bargaining power at home. With the fledgling labour market, there is a tendency for Chinese women (as in other societies) to be the last hired and first fired. Although open unemployment is not a major problem in the growing Chinese economy, there is enough underemployment or surplus labour to make it a potential problem for the future. If so, women can be expected to have a larger share in the unemployment figures than men; according to the One Per cent Sample Survey of 1987, women accounted for 65 per cent of the unemployment at the time.

State firms are compelled to become more competitive, and women are disproportionately identified as those who will lose their jobs (*Beijing Review* 1988: 19–20). Women who have been sent home at partial wages may appreciate their lighter burden, but their skills may become obsolete as new technology is introduced; they are well aware that they may never regain employment and that the funding for staying home is temporary. Most urban women questioned in a recent survey said that they preferred to stay employed, and many report that they are treated worse by their husbands when they are sent home from work (interviews; *Zhongguo Funu Bao* 1988a: 3).

Human development issues

In addition to problems with the education of rural girls mentioned above, other areas of human development merit attention for their impact on well-being, specifically those that affect health and life expectancy. Problems appear mostly in rural areas where many of the policy conflicts occur and where traditional biases are most strongly embedded.

Although not an *economic* reform, the one-child policy deserves examination as a major reform and as the only one explicitly directed at women. Chinese planners had already promoted birth control measures for the Han majority before the reform period. By 1978, the average number of births per woman in the cities was only 1.55, but the fertility rate in the countryside was still around 3 (compared to 6.4 in 1970). With projections of reaching a population of 1.5 billion people if couples continued to have as many as two children each, reformers instituted the one-child policy in 1979. The urban fertility rate dropped to 1.3 births per woman during the 1980s, but rural families have resisted the pressure to reduce births and the rural fertility rate exceeds 2 (Banister 1991: 238–9). Though the population growth rate has slowed, in 1991 China had 1.15 billion mouths to feed (World Bank 1993b).

The one-child policy includes both positive and negative incentives to persuade parents to have a single child. These incentives, however, contradict those produced by the household responsibility system which result in greater accumulation of wealth by families with more sons. As a result, rural women are discriminated against; the most extreme form of this discrimination manifests itself through infanticide, neglect and other acts that result in death.

In 1992, the sex ratio in China reached 118.5 boys for every 100 girls; in five of the thirty provinces, the sex ratio exceeded 120 boys for every 100 girls (*New York Times* 1993: 1). Since typically around 105 boys are born to every 100 girls (the ratio usually reverses by adulthood), these figures are higher than would be expected from random variation. The missing girls are not all being killed; some are hidden at relatives' homes. And some female births are averted after ultrasound is used to detect the sex of the foetus. The implications for the well-being of girls and women are obvious.

Other policies have targeted social expenditure; one of the most significant is the reduction of state funds for health care in the countryside. Pressure for health institutions to earn income reduces the time staff can devote to preventive work. Basic health care coverage is also changing under the reforms. In 1975 about 85 per cent were covered; by the early 1990s the majority of those living in rural areas had no coverage (World Bank 1992a: 97–8). Private insurance arrangements are gradually replacing the state-funded system but problems exist in the interim.[9]

These problems have led to stagnating or falling indicators of human development (or well-being) during a period when income was doubling. Although a slower rate of improvement is expected at high levels of development, the indicators basically show stagnation. Official statistics show that life expectancy and infant mortality figures have remained approximately constant over the 1980s, but the declining sex ratio for newborn girls compared to boys indicates that female infant mortality has been climbing (Banister 1991: 236; World Bank 1992a: 5).

CONCLUSION

The post-Mao economic reforms in China have achieved impressive rates of growth. The gains have been broadly distributed since most people in rural areas have access to land and most urban residents have jobs; poverty has been significantly reduced except in isolated pockets.

Many Chinese women have benefited from the growth in family incomes. The economic reforms have also expanded job opportunities for women in the Special Economic Zones, and in rural and urban industries.

The adverse impact of reforms on women, however, are serious and merit attention. Women are often concentrated in traditional, low-level jobs with little chance of promotion. They are discriminated against in hiring and layoff decisions;[10] the threat of female job losses looms as planners discuss the need to make state firms more cost-effective. With the return of farming to the patriarchal household, rural women may experience reduction in their bargaining power. In addition, traditional preference for male children and cutbacks in social services have resulted in significant costs for women during the reform period; girls who are pulled out of schools have lost an array of future opportunities.

The death (or abandonment) of newborn girls is especially disturbing. The resulting imbalance in the male/female sex ratio will soon exacerbate the already existing shortage of women of marriageable age. Such a shortage may in fact augment the value of women; there are reports that the amount of money a man is expected to spend on the marriage ceremony (frequently around $1,000) has increased beyond the means of poor rural men. The shortage may, on the other hand, increase the abduction and sale of women; in some areas, a wife can be bought, through a slave market, for $350. Between 1991 and 1992, the police solved over 50,000 cases of abduction (Kahn 1993); but many more women remain in virtual slavery since only a small percentage of such crimes are solved.

The future of women in China remains uncertain given the lack of gender-oriented policies. Women's well-being depends on numerous factors, not all of which can be automatically resolved by an increase in the role of markets. Economic growth, surplus labour pressures, population policies and traditional biases will continue to create a complex web of contradictory outcomes. As a result, it is imperative that women take a leadership role in voicing their demands through various organizations. The Women's Federation is already addressing some of the problems associated with literacy, availability of credit and training in new technology. Some women have begun to participate actively in politics by running for office. Non-governmental organizations also offer a new means of reducing the negative impact of economic reforms. For Chinese women, the next decade offers both opportunity and danger.

NOTES

1 For a fuller discussion of the problem, see Stacey (1983).
2 Because the one-child policy is only indirectly an economic reform, it is discussed in the section on human development issues in terms of its interaction with the other reforms rather than as a separate section.
3 In 1985, it became clear that the zones used more foreign exchange than they brought in; this happened while scarce foreign exchange reserves for the whole country fell from $16.6 billion to $11.3 billion between September 1984 and March 1985 (Fewsmith 1986: 80). Of the $2.3 billion in foreign contracts, just $525.5 million had actually been invested by 1984. Most of the foreign investment had been from Hong Kong instead of from developed countries; most of this investment was for low technology, labour-intensive assembly work. Output-value figures had been misleading because of the inclusion of extensive infrastructure construction. The extent of necessary infrastructure greatly exceeded expectations. Moreover, two-thirds of the work had been financed by China instead of the anticipated foreign sources (Pepper 1986: 7). Corruption and social problems became sensitive issues nationally. The zones were accused of prospering at the expense of the rest of the economy.
4 The demonstration effect refers to the influence on domestic production and attitudes toward trade liberalization that results from the success of an export-processing zone. These changes include convincing domestic businesses that they can successfully export to the developed countries; increasing the discipline of the local workforce; and improvement of infrastructure (ILO/UNCTC 1988: 132).
5 Due to inflation and austere measures to control it, income growth in the second half of the 1980s was much slower than at the beginning of the decade. Between 1981 and 1987 real urban income grew 45 per cent, but it then stagnated until 1990 when it increased 6 per cent above the 1987 level. Real rural income grew more than 130 per cent between 1978 and 1984 but gained less than 3 per cent between 1985 and 1990 (World Bank 1992a: 9).
6 Since the zones employ people in the tourist industry, construction, and services, the number doing processing work must be well below the total working in the zones (a few million at present); at the same time the figure of approximately 200,000 given for 1988 is clearly too low (see *Beijing Review* 1988: 18).
7 Recently there has been some experimentation with national insurance programmes for maternity leave and health care that would reduce the differential for individual firms.
8 In addition to financial problems in providing education to rural girls, there are cultural and language problems, especially among China's many minorities. Education of Yao girls in Guanxi, for example, has been limited by the scarcity of Yao female teachers. Much time is spent trying to teach the standard national language in the countryside when most of the students will never use it outside of school, but without the capability to speak and write the standard language, opportunities for secondary education will be almost non-existent (World Bank 1992a: 84).
9 The gender effects of private insurance programmes depend on the particular form they take; if there is an incremental cost for each use to prevent the moral hazard effect (or discourage unnecessary use), families may choose to take boys to the doctor but not the girls.

10 Discrimination against women in the labour market conflicts with the goals of the one-child policy because children still provide most of the income for elderly parents in China. If a daughter cannot provide as much as a son, people will clearly be reluctant to have only a daughter. Improving the social security network can reduce the policy conflict but cannot completely alleviate it.

9

ECONOMIC RESTRUCTURING IN SINGAPORE AND THE CHANGING ROLES OF WOMEN, 1957 TO PRESENT

Jean L. Pyle

INTRODUCTION

The island city-state of Singapore in South-East Asia has captured the attention of social scientists and planners interested in the process of economic growth and development. Singapore is one of four Pacific Asian nations commonly referred to as the newly industrialized countries (NICs), which have been widely studied for a number of years.[1] These countries have exhibited exceptionally high rates of growth since the 1960s and are considered examples of successful export-oriented growth, the type of development strategy currently advocated throughout the world by major international institutions such as the World Bank and the International Monetary Fund. Singapore, in particular, has received international prominence. Although its population is only 3 million, this small country has been the subject of global debates over critical political and economic issues important to the future of most economies – the sources of continued high rates of growth and rapidly rising per capita incomes, the appropriate role of the state versus market forces in fostering economic development, and the relationship between political authoritarianism and sustained economic growth.

Another critical dimension of the Singaporean case, with relevance to other countries, concerns the importance of women in the development process. This chapter examines the impact of structural changes in Singapore on the economic roles of women relative to men. It also focuses on how state policies have shaped this impact, and on the subsequent implications for the country's continued growth as well as for women's future position in the economy. Although the use of female labour has been mentioned in some of the literature examining Singapore's development (Pang 1988), and although a few articles (Wong 1981, 1980; Salaff 1986) examine changes in women's roles in Singapore's development process, the interrelationship among economic restructuring, growth and women's roles in Singapore has not been fully recognized. Understanding these effects and their implications is important for a range of other countries – those that are adopting the export-oriented development strategy and others that must make optimal use of labour.

The next section of this paper outlines the economic changes in Singapore since the late 1950s. In light of domestic and international events and trends, Singapore's government has implemented policies to significantly restructure and reorient the focus of the economy several times during the past thirty-five years. Most fundamental was the shift to export-oriented industrialization in 1965 after a brief period of import-substitution industrialization. This was followed by attempts to significantly modify export-oriented development in late 1970s and mid-1980s.

The following section compares the disparate effects of these changes on the roles of women and men in the workforce. The export-oriented approach to development depended heavily on the role of Singaporean women in the paid workforce and the household; modifications to this strategy have also affected women. In particular, since 1985, women have been the central factor in Singapore's effort to augment its workforce. Throughout the entire period, there have been dramatic increases in women's workforce participation. The demand for female labour was directly increased through policies designed to attract foreign direct investment in export-oriented industries which typically employed women. However, while women experienced some improvement in their limited share of higher level occupations and some improvement in their relative wages, in 1989 they still remained largely in subordinate positions, disproportionately vulnerable to layoffs, and earned much less than men.

The paper concludes by discussing two related issues – how the economic restructuring of the past three decades is likely to affect women's future roles and how Singapore's utilization of women is likely to affect its future economic growth. It is suggested that Singapore's future growth will depend on the success of policies that increase female workforce participation and whether women are fully incorporated into the national economy.

STRUCTURAL CHANGE IN THE SINGAPORE ECONOMY, 1957–PRESENT

Singapore has changed dramatically over the past thirty-five years. Controlled by Britain from 1819 to 1959, Singapore became a naval shipbuilding and repair base and an entrepôt economy, a site to ship products into and out of South-East Asia. This necessitated certain processing functions as well as banking, insurance and storage activities. Local manufacturing was not encouraged by the British.

Since attaining self-rule in 1959 and independence in 1965, an activist state policy and the presence of transnational corporations (TNCs) have trans-formed Singapore into a highly open, modern international economy. Exports have grown from 123 per cent of gross domestic product (GDP) in 1965 to 191 per cent in 1989, changing also in composition. As of 1990, Singapore's exports largely consisted of machinery and equipment (office machines, electronic, radio and TV components), mineral fuels (petroleum refining) and chemicals, all of which are produced by TNCs (Ministry of Trade and Industry, Singapore 1991).

Singapore's government actively shaped the country's economic de-velopment throughout the past thirty-five years, implementing policies that altered the structure of the economy. First, the newly independent nation switched from an import-substitution industrialization policy to an export-oriented strategy in 1965. Secondly, although Singapore had been attempting to shift into less labour-intensive industries during the 1970s, it made a dramatic move in this direction in 1979 when the government mandated substantial wage increases. Thirdly, when it became clear in 1985 that this approach was not working and that the economy was experiencing its first recession, the national economic strategy was re-evaluated. The government urged wage restraint and planned to develop the country as a hub for production, marketing and financial services in the region.

To elaborate, in 1961, expecting to be granted full independence as a member state in the Malaysian Federation, Singapore's government decided to pursue import-substitution industrialization in order to serve the needs of the large domestic market the Malay Federation offered. This strategy involved tariffs and tax incentives to protect, and thereby spur the development of, domestic industries. However, the plan to incorporate Singapore into the Malaysian Federation was abandoned in 1965 because of the conflict among political groups in the two countries. With the loss of the large Malaysian market, import-substitution industrialization was no longer a rational strategy.

After assessing both domestic conditions and international trends, the government decided to pursue export-oriented industrialization. Domestic-ally, Singapore had few resources, a limited local manufacturing base and unemployment of over 9 per cent. Internationally, world trade was increasing and TNCs in labour-intensive industrial sectors were moving into low-cost production sites in the Third World. Given these circumstances, the govern-ment chose to provide employment through export-oriented industrialization based upon production by TNCs in Singapore rather than by encouraging domestic entrepreneurs.

Consequently, the institutional structure of Singapore changed sub-stantially over the next few years – the government took a much more interventionist role, the power of labour unions was deliberately diminished and, attracted by a variety of incentives, the TNCs flowed into the country. Before independence, the government had a limited role in the economy. However, in the 1960s, its role was expanded through the development of a relatively large state enterprise sector, increases in public employment, investment in infrastructure and human resources, attraction of TNCs, and intervention in product, financial and labour markets as well as in socio-economic life in general.[2]

Given its favourable geographic location and port, the government courted TNCs in labour-intensive industries by offering an array of financial incentives, a stable political environment and an adequate supply of workers. It allowed 100 per cent foreign ownership of enterprises and permitted full repatriation of profits, both more generous incentives than offered by many other developing nations. The government also provided low-cost sites for production, accelerated depreciation, duty-free import of inputs, and export-tax reduction on targeted products.

The state also took measures to ensure political and labour stability, important factors in the investment decisions of TNCs. The Left had been politically defeated in the early 1960s. In 1968, two legislative acts reduced workers' benefits and gave management increased discretion in all aspects of employment policy; this severely diminished the power of labour. Unlike many other developing countries, where labour conflicts occurred frequently, unions in Singapore essentially became a junior partner with the government in facilitating export-led development.

In contrast to earlier foreign direct investment, which focused on capital-intensive industries such as petroleum refining and chemicals, the flow of foreign investment that began in 1967 was largely in the fabricated metal products, machinery and transport equipment sector (a category that included the electronics industry, and shipbuilding and repair). There was also a substantial inflow of firms in the textile and garment industry during the 1960s, as firms from other NICs circumvented US quotas by relocating production to Singapore. Both the electronics and textile/garment industries relied heavily on female workers because they could be paid lower wages and were deemed dexterous and obedient.

The government developed a wide range of policies to influence the labour market and provide an adequate supply of workers with appropriate skills. For example, policies were designed to increase the workforce participation of women, regulate the flow of immigrant workers, educate workers in needed skills, and develop areas zoned for both housing and production facilities.

The government's export-oriented approach altered the growth rate of the economy and the structure of output and employment. Singapore's internationally renowned economic growth, a 10 per cent average annual increase in GDP during the 1965–80 period, was propelled by a 13.2 per cent yearly increase in manufacturing (World Bank 1991). TNCs were a major reason for this success since public policy emphasized production by foreign corporations rather than by domestic entrepreneurs. According to Deyo (1991), foreign firms produced nearly three-quarters of all manufacturing output by

1975. Employment generation was substantial. Growth in the electronics industry, almost wholly foreign firms, accounted for one out of three manufacturing jobs created in the 1970s (Pang 1988). By the mid-1980s, foreign firms employed over one-half of the manufacturing workforce.

Three types of problems arose with Singapore's export-led development strategy during the 1970s. First, the economy began to experience a shortage of labour, a problem which, it was felt, could undermine future growth. Unemployment dropped to levels considered full employment in the more developed countries (see Table 9.1). This was compounded by Singapore's guided-wage policy – annual guidelines for wage increases that covered all industries, irrespective of changes in productivity. This policy recommended only modest wage increases, resulting in the continued growth of largely labour-intensive production (Pang 1988).[3] Secondly, other countries in the region (Malaysia, the Philippines, Thailand and Indonesia) with plentiful supplies of low wage labour were now becoming competitors for foreign direct investment in Pacific Asia. Thirdly, the global recession of 1974–5 clearly revealed the vulnerability of an export-oriented strategy to worldwide downturns or to rising protectionism in major export markets.

Table 9.1 Unemployment rates by sex, various years, 1957–89

	Total	Female	Male	Ratio of female to male
1957	4.9	5.5	4.7	1.17
1970	10.1	16.2	7.7	2.10
1973	4.5	6.7	3.6	1.86
1974	3.9	5.0	3.4	1.47
1975	4.6	6.4	3.7	1.73
1976	4.5	5.8	3.9	1.48
1977	3.9	5.0	3.4	1.47
1978	3.6	4.1	3.3	1.24
1979	3.4	4.1	2.9	1.41
1980	3.5	3.9	3.4	1.15
1981	2.9	3.1	2.8	1.11
1982	2.6	2.9	2.4	1.21
1985	4.1	4.1	4.2	0.98
1989	2.2	1.9	2.3	0.83

Sources: *Report on the Labour Force Survey of Singapore* (1985, 1989); Department of Statistics, Singapore (1983).

The above trends and problems spurred a major effort to restructure the economy. Throughout the decade, the government had tried to reorient its export-oriented strategy by focusing on industries that added greater value or that transferred more research and development to Singapore. It had hoped to reduce its reliance on a limited number of exports and on too few markets. In 1979, however, the government decided drastic action was required.[4] It mandated 20 per cent compulsory wage increases, hoping to force an upgrading of the industrial structure. These substantial increases were maintained from 1979 to 1981. However, in the early 1980s, increases in wages exceeded productivity gains, eroding Singapore's competitiveness.

The TNCs did not respond as the government had expected. Few brought significant amounts of research and development or higher technology industries into Singapore. Some relocated to the lower-cost production sites in other South-East Asian economies (Kumar and Lee 1991). The early 1980s growth in Singapore was solely due to construction and services rather than manufacturing. Even more shocking, in 1985, recession in the industrialized countries led to the first negative growth in GDP for the economy (−2 per cent) in two decades.

Stunned by these events, and recognizing once again problems with its export-oriented development, the government established the special Economic Committee in 1985 to reassess national economic policy. The committee's report, *The Singapore Economy: New Directions* (Ministry of Trade and Industry, Singapore 1986), recommended changing business incentives, restructuring Singapore in the regional and global economy, and policies to increase the supply of labour.

First, the government reduced business taxes and reversed the wage policy adopted in 1979. It readopted a policy of wage restraint to try to restore wage competitiveness.

Secondly, the committee recommended making Singapore a hub in South-East Asia for production, marketing and financial services. This newest strategy for restructuring the economy would build on the country's existing strengths relative to other countries in the region – its location, its infrastructure (harbour, airport and telecommunications), and the rising skills of the workforce. TNCs would be encouraged to place regional headquarters in Singapore rather than simply locating production facilities there. In addition, the 'Growth Triangle' concept was developed, whereby Singapore and neighbouring parts of Malaysia and Indonesia would jointly pursue development. This would provide the dual advantages of low-cost production sites in Indonesia and Malaysia that offered cheap female labour, along with the more sophisticated administrative, marketing and financial services offered in Singapore. The biotechnology industry was to be encouraged, and Singapore was to become a regional centre for both agribusiness and financial services. Given the uncertainty regarding the future of Hong Kong, a major financial and trading centre in Pacific Asia, the latter was particularly favoured.

Thirdly, recognizing that the supply of labour depended on workforce participation rates, net migration and the rate of natural increase, the government developed initiatives in all three areas (Ministry of Trade and Industry, Singapore 1986: 105–9). The cornerstone of the Economic Committee's recommendations was increasing the female workforce participation rate by providing affordable childcare, and by encouraging part-time employment, job-sharing and homework. The committee also suggested policies that would encourage working beyond the retirement age of 55. Although very reluctant to permit long-term use of immigrants, it advocated continued use of foreign workers and suggested tailoring immigration policies to needed sectors and skill levels.

The plan to increase women's workforce participation was constrained by the fact that previous policies designed to reduce fertility and thereby increase female workforce participation were altered in the early 1980s. Fertility reduction policies had been selectively reversed because such anti-natalist strategies were found to decrease the supply of workers in subsequent generations. Now substantial financial incentives were constructed to encourage educated women in younger age-groups to increase their fertility. However, the efforts to both augment fertility rates and increase female workforce participation in the 1980s were contradictory because of the intense demands they placed on women's limited time.

In short, Singapore's export-oriented development strategy during this entire period relied heavily on TNCs in industries that hired large proportions of women. Since the mid-1960s, women have therefore been central to the development strategy. Moreover, since the mid-1980s the state has explicitly relied upon women (as workers and as procreators of future labourers) as a major component of Singapore's revised growth strategy. The next section examines the differing effects that economic development and restructuring have had on women relative to men.

DISPARATE EFFECTS OF ECONOMIC RESTRUCTURING ON WOMEN AND MEN

Economic restructuring has affected men and women quite differently. This can be documented through changes in workforce participation rates of men and women, changing sectoral and occupational employment patterns by gender, and changes in relative wages.

Although it would be desirable to examine overall trends during the entire period, as well as changes in women's roles in the economy during the major periods of restructuring, this analysis is somewhat constrained by the lack of census and workforce survey data. For example, the import-substitution strategy was operational in 1961–5 but, because census data are only available for the years 1957 and 1970, the impact of import-substitution strategy on female employment cannot be gauged. Unemployment data will be used instead to suggest some effects of changes in later years.

Overall, census data show that women dramatically increased their presence in the workforce since 1957, while the participation of men actually decreased. Women were a critical part of Singapore's economic success. However, they remained in distinctly disadvantaged positions.

Table 9.2 shows that the effect of export promotion on women's employment was substantial, particularly in contrast to the changes that occurred in male employment. The female workforce participation rate more than doubled from 1957 (21.6 per cent) to 1989 (48.4 per cent), with the largest portion of the increase (29.5–48.4 per cent) occurring in 1970–89, a period of time after the initiation of export-oriented industrialization. By contrast, the workforce participation rate of men fell from 87.6 per cent in 1957 to 78.6 per cent in 1989, a decrease of 10 per cent.

Table 9.2 Workforce participation rate by sex, 1957–present

	1957	1970	1975	1980	1985	1989
Economically active women as % total female population aged 15+	21.6	29.5	35.2	44.3	44.9	48.4
Economically active men as % total male population aged 15+	87.6	82.3	79.3	81.5	79.9	78.6
Economically active persons as % total population aged 15+	57.0	56.5	58.2	63.2	62.2	63.1

Sources: Report on the Labour Force Survey of Singapore (1975, 1985, 1989); *Census of Population, Singapore* (1980); Department of Statistics, Singapore (1983).

These dramatically different trends in male and female workforce participation rates sharply altered the proportion of the workforce that was female. The female share of the total workforce more than doubled during this period, rising from 17.6 per cent in 1957 to 39.3 per cent in 1989. Again, the major portion of this increase occurred after 1970.

Greater female employment in manufacturing and two service sectors, areas targeted by the export-oriented strategy, were major factors increasing the female workforce participation. The female workforce grew from 84,000 in 1957 to 503,000 in 1989 with increased employment in manufacturing providing 153,000 or 36.5 per cent of the increase. As mentioned earlier, the influx of foreign firms was responsible for a substantial portion of the increase in manufacturing employment (Deyo 1991: 54). In particular, the electronics industry, employing chiefly young women and dominated by TNCs, accounted for one-third of all new manufacturing jobs created since the 1960s (Pang 1988: 219). Therefore, women were pulled into the manufacturing sector largely because of the influx of foreign firms in industries that desired female workers. In sharp contrast to their 17 per cent share of the manufacturing workforce in 1957, large proportions of the new manufacturing jobs since that time were filled by women. Women accounted for

46 per cent of the increase in manufacturing employment in 1957–70, 41 per cent of the increase in 1970–5, and over 50 per cent of the increase in 1975–80.

As Table 9.3 shows, by 1975 the manufacturing sector was the largest employer of women; and it remained the largest employer of women throughout the 1980s. In 1957, under one-fifth of women in the workforce were employed in manufacturing; by 1989 the proportion was over one-third. In contrast, the proportion of the male workforce employed in manufacturing rose only to one-quarter. Furthermore, as Table 9.4 reveals, there were substantial increases in the proportion of the workforce that was female in most sectors of the economy. The percentage of the workforce in manufacturing that was female rose from 17 per cent in 1957 to 45.8 per cent in 1989. Looking at other sectors where large percentages of women work, we find that the female share of employment in community, social and personal services rose from one-quarter to 46.6 per cent during this period. Even more dramatically, women comprised less than 7 per cent of the workforce in the commerce sector in 1957, but 39.1 per cent in 1989.

Restructuring affected particular groups of women differently than their male counterparts. Table 9.5 shows that the export-promotion strategy initially drew upon large numbers of young female workers. The workforce participation rates of women in the 15–29 age-group dramatically increased from 1957 to 1970 (doubling or nearly doubling), with substantial further increases in 1970–4 for the 20–29-year-olds. Over the entire 1957–89 period, the workforce participation of women aged 20–44 sharply increased. (After

Table 9.3 Distribution of the workforce by sex and industry, 1957–89

	1957		1970		1980		1989	
	F	M	F	M	F	M	F	M
Manufacturing	19.4	17.0	31.3	19.1	40.5	24.6	33.7	25.9
Construction	2.1	16.3	1.8	8.1	1.4	9.5	1.4	10.0
Commerce	15.7	14.5	18.9	24.9	21.2	21.4	22.6	22.9
Transport, storage, communication	1.3	8.3	2.6	15.1	5.1	14.3	5.1	13.0
Finance, insurance, real estate and business services	2.4		3.5	3.6	8.9	6.6	11.5	7.7
		19.0*						
Community, social, personal services	47.0		38.3	23.8	21.7	20.4	25.3	18.9
Other†	12.1	25.0	3.6	5.4	1.2	3.2	0.4	1.6
Total	100	100	100	100	100	100	100	100‡

Sources: Wong (1981); *Census of Population, Singapore* (1970, 1980); *Report on the Labour Force Survey of Singapore* (1975, 1985, 1989).
* Data for males in these two categories were not separated in 1957.
† Other includes 'agriculture, forestry and fishing', 'mining and quarrying', 'utilities', and others.
‡ Columns may not total exactly 100 due to rounding.

rising until 1980, the workforce participation rate of women aged 15–19 fell, due to increased government emphasis on further education.) This contrasts to changes in the participation rates for similar groups of men. As Table 9.5 shows, men aged 20–24 reduced rather than increased their levels of economic activity. Workforce participation rates remained relatively constant for men aged 25–50 throughout the period, and men aged 15–19 exhibited no spike in their workforce participation rates, with rates declining throughout the period.

Further, as Table 9.6 shows, there were dramatic increases in 1957–89 in the workforce participation rates of single and married women, both of which almost tripled. However, export promotion initially involved single women. Their workforce participation rate jumped from 24.8 per cent in 1957 to 35.6 per cent in 1970, while the rate of married women remained constant at just under 15 per cent. It was only after 1970 that married women's participation increased substantially. Although data on men's workforce participation by marital status are only available from 1970 to 1989, clear differences can nevertheless be discerned. Married men's participation actually fell, and single men increased their participation by 39 per cent, substantially less than the 91 per cent increase for single women.

Patterns of female and male workforce participation also differed by ethnic group. While the workforce participation rate of Chinese women more than doubled in 1957–89, that for Malay and Indian women (the minority groups) increased more than sevenfold. Percentage changes in female workforce participation were substantially larger in each ethnic group from 1970 to 1989 than for males.[5]

Finally, there are distinct differences in changes in the workforce participation rate for males and females based upon citizenship status. The available data, from 1975 to 1989, show that the workforce participation rate of female

Table 9.4 Female share of those employed by industry, 1957–89

	1957	1970	1980	1989
Manufacturing	17.1	33.6	46.3	45.8
Construction	3.7	6.6	7.4	8.3
Commerce	6.7	19.0	34.2	39.1
Transport, storage, communication	NA	5.0	15.7	20.5
Finance, insurance, real estate and business services	NA	23.0	41.6	49.2
Community, social, personal services	25.7	33.2	35.8	46.6
Other*	46.8	17.2	16.4	13.3

Sources: Wong (1981); *Census of Population, Singapore* (1970, 1980); *Report on the Labour Force Survey of Singapore* (1975, 1985, 1989).
NA = Not available.
*Other includes 'agriculture, forestry and fishing', 'mining and quarrying', 'utilities', and others.

Table 9.5 Workforce participation rate by sex and age, 1957–present

	1957		1970		1980		1989	
	F	M	F	M	F	M	F	M
15–19	23.4	59.4	43.0	55.7	50.7	47.5	28.2	25.5
20–24	22.9	92.3	53.6	92.9	78.4	93.4	81.3	84.8
25–29	16.5	98.0	30.8	98.0	58.7	97.2	74.1	96.6
30–34	17.3	98.6	22.7	98.3	44.2	97.9	59.8	98.3
35–39	20.8	98.5	19.3	98.4	37.1	98.0	53.3	99.0
40–44	26.3	98.0	17.8	98.1	33.2	97.6	50.2	97.8
45–49	30.1	97.0	17.5	96.2	26.5	95.7	41.3	96.1
50–54	28.8	93.5	17.5	88.1	20.4	89.6	30.7	89.2
55–59	24.7	85.1	16.2	73.9	14.5	70.7	19.4	66.6
60+	10.0	52.4	9.1	42.6	8.0	37.4	7.0	31.2

Sources: *Report on the Labour Force Survey of Singapore* (1985, 1989); Department of Statistics, Singapore (1983).

Table 9.6 Workforce participation rate by marital status and sex, 1957–present

	1957	1970	1975	1980	1985	1989
Females						
Single	24.8	35.6	39.1	53.1	68.1	68.1
Married	14.0	14.7	22.1	29.8	33.1	40.3
Widowed	25.8	15.5	14.8	16.1	18.2	26.2
Divorced	46.5	47.6	50.0	61.7	68.6	
Males						
Single	NA	51.0	51.0	59.0	72.9	70.8
Married	NA	89.2	87.3	87.8	86.7	85.7
Widowed	NA	45.7	43.0	37.0	37.4	49.3
Divorced	NA	85.0	83.3	83.8	82.6	

Sources: *Census of Population, Singapore* 1970, 1980; *Report on the Labour Force Survey of Singapore* (1975, 1985, 1989).
NA = Not available.

Singaporeans increased 30 per cent while that for of non-Singaporean women increased almost threefold. While Singaporean women had the higher rate in 1975, this was no longer the case in 1985. The pattern for women contrasts sharply to the relatively unchanging rates for both Singaporean and non-Singaporean males. These figures suggest that immigrant women were increasingly relied upon to alleviate labour shortages in Singapore.

As mentioned earlier, because of data limitations it is not possible to provide detailed examination of how the two modifications to the export-oriented strategy affected women. However, unemployment data can shed some light on this issue. Table 9.1 shows that female unemployment rates rose sharply relative to male unemployment rates during the international recession of 1975. Although the female/male ratio declined over the next three years, it rose again in 1979 when the government increased wages by 20 per cent in an attempt to upgrade to higher-tech industries. This suggests that such a strategy was relatively disadvantageous to female workers in export industries facing competition from the lower wages paid in other Asian countries. It corresponds to other research that suggests that as industrial sectors become more highly skilled, the female share of the workforce declines (Pyle and Dawson 1990).

After the development strategy was revised in 1985 (to focus on turning Singapore into a regional production, marketing and financial services site and making women central to alleviating the labour shortage), female unemployment rates fell below male unemployment rates. The female/male ratio continued to decrease. This suggests that abandoning the higher wage strategy and emphasizing the use of female labour bolstered women's employment.

Throughout this period, the state undertook to increase women's workforce participation rate only; it was not trying to provide women with rights equivalent to men's or move them into equal positions in the workforce. According to Wong (1980), although women's work contributed significantly to Singapore's industrial success, the society has long regarded women's access to employment as less of a right than men's. Women's work has been considered supplementary to men's and/or dispensable when they are not needed by the economy. Furthermore, according to *The Singapore Woman* (1988: 22), there is no guarantee of equality in employment by either the Constitution or labour laws. Article 12 of the Constitution protects people from discrimination in employment only on the grounds of religion, race, descent or place of birth. Therefore, there is no protection from gender biases in hiring, access to training, promotion or pay. In addition, Singapore has not ratified three United Nations Conventions which protect women (*Legal Status of Singapore Women* 1986: 29–31).[6]

Although export-oriented industrialization depended critically upon the work of women, and although the female employment share of all industrial sectors has risen over the past three decades, women in Singapore remain in subordinate positions. This can be assessed in terms of their distribution across occupations, relative gross monthly incomes, vulnerability during economic downturns, and disproportionate responsibility for childcare and household duties.

While there has been some improvement over the years, women still constitute a very low percentage of the higher level occupations. In 1989, over one-third of the female workforce was in manufacturing, mainly in production jobs where women made 69 per cent of men's median gross monthly income.

Table 9.7 provides information on the median gross monthly incomes for men and women in different occupational categories. Overall, the ratio of female to male median gross monthly income rose from 63 per cent to

73 per cent. However, the *Report on the Labour Force Survey* (1989: 19) states that female median income as percentage of male median income fell from 74.2 per cent in 1980 to 73.4 per cent in 1989. Table 9.7 reveals that for professional and technical workers, the ratio fell substantially. For all other occupations, the female/male ratio rose but women's median gross monthly income was still well below men's.

Similarly, Table 9.8 examines median gross monthly income by sex and educational attainment. Across all educational levels, women earned sub-stantially less than men in 1978 and 1989. More surprisingly, during this period, the female/male ratio *fell* for more educated workers while it rose to about 70 per cent for workers with no schooling, no qualifications, or less than secondary education. This problem is compounded by the fact that women workers are better educated than male workers. According to Pang (1988), who constructed profiles of the female and male workforce in each educational level, women are better educated than men. *The Singapore Woman* (1988: 15) states that in 1986 over 53 per cent of female workers had at least a secondary education while only 44 per cent of male workers did.

Due to the manner in which they were incorporated into the economy during economic restructuring, women were also more vulnerable than men in two global recessions that affected Singapore. Although female workforce participation rates increased sharply during this period, women's jobs were disproportionately affected by recessionary conditions. According to Wong (1981: 440), 16,900 workers were retrenched in 1974 – 79 per cent of whom

Table 9.7 Median gross monthly income by sex and occupation in Singapore dollars (S$)

	1978			1989		
	M	F	F/M	M	F	F/M
Professional and technical workers	493	510	1.03	1,804	1,419	0.79
Administrative and managerial workers	1,019	584	0.57	2,726	1,958	0.72
Clerical and related workers	355	309	0.87	859	774	0.90
Sales workers	313	138	0.44	951	632	0.66
Service workers	297	150	0.51	692	385	0.56
Production and related workers, transport equipment operators and labourers, agricultural workers	290	134	0.46	741	511	0.69
Workers not classifiable by occupation	157	230	1.46	261	1,181	4.53
Overall	314	197	0.63	865	635	0.73

Sources: *Report on the Labour Force Survey of Singapore* (1978, 1989).

Table 9.8 Median gross monthly income by sex and highest qualification attained (S$)

| | 1978 | | | 1989 | | |
	M	F	F/M	M	F	F/M
Never attended school	342	200*	0.584	627	444	0.708
No qualifications	348	200*	0.575	680	476	0.700
Primary/post-primary	332	221	0.665	756	523	0.692
Secondary	405	315	0.778	969	732	0.755
Post-secondary	568	437	0.769	1,411	1,019	0.722
Tertiary	1,547	1,063	0.687	3,000+	2,028	0.676

Sources: Report on the Labour Force Survey of Singapore (1978, 1989).
* The median could not be calculated because the category 'less than 200' in the data was open-ended.

were women. During the 1974–5 recession, 50 per cent of those laid off from work were female, yet women were only 30 per cent of the workforce (*Straits Times* 1985). In 1980, the recession in the United States resulted in 'massive layoffs of female electronics workers in large U.S. firms in Singapore' (Wong 1981: 440). In 1985, despite the fact that women made up 34.6 per cent of the workforce, at least 60 per cent of all workers laid off in the first six months of the year's recession were female (*Straits Times* 1985: 6). Almost 90 per cent of the layoffs were production workers, who were largely female.

Another critical aspect of the disadvantaged economic status of women in Singapore is the fact that women bear disproportionate responsibility for childcare and work in the home. This is often a constraint on female workforce participation, and in many ways serves to reinforce their subordinate status in the labour market. Seen in this light, the government's approach since the mid-1980s – to increase the female workforce participation while simultaneously raising the fertility rate – has placed nearly impossible demands on the limited time and energies of many women. This occurs because increased female participation must come largely from married women, the group with lower participation rates. However, many of these married women are in the age-groups targeted for increased childbearing and have the chief responsibility for home duties.

This problem is compounded by government policies toward immigrants. The country has been extremely reluctant to allow any additional ethnic groups to establish themselves in Singaporean society. Reliance on immigrant labour has been considered a temporary and less-desirable method to alleviate the labour shortage, and has been carefully controlled. However, immigrants could provide more workers for the formal labour market (relieving the need to increase female workforce participation) or for the household sector (reducing household and childcare duties that constrain women's participation).

The government has recognized the problems women face in combining paid work in the labour force with home duties. In the hope of alleviating the problem, the government has proposed a number of wide-ranging policies over the last few years – incentives for provision of childcare by corporations or the state, encouragement of flexible work schedules and part-time work, recommendations that males share more home duties, and strategies to encourage grandparents to live next door and provide childcare.

CONCLUSION

This paper has compared the effect of structural change in the Singapore economy on the labour-market experiences of women and men. It has examined policy changes instituted by the government to achieve its economic goals – abandonment of import-substitution industrialization, adoption of an export-promotion strategy based upon foreign direct investment, and modifications to this strategy deemed necessary for continued high growth rates. It has shown that economic development in Singapore has depended heavily on the role of women – in providing the supply of labour necessary for export-led development (as workers themselves and as pro-creators of the next generation of workers).

Although women's workforce participation rate and the proportion of the workforce that is female have both more than doubled, women remain in distinctly subordinate positions in the economy. Furthermore, in trying to simultaneously increase fertility rates of educated women and female workforce participation rates, the government pursues two contradictory objectives. Because the state has given both precedence, and considers both to be central elements of its development strategy, resolving this contradiction will be critical to the future economic role of women and to sustaining high rates of economic growth.

With the publication of 1990 census volumes and newer Labour Force Surveys, it will be possible to examine the impact of current restructuring efforts on women's workforce participation.[7] Further study is certainly needed regarding the gender impact of the recently enacted social policies mentioned at the end of the preceding section. These policies have not fully resolved the contradictions that women face when simultaneously increasing their workforce participation and fertility rates. It may be necessary to revise existing policies or develop new ones. Data in existing workforce surveys could be analysed to understand the reasons why women leave the workforce, why people work part-time or are economically inactive, and what factors might induce them to enter the workforce full-time (see for example *Report on the Labour Force Survey* (1989: 11, 21–2, 24–6)).

In addition, the lack of state policy addressing employment equality for women has serious implications for Singapore's future economic growth and for the economic roles of women. For Singapore to restructure and remain competitive in the 1990s, women must be incorporated into more equal roles in the economy. Past policies have focused only on increasing their workforce participation rates. For a labour-short economy which has a long-term stated interest in providing a skilled workforce to attract TNCs, the failure to draw fully on women's capabilities reduces potential growth rates. Women's status as more educated must translate into greater equality in jobs and pay. Finally, an important component of enhancing the economic position of women is the effort some women are making to gain empowerment. This is a difficult, but not impossible, task in a society that has long been authoritarian and male-dominated.[8]

NOTES

1 The NICs – Singapore, Hong Kong, Taiwan and South Korea – are also referred to as the NIEs (the newly industrialized economies), the Four Dragons or the Mini-Dragons. For an overview of the economic development of these countries, the similarities and the differences between them, and the main issues regarding their development see Goldstein (1991); Vogel (1991); Bello and Rosenfeld (1990); Pang (1988); and Deyo (1987).

2 This aspect of Singapore's development will be explored more fully in my forthcoming book. For more information see Deyo (1991); and Pang (1988).

3 The growing labour shortage was somewhat alleviated by liberal policies toward immigration. It was also lessened by earlier policies designed to decrease fertility and the subsequent increases in female workforce participation rates.

4 Incentives were altered to attract TNCs in consumer electronics, precision instruments, pharmaceuticals and non-manufacturing sectors such as engineering, communications, finance and health care.

5 Data are available from the author upon request.

6 These consist of the Convention on the Elimination of all Forms of Discrimination Against Women, the Convention Concerning Equal Remuneration for Men and Women Workers for Work of Equal Value, the Convention Concerning Equal Opportunities and Equal Treatment for Men and Women Workers: Women with Family Responsibilities.

7 As of August 1993 there was no projected publication date for the 1990 census volume on economic characteristics.

8 See also *The Singapore Woman* for suggestions on policies regarding discrimination, education, women and work, and labour law.

10

GOVERNMENT REFORMS, ECONOMIC RESTRUCTURING, AND THE EMPLOYMENT OF WOMEN: SOUTH KOREA, 1980–92

Scott M. Fuess, Jr. and Bun Song Lee

INTRODUCTION

South Korea's rapid and sustained growth since the mid-1960s is well-known and has been well-documented. Much attention has focused on the government's export-promotion policies and the economic restructuring they have led to. Rapid development has required changes in the composition of jobs, especially the reallocation of labour-intensive activities from agriculture to export-oriented manufacturing. This process can result in a dualistic pattern of development, a growing, high-wage industrial sector coexisting with a stable, low-wage agricultural sector. Such dualistic development opens the door to job discrimination.[1]

At present, there is controversy over whether women have in fact gained from industrialization in South Korea. Some analysts have argued that economic development has created new opportunities for women, providing job openings in industries and occupations where previously there had not been much female employment. Conversely, others have argued that industrialization has reinforced historical patterns of sex discrimination. Many have maintained that female employment has been skewed toward 'declining' industries (e.g. agriculture) and lower-status jobs (e.g. unpaid family work), while men tend to work in 'targeted growth' industries like heavy manufacturing and in higher status jobs, such as salaried work.[2]

Prior studies of rapid industrialization and female employment in South Korea have focused mostly on the period up to 1980. These accounts of the 1960s and 1970s suggest that as the manufacturing sector expanded, the agricultural sector became feminized. Moreover, it has been argued that much of the female employment growth in manufacturing has involved menial jobs. Further, in the growing urban centres women often worked in temporary manufacturing or service work. The overall impression is one of job segregation – the 'crowding' of women into 'secondary' work.[3]

145

During the 1960s and 1970s the South Korean government intervened widely in the economy, setting export targets and supporting manufacturing with subsidized credits and protection via import substitution.[4] There was rapid economic growth, but there were also relatively high rates of inflation. Oil shocks, interest rate shifts, instability in export markets and poor agricultural harvests threatened to undermine the economy's performance.

By 1980 South Korea was experiencing a deep recession, inflation of nearly 30 per cent and social strife following the assassination of President Park Chung-Hee. In response, the government shifted its focus from economic growth, with a heavy emphasis on manufactured exports, to policies aimed at achieving steady growth with lower inflation. To stabilize macroeconomic conditions, reforms were introduced to reduce the country's external debt and current account deficit. To improve microeconomic performance, the government implemented a number of 'competitiveness' measures, intervening less in the day-to-day operation of private sector industries. Thus, the government pursued the twin objectives of stabilizing aggregate demand and stimulating aggregate supply.[5]

This chapter examines the impact of the above economic reforms on labour market segregation. We compare employment data across industrial and work-status classifications for the 1980–92 period with figures for earlier years. This allows us to examine how the representation of women in various occupations and economic sectors changed as government reforms drove for more stable development. Our analysis helps to determine whether the concentration of women in declining sectors and in lower status jobs changed after reforms were implemented to stabilize economic growth.[6]

ECONOMIC REFORMS AND RESTRUCTURING

Government reforms can be traced back to the announcement of the Comprehensive Measures for Economic Stabilization (CMES) in April 1979. These measures aimed to control inflation with tighter monetary and fiscal policies. As reported by Kwack (1990b), money supply growth was slowed substantially over the period 1981–4, as was government spending. A key element in the government plan was to control subsidized credit for favoured industrial sectors.

Following another oil shock and the death of President Park in 1980, the CMES stabilization programme was modified by the new government of President Chun Doo-Hwan. To spur exports, the Korean won was devalued. The government held down public sector wage increases in an attempt to control wage inflation in the private sector. To open the economy to more competition and improve economic efficiency, microeconomic reforms focused on deregulation, trade liberalization and anti-monopoly legislation. Reforms included deregulation of foreign investment in South Korea and denationalization of banks. Further, the government used agricultural price supports and a programme of farm diversification to stabilize fluctuations in food production.[7]

As the 1980s closed, there was slower economic growth in the world economy, and energy prices were again rising. The Korean won started to appreciate, which threatened exports. Labour strikes and demands for democratization created social unrest. These developments slowed economic growth and inflation rates began to rise again. To keep inflation under control, the government of President Roh Tae-Woo responded with restrictive monetary and fiscal policies in 1988.

South Korea's economic performance

The South Korean economy was able to sustain economic growth with lower inflation after the CMES programme was implemented. From 1965 to 1980, real gross domestic product (GDP) reached an annual growth rate of 8.8 per cent; but the consumer price index measured 15 per cent inflation per year. From 1981 to 1992, average annual real GDP growth was 9 per cent while inflation averaged less than 7 per cent.[8]

The performance of the economy since 1980, however, masks several distinct phases. Annual real GDP growth accelerated from 1981 to 1983, but then slowed during 1984 and 1985. Meanwhile, inflation fell from 21.3 per cent in 1981 to less than 2.5 per cent in 1985. GDP growth boomed again between 1986 and 1988, nearly reaching 12 per cent annually, but was more erratic thereafter – slowing to 6.2 per cent in 1989, rebounding in 1990 to 9.2 per cent, and then falling to 4.8 per cent in 1992. As the economy boomed in the later 1980s, inflation rates rose from 2.7 per cent in 1986 to 7.1 per cent in 1988; inflation then escalated to 9.7 per cent in 1991 before falling to 6.2 per cent in 1992. Although inflation climbed, it failed to reach the double-digit rates that occurred consistently in the initial phase of rapid industrialization.

One source of volatility in the late 1980s was labour unrest. According to the Korean Statistical Association (1991: 93), during 1981–6 about 34,600 working days per year were lost due to strikes; in contrast, during 1987–90 strikes took more than 5,135,000 working days per year. This discord resulted in substantial wage inflation. Nominal wage growth slowed from 20.2 per cent in 1981 to 10.1 per cent in 1985 (see Kwack 1990b: 226). In contrast, between 1986 and 1990, nominal labour earnings increased quickly, more than 20 per cent annually (see Ministry of Labour, South Korea 1991: 180).

Structural changes continued during the 1980s, but followed a different pattern from earlier years. In 1965 only 10.3 per cent of employment was in mining and manufacturing. By 1980 the sector's employment share had more than doubled, to 22.5 per cent. The percentage of workers in mining and manufacturing continued to rise in the 1980s, but much more slowly than in the 1960s and 1970s. The sector's employment share in 1992 was 25.5 per cent.

Between 1965 and 1980 the sector encompassing services, utilities and construction also increased its employment share – from 31 per cent to 43.5 per cent. This growth was slower than the growth of manufacturing; during the 1980s, growth in this sector exceeded that of manufacturing. In fact, by 1985 the services, utilities and construction sector employed more than half of South Korea's workers, and by 1992 employment in this sector was 58.5 per cent of South Korea's workers.

Growing employment shares in manufacturing and services occurred at the expense of the agricultural sector. While 59 per cent of the workforce was employed in the agricultural sector in 1965, this dropped to 34 per cent in 1980 and to 16 per cent in 1990.

EMPLOYMENT PATTERNS FOR WOMEN AND MEN

To compare recent employment developments with employment changes during the years of rapid industrialization, we examine workforce participation and employment patterns by industries and job status for the 1965–92 period. A summary of the evidence follows.

Workforce participation

As South Korea industrialized between 1965 and 1980, female workforce participation increased while male participation fell (Table 10.1). In the early 1980s participation dropped overall, but rebounded after 1985, especially for women. According to Kwack (1990b) and Castañeda and Park (1992), in the early 1980s the number of people in housekeeping or going to school sharply increased, which would account for falling workforce participation rates during this period. As the economy started to boom again in 1986, however, workforce participation increased, with a more pronounced jump for women.[9]

Table 10.1 Workforce participation rates in South Korea

	Female (%)	Male (%)
1965	37.2	78.9
1970	39.3	77.9
1975	40.4	77.4
1980	42.8	76.4
1985	41.9	72.3
1990	47.0	73.9
1992	47.3	75.3

Sources: Workforce participation rates for 1965–90 were taken from Lee (1993: table 1a). The 1992 data were taken from National Statistical Office, Republic of Korea (1993).

Employment patterns across industries

Given this upward trend in female workforce participation, we examine whether female employment grew to the same extent across industries. The National Statistical Office of South Korea classifies industries in three broad categories: (i) agriculture, forestry, hunting and fishing, (ii) manufacturing and mining, and (iii) social overhead capital and services (SOCS). 'Social overhead capital' includes construction and utilities (electricity, gas and water). 'Services' consist of wholesaling and retailing (including restaurants and hotels); transport, storage and communication; financial and business services (including insurance and real estate); and community, social and personal services.[10] Employment levels for women and men across industries are reported in Table 10.2. The figures indicate growing female representation in work economy-wide.

As production expanded in mining and manufacturing, employment grew substantially for both women and men. Until 1990, employment increased more rapidly among women, causing the ratio of females to males to rise. The increase in female representation was most pronounced for the 1985–90 period, when the sector experienced especially rapid expansion. But as manufacturing growth slowed in the early 1990s, female employment and representation in the sector receded.

Table 10.2 also reveals a growing female presence in social overhead capital and services. The number of women and men working in the SOCS sector consistently increased, with faster growth for women. Consequently, female representation in the sector expanded throughout the 1965–92 period. This expansion was the most pronounced after 1980.

Female representation also grew in agriculture between 1965 and 1975. Agricultural employment declined after 1975, with sustained reductions for both women and men. Because more men left agricultural work than women, the female–male ratio in the sector continued to rise.[11]

In mining and manufacturing and social overhead capital and services it appears that job opportunities opened for women, especially in the 1980s. But it would be hasty to conclude that job segregation declined in South Korea as the economy drove for more stable development. In manufacturing, female employment, especially for those under the age of 30, has been concentrated in relatively low-wage areas like wearing apparel, footwear and textiles, while men dominated employment in higher wage areas like steel and metals, machinery and transport equipment.[12] According to the Korean Statistical Association (1991: 84–7), in the 1984–90 period average monthly earnings of regular employees in machinery (excluding electrical machinery), iron and basic steel exceeded average manufacturing earnings by 15–50 per cent. In contrast, average earnings in wearing apparel and textiles were 20–35 per cent less than the manufacturing average.

The volatility in female manufacturing employment in the 1980s and 1990s

Table 10.2 Employment in South Korean industries, 1965–92

	Number of females (million)	Growth rate* (%)	Number of males (million)	Growth rate* (%)	Female–male job ratio
Mining and manufacturing					
1965	0.238		0.611		0.390
1970	0.435	16.555	0.960	11.424	0.453
1975	0.760	14.943	1.505	11.354	0.505
1980	1.166	10.684	1.913	5.422	0.610
1985	1.356	3.259	2.303	4.077	0.589
1990	2.058	10.354	2.871	4.933	0.717
1992	1.921	−3.328	2.907	0.627	0.661
Social overhead capital and services					
1965	0.803		1.744		0.460
1970	1.097	7.323	2.337	6.800	0.469
1975	1.328	4.211	2.812	4.065	0.472
1980	2.022	10.452	3.929	7.945	0.515
1985	2.858	8.269	4.720	4.026	0.606
1990	3.785	6.487	6.031	5.555	0.628
1992	4.304	6.856	6.764	6.077	0.636
Agriculture, forestry, hunting and fishing					
1965	1.843		2.967		0.621
1970	2.046	2.203	2.870	−0.654	0.713
1975	2.253	2.023	3.172	2.105	0.710
1980	2.034	−1.944	2.620	−3.480	0.776
1985	1.619	−4.081	2.114	−3.863	0.766
1990	1.499	−1.482	1.793	−3.037	0.836
1992	1.384	−3.836	1.641	−4.239	0.843

Sources: Female employment figures for 1965–90 and male employment figures for 1980–90 were taken from Lee (1993: tables 12 and 14). The 1965–75 data for males and 1992 figures were taken from National Statistical Office, Republic of Korea (various years).
* The simple percentage change between observations is divided by the appropriate number of years to obtain the maximal annual growth rate for the period.

suggests that female labour may have come to be used as a buffer to absorb cyclical shocks.[13] The figures in Table 10.2 also support the view of female 'crowding' in the agricultural sector. As the number of agricultural workers fell after 1980, the representation of women in the sector became more pronounced.

The employment figures in the SOCS sector deserve further clarification. Wages in utilities and construction have been relatively high, with male workers far outnumbering females. Between 1982 and 1990, average monthly earnings of regular employees in utilities (electricity, gas and water) exceeded the average for all industries, in the range of 71 per cent (in 1982) to 48 per cent (in 1990). Earnings in construction were higher than the overall average by 49 and 16 per cent in the same period (Korean Statistical Association 1991: 82–3).

Women are heavily concentrated in services, which provide above average pay; but it is not clear that they hold higher paying jobs in services. Women are most heavily concentrated in low paying service areas. For example, in 1990 the ratio of females to males in SOCS work was 0.628. In financial services the ratio was 0.615; and in community, social and personal services, the ratio was 0.753. In the financial sector, average monthly earnings of regular employees were higher than the average for all industries between 1982 (58 per cent) and 1990 (32 per cent). Over the same period, earnings in community, social and personal services exceeded the overall average by 66 and 28 per cent.

Regular employees in wholesale–retail trade earned between 16 (1982) and 2 per cent (1990) more than the overall average (see Korean Statistical Association 1991: 82–3). Women outnumbered men in wholesale–retail trade, where the female–male ratio was 1.125, but in finance and in wholesaling–retailing, women predominantly worked in clerical and sales positions, not higher wage professional and technical jobs. In contrast, in community, social and personal services, women outnumbered men in professional and technical jobs. In this service area, women held more than 20 per cent of administrative and managerial jobs, although they occupied only 4 per cent of the administrative and managerial jobs overall (National Statistical Office, Republic of Korea 1992: 231).

Employment by work status

Employment figures at the industry level say nothing about the status of work. To determine whether women have been concentrated in less favourable working situations than men, we examine employment patterns across industries by work status. The South Korean government classifies work according to three status categories – unpaid family work, self-employment and paid employment.

The first category represents work performed within a household or a family unit. To qualify as an unpaid worker, a person must work at least 18 hours, during a survey week, in a family-owned enterprise. Because such work is performed without pay, it is considered to be of relatively low status. Korean women have traditionally been concentrated in this type of work (see Hyoung Cho 1987; Yu 1987). The other two categories represent work performed outside the home or family unit. A self-employed person operates an enterprise for profit. Paid workers are employed by firms and receive wages. Because this last category includes salaried employees and other wage earners, it encompasses higher status work.

Unpaid family work

Table 10.3 looks at employment growth in unpaid family work. Although men outnumbered women in each sector, more women performed unpaid work than men in each sector. The number of women in unpaid family work rose during the 1965–80 period, while the number of men performing such work fell. This left the number of unpaid workers approximately the same in 1980 as in 1965. During the 1980–92 period, unpaid work became less prevalent for both women and men. Overall, unpaid work declined from 18.8 per cent to 10.4 per cent of Korean workers. But there was also a dramatic increase in the concentration of women performing this less favourable type of work.

Female representation in unpaid family work grew the most in mining and manufacturing. The number of women performing such work increased continuously, accelerating as the sector boomed in the second half of the 1980s. Unpaid work among women continued to expand from 1990 to 1992, although total female manufacturing employment dropped. Men, in contrast,

Table 10.3 Women and men in unpaid family work

	Number of females (million)	Growth rate* (%)	Number of males (million)	Growth rate* (%)	Female–male job ratio
Mining and manufacturing					
1965	0.040		0.039		1.026
1970	0.056	8.000	0.043	2.051	1.302
1975	0.061	1.786	0.033	−4.651	1.848
1980	0.083	7.213	0.037	2.424	2.243
1985	0.085	0.482	0.022	−8.108	3.864
1990	0.149	15.059	0.021	−0.909	7.095
1992	0.160	3.691	0.018	−7.143	8.889
Social overhead capital and services					
1965	0.184		0.065		2.831
1970	0.225	4.457	0.079	4.308	2.848
1975	0.334	9.689	0.085	1.519	3.929
1980	0.463	7.725	0.082	−0.706	5.646
1985	0.608	6.263	0.065	−4.146	9.354
1990	0.663	1.809	0.081	4.923	8.185
1992	0.677	1.056	0.094	8.025	7.202
Agriculture, forestry, hunting and fishing					
1965	1.445		0.779		1.855
1970	1.519	1.024	0.706	−1.874	2.152
1975	1.689	2.238	0.813	3.031	2.077
1980	1.409	−3.316	0.496	−7.798	2.841
1985	1.092	−4.500	0.316	−7.258	3.456
1990	0.992	−1.832	0.165	−9.557	6.012
1992	0.895	−4.889	0.130	−10.606	6.885

Sources: The 1965–90 employment figures for females and the 1980–90 figures for males were taken from Lee (1993: tables 13a–c and tables 15a–c). The 1965–75 data for males and 1992 figures were obtained from National Statistical Office, Republic of Korea (various years).

* The simple percentage change between observations is divided by the appropriate number of years to obtain the maximal annual growth rate for the period.

left family work in the early 1970s as well as throughout the 1980–92 period. As a result, the ratio of women to men increased from 1.026 to 2.243 between 1965 and 1980, and by 1992 the ratio had jumped to 8.889. Since the number of women has tended to grow while the number of men engaged in unpaid work has declined, it appears that women have replaced men in this low status manufacturing work.

In social overhead capital and services, there have also been increases in the number of unpaid working women, and a growing female–male job ratio. But in one respect the SOCS sector has been different. In the late 1980s and early 1990s, as services expanded (especially financial and community social and personal services and wholesale and retail trade), there was slower, not faster, growth in the number of unpaid women in SOCS labour. Female representation in lower status SOCS work actually declined after 1985.

The representation of women in unpaid work also increased consistently in agriculture, accelerating after 1980. As agricultural employment declined, men left unpaid family farming more quickly than women.

Self-employment

Table 10.4 shows that the number of self-employed women and men increased in the mining and manufacturing and social overhead capital and service sectors. Lee (1993) has conjectured that in some types of manufacturing and services, women have been more likely than men to be self-employed in casual or informal endeavours. If this conjecture is correct, then relatively wide fluctuations should be observed in the number of women performing such work.

Table 10.4 indicates that self-employment in mining and manufacturing indeed varied much more among women than men: female representation more than doubled between 1965 and 1980 and then fell more than 60 per cent after 1980. In the SOCS sector, however, self-employment grew at similar rates for women and men: the concentration of women in such work did not alter greatly.

Men have tended to outnumber women in self-employed agricultural work and this trend held throughout the 1980–92 period. Nevertheless, after 1980 there was a greater representation of women in this type of farming, as the number of self-employed males dropped while the number of women varied little.

Paid employment

Table 10.5 reports figures for women and men in paying jobs. Between 1965 and 1980 in the three industrial sectors, paid employment increased from 32.1 per cent to 47.3 per cent of workers. The percentage of workers with paying jobs continued to increase between 1980 and 1992, but at a slower rate than

Table 10.4 Women and men in self-employment

	Number of females (million)	Growth rate[*] (%)	Number of males (million)	Growth rate[*] (%)	Female–male job ratio
Mining and manufacturing					
1965	0.046		0.161		0.286
1970	0.099	23.043	0.203	5.217	0.488
1975	0.188	17.980	0.201	−0.197	0.935
1980	0.184	−0.426	0.317	11.542	0.580
1985	0.086	−10.652	0.317	0.000	0.271
1990	0.089	0.698	0.395	4.921	0.225
1992	0.104	8.427	0.467	9.114	0.223
Social overhead capital and services					
1965	0.321		0.582		0.552
1970	0.356	2.181	0.725	4.914	0.491
1975	0.428	4.045	0.949	6.179	0.451
1980	0.648	10.280	1.304	7.482	0.497
1985	0.815	5.154	1.575	4.156	0.517
1990	0.902	2.135	1.834	3.289	0.492
1992	1.011	6.042	2.080	6.707	0.486
Agriculture, forestry, hunting and fishing					
1965	0.242		1.667		0.145
1970	0.298	4.628	1.650	−0.204	0.181
1975	0.354	3.758	1.892	2.933	0.187
1980	0.387	1.864	1.814	−0.825	0.213
1985	0.339	−2.481	1.548	−2.933	0.219
1990	0.388	2.891	1.491	−0.736	0.260
1992	0.382	−0.773	1.399	−3.085	0.273

Sources: The 1965–90 employment figures for females and the 1980–90 figures for males were taken from Lee (1993: Tables 13a–c and Tables 15a–c). The 1965–75 data for males and 1992 figures were taken from National Statistical Office, Republic of Korea (various years).

* The simple percentage change between observations is divided by the appropriate number of years to obtain the maximal annual growth rate for the period.

before. By 1992, 60.8 per cent of workers were in paid employment. Men consistently outnumbered women in each industry, but female representation in paid employment increased in each sector.

The number of paying jobs in mining and manufacturing increased for women and men until 1990, with consistently faster growth for women. As the sector expanded and female workforce participation increased, the representation of women in paid manufacturing employment doubled. But as manufacturing growth slowed after 1990, the number of women in paying jobs dropped, as did the ratio of females to males.

Paid work increased steadily in social overhead capital and services, growing faster for women than men. In the 1980s there was a sustained, rapid increase in the number of women in paying service jobs. Although employment growth decelerated after 1990, female representation in this sector continued to rise. Paid employment has declined for both women and men in agriculture. But, as with other types of agricultural work, the decline in the number of females was comparatively small, so the concentration of women increased.

The fast growth of female representation in paying service sector jobs after 1980 is consistent with the claim that opportunities in higher status jobs opened for women as the economy continued to develop. Increases in the number of women in paid manufacturing employment also might support this claim. But the observation that women have been clustered in relatively low-wage manufacturing jobs indicates that figures for paid employment must be interpreted with care.

Paid employment encompasses high-status and well-paid technical, administrative and managerial positions, but the category also includes some less

Table 10.5 Women and men in paid employment

	Number of females (million)	Growth rate* (%)	Number of males (million)	Growth rate* (%)	Female–male job ratio
Mining and manufacturing					
1965	0.152		0.411		0.370
1970	0.280	16.842	0.714	14.745	0.392
1975	0.511	16.500	1.271	15.602	0.402
1980	0.899	15.186	1.561	4.563	0.576
1985	1.187	6.407	1.964	5.163	0.604
1990	1.820	10.691	2.453	4.980	0.742
1992	1.658	−4.451	2.422	−0.632	0.685
Social overhead capital and services					
1965	0.298		1.097		0.272
1970	0.516	14.631	1.533	7.949	0.337
1975	0.566	1.938	1.778	3.196	0.318
1980	0.911	12.191	2.544	8.616	0.358
1985	1.436	11.526	3.081	4.222	0.466
1990	2.219	10.905	4.115	6.712	0.539
1992	2.617	8.968	4.591	5.784	0.570
Agriculture, forestry, hunting and fishing					
1965	0.156		0.521		0.299
1970	0.229	9.359	0.514	−0.269	0.446
1975	0.210	−1.659	0.467	0.182	0.450
1980	0.239	2.762	0.312	−6.638	0.766
1985	0.188	−4.268	0.250	−3.974	0.752
1990	0.119	−7.340	0.136	−9.120	0.875
1992	0.106	−5.462	0.112	−8.824	0.946

Sources: The 1965–90 employment figures for females and the 1980–90 figures for males were taken from Lee (1993: Tables 13a–c and Tables 15a–c). The 1965–75 data for males and 1992 figures were obtained from National Statistical Office, Republic of Korea (various years).
* The simple percentage change between observations is divided by the appropriate number of years to obtain the maximal annual growth rate for the period.

prestigious work. The National Statistical Office distinguishes between two types of paying jobs – regular employment and daily work. A person is counted as a regular employee if her (his) employment contract exceeds one month and if she (he) has worked at the job for more than 45 days during the past three months; otherwise a person is classified as a daily worker (see Korean Statistical Association 1991: 83). The shorter-term employment embodied by 'daily work' can be considered lower status paying work than the longer-term, more permanent attachment associated with 'regular employment'. If the growth of female paid employment is centred around daily work, then it is not clear that higher status jobs have been opened to women.

Table 10.6 shows that the percentage of female paid workers in regular work increased between 1965 and 1980. During the initial phase of rapid industrialization, the percentage of women in regular paid work increased, indicating that more favourable employment opportunities did open for women.

As the South Korean economy adjusted to development with lower inflation and increased competition, the representation of women in longer-term jobs did not improve – a smaller percentage of women worked in regular employment. This trend was reversed from 1990 to 1992, when the proportion of women in regular paid work increased. These compositional changes suggest that the female workforce has been used to absorb cyclical shocks.

Table 10.6 Compositional change of female paid employees, 1965–92

	Percentage employed in regular work (economy-wide)	Percentage employed in regular work (non-farming)
1965	65.15	71.49
1970	68.48	80.14
1975	77.05	82.11
1980	78.81	83.15
1985	77.29	79.14
1990	77.25	78.28
1992	81.03	81.95

Sources: Figures for 1965–90 were taken from Lee (1993: table 9a). The 1992 figures were derived from National Statistical Office, Republic of Korea (1993).

Summary of employment patterns

When the share of agricultural employment fell over the 1965–80 period, female representation in this sector increased. With agricultural employment contracting between 1980 and 1992, the concentration of women (especially in unpaid and thus lower status work) became even more pronounced.

As economic reforms were implemented by the government and as the economy moved away from relying exclusively on manufacturing development, the employment circumstances of women in this sector became less favourable. Not only did the number of women in unpaid work increase, but it appears that paid employment among women in the sector became more oriented toward daily work. Young female labour, especially, became a buffer, absorbing cyclical fluctuations in manufacturing.

In contrast to the other two industrial sectors, more favourable employment opportunities opened for women in the SOCS sector. The female share of unpaid family work fell. Further, the representation of women in paying jobs – apparently centred around regular, longer-term employment – increased.

CONCLUSION

Several analysts have claimed that rapid industrialization in South Korea during the 1960s and 1970s resulted in the segregation of women in the less desirable jobs, reinforcing past patterns of discrimination against women. Specifically, employment patterns suggest that women were concentrated in agriculture, and tended to work in menial jobs in the manufacturing sector.

This chapter reviewed more recent employment patterns in South Korea, focusing on the years 1980–92 – a period that encompasses government reforms aimed at sustaining economic growth but with lower inflation. We also compared the recent trends with those of the earlier years of industrialization.

Our analysis indicates that the conclusions drawn about the effects of industrialization on job segregation must be modified somewhat. The rapid industrialization of the 1960s and 1970s did result in the greater concentration of women in agriculture and in lower status, unpaid work. But there also was growth in the number of women in paid employment, with an increased percentage of women holding longer-term, regular paying jobs.

South Korean economic reforms to stabilize macroeconomic conditions, improve the allocation of financial resources, de-emphasize the exclusive development of heavy manufacturing and increase competitiveness had a mixed impact on the economic status of women. There was an increase in the number of women performing low status, unpaid work. Further, female labour in mining and manufacturing came to be used as a buffer stock to absorb cyclical shocks. But in social overhead capital and services (SOCS), the representation of women in unpaid work fell and it appears that opportunities in longer term, regularly paying jobs opened for women.

The growth of female paid employment in the service sector was greater than the increase in the number of women in unpaid family work and paid manufacturing employment. The tables show that the share of employed women in unpaid family work and paid manufacturing fell – from 63.1 per cent in 1965 to 54.7 per cent in 1980, and dropped further to 44.6 per cent in 1992. Meanwhile, the percentage of women in paying SOCS jobs increased – from 10.3 per cent in 1965 to 17.4 per cent in 1980, nearly doubling to 34.4 per cent in 1992.

On the whole, women appear to have benefited from South Korea's economic development; women's increased share of employment in paid SOCS work as well as their decreased share in unpaid work may compensate for the decline in their share of paid manufacturing. However, an asymmetric distribution of female employment remains in South Korea, as evidenced by the fact that in 1992 the percentage of women in unpaid work and paid manufacturing was still greater than the share of women in regular, paying service sector jobs.

NOTES

1 On dualistic economic development, see Kelley et al. (1972). On labour segmentation and economic development, see Taubman and Wachter (1986: 1190–2). More recent research on dualistic labour markets and discrimination is discussed by McConnell and Brue (1992).
2 For historical and sociological background on women and work in Korea, see Yu and Phillips (1987); also see Cho and Koo (1983). Discussion of employment trends is also provided by Castañeda and Park (1992) and Galenson (1992).
3 Among those reporting such trends are Haejong Cho (1987), Hyoung Cho (1987), Oakla Cho (1987), Cho and Koo (1983), Koo (1987), and Yu (1987).
4 For background on South Korea's development in the 1960s and 1970s, including summaries of government policies, see Corbo and Suh (1992); also see Balassa (1985, 1988), Cho and Koo (1983), Kim and Roemer (1979), Koo (1984), Kuznets (1988), Kwack (1990a), Lee and Naya (1988), Oshima (1986, 1988), Scitovsky (1990) and Song (1990).
5 For general background on government reforms and economic restructuring, see Corbo and Suh (1992); also see Balassa (1985), Kwack (1990b), and Song (1990).
6 For the years 1970 and 1989, Galenson (1992) reported data on the distribution of female workers across South Korean industries and the representation of women in those sectors. For the years 1963 and 1989 he presented aggregate employment figures for women according to job status. He did not cover work status by industry. Further, he did not report data for intervening years, so more recent work patterns cannot be distinguished from those of earlier years of economic development. Castañeda and Park (1992) reported employment figures by industry through 1985, as did Song (1990) through 1988, but neither distinguished between male and female employment.
7 On the effects of stabilization policies on aggregate demand, see Corbo and Nam (1992a, b) and Dornbusch and Park (1992). Cho and Cole (1992) have examined the impact of structural adjustments in the financial sector. On the aggregate supply side, the effects of trade liberalization and anti-monopoly measures have been discussed by Young (1992) and Lee et al. (1992), respectively. Adjustment in the agricultural sector has been recounted by Song and Ryu (1992).
8 Real GDP figures (in 1985 prices) reported by the International Monetary Fund (1993) were used to calculate output growth rates. CPI data reported by the IMF were used to calculate inflation rates for 1981–92. The CPI data reported by the IMF only extend back to 1966. Kwack (1990a: 80) presented CPI inflation rates for 1965–80, which we used to calculate inflation over that period. Using the IMF data, annual CPI over 1967–80 measured 15 per cent inflation.
9 The increase in housekeeping was attributed by Kwack (1990b) to exceptionally

rapid rural–urban migration over 1982–5. Kwack argued that the migrants of the early 1980s tended to be older and less educated than previous migrants, which made it more difficult for them to enter the workforce. Castañeda and Park (1992) also attributed the drop in participation to rural–urban migration, noting that there was a comparatively higher rate of participation in the shrinking rural sector.

10 The National Statistical Office surveys the South Korean population on work activities. For a description and summary of the survey (in Korean and English), see the *Annual Report on the Economically Active Population Survey* for 1991.

11 Employment in the different industrial sectors also tend to be age dependent. For example, in 1991 more than half of the workers in manufacturing – both male and female – were younger than 35 years of age (see the National Statistical Office, Republic of Korea 1992: 240). In the SOCS sector, the median age was between 35 and 39 years in the areas of utilities, construction, wholesale–retail trade and transport. The median age was younger, under 35 years, in financial, social and personal services. Agriculture was centred around workers older than 50 years.

12 For a description of female manufacturing employment, see Hagen Koo (1987).

13 See Lee (1993) for more discussion of the incentives of Korean employers to use female labour as a buffer stock.

11

NEO-LIBERAL ECONOMIC REFORMS AND WOMEN IN CHILE

Verónica Montecinos[1]

INTRODUCTION

Since the late nineteenth century, Chile's rich mineral deposits have provided funds for development, urban growth and industrial expansion. With an urbanization rate exceeding 80 per cent and a 6 per cent illiteracy rate, Chile's economic and social development rank relatively high in Latin America.

Until the military coup of 1973, Chile was also among the most democratic countries in the world. The political instability that characterized nineteenth-century Latin America was distinctly absent in Chile. From the 1900s, the Chilean armed forces espoused a doctrine of non-intervention in political affairs. This reinforced internal discipline, strict hierarchy and subordination to civilian authority. A sophisticated multi-party system included strong centrist, conservative and Marxist parties. From the early 1930s, competitive electoral politics meant uninterrupted civilian rule. Democratically elected governments succeeded each other every six years, conforming to legal and constitutional traditions. Chilean politics stressed coalition, negotiation and compromise. This allowed a large middle class as well as other social classes to benefit from public policies and to be included in political decision-making.

In the 1960s and early 1970s, Christian Democrats under President Frei and Socialists under President Allende sought to reduce income disparities, hasten economic modernization, and promote political participation through a series of state-led reforms in the productive and social service sectors. The reforms, however, also led to administrative centralization, economic instability, low investment rates and chronic inflation. At the time of the military coup in 1973, the government was heavily involved in the regulation of economic and social activities. State agencies intervened in international trade, labour markets, capital accumulation, and creation of infrastructure, and mediated in distributive conflicts.

Soon after the coup, the government's economic team (known as the 'Chicago boys') gained control over the state bureaucracy. Articulate and ambitious, they argued that the state should only remove market distortions and inefficiencies, and that competitive markets should be allowed to operate free of government intervention. With the support of General Pinochet, neo-liberal economic policies were launched in conjunction with administrative political reforms (Montecinos 1988; A. Valenzuela 1991). Hence, long before the debt crisis erupted in Latin America, the structural reforms of the kind recommended and promoted by the International Monetary Fund (IMF) were already in place in Chile. By the end of the 1970s, deregulation policies had substantially dismantled the mixed economy and one of the most progressive social welfare systems in the region. The massive economic changes implemented in the 1970s and 1980s under an authoritarian political regime – and the continuation of these policies by the democratically elected government since 1990 – have persuaded the international agencies that Chile is an exemplar of successful reform.

Following two decades of authoritarian rule, elections were held again in December 1989. Hernan Buchi, General Pinochet's last finance minister and a member of the Chicago group, lost to a coalition of centre and left parties supporting the Christian Democrat Patricio Aylwin, and the transition to civilian rule began.

The newly elected government pledged to consolidate democracy while combining economic growth with redistribution. Aylwin's officials emphasized their commitment to maintaining fiscal prudence, an open economy, export growth, a strong private sector, and other economic reforms initiated by the military regime. However, they stressed the need to alleviate the burden placed on the poor, and the convenience of restoring some of the economic and regulatory powers of the state.

Aylwin's policy agenda also included some proposals made by women's organizations in the 1980s. Paradoxically, the collapse of democratic institutions led to the creation of a variety of women's groups that mobilized with unsuspected political vigour (Silva 1987; M.E. Valenzuela 1991). During the 1973–90 authoritarian interregnum, demands for the restoration of civil and political rights and the simple struggle for subsistence led women to actively search for new identities, new role definitions and new forms of collective action. In the void left by parties, traditional union leaders and politicians, women opened up the private world of homes and neighbourhoods, carving out a new social and political space.

After a detailed account of the economic reforms under the authoritarian rule of Pinochet, this chapter examines their impact on women. Special attention is paid to policies addressing poverty, labour, social security and health. The specific conditions that brought gender issues to policy agenda are examined next. A summary of the main findings concludes the paper.

ECONOMIC REFORMS UNDER PINOCHET (1973–90)

Reducing inflation was one of the first tasks facing the military government when it took power in 1973. Toward this end, a monetarist stabilization programme was set up to reduce government expenditure and decrease the growth of money supply. Severe cuts in the public sector and the privatization of state enterprises were mechanisms of fiscal adjustment (Marcel 1989).[2] By the late 1970s Chile had a fiscal surplus for the first time in more than twenty years.

A second problem area involved international economic relations. The rise in oil prices, and a drastic drop in copper prices in the early 1970s, created an external financial crisis that prompted the monetarist team to accelerate the opening of the economy to world trade, foreign investors and capital inflows. The government devalued the peso, abolished the system of multiple exchange rates, eliminated non-tariff barriers, simplified customs regulations, and established lower and uniform tariffs. Non-discriminatory policies toward foreign investors, deregulation of foreign exchange transactions, exchange-rate devaluations, and easier access to foreign credit led to a significant increase in trade and external banking activity.

Following a free-market ideology, the authorities also abandoned the industrialization policies that successive governments had followed since the 1930s. The manufacturing sector lost its privileged status. Comparative advantage placed agricultural exports at the centre of a new development strategy. Special government incentives, trade liberalization and low wages allowed agricultural exporters to modernize their technology.[3] Simultaneously, the state reduced its involvement in the rural sector and in 1978 the agrarian reform law, implemented under Frei and Allende, was repealed. Public expenditure in agriculture fell by more than 50 per cent between 1969 and 1979 (Silva 1987: 199). Agribusinesses, service agencies and all the capital equipment owned by the government were sold to the private sector. Almost 30 per cent of the expropriated land was returned to their previous owners. Peasants received individual lots, but a high percentage of their land was eventually sold or rented. More than 54,000 families did not have access to land or had it only temporarily (Ortega 1987: 40). Government policies also broadened the gap between commercial agriculture and small producers (Gómez and Echenique 1988: 275). The traditional agricultural sector, which satisfied domestic needs, lost state subsidies, tax exemptions, selective loans and technical assistance. Land began to be treated as an additional capital good (Sanfuentes 1987: 118).

In 1979, the peso was pegged to the dollar at a fixed exchange rate for the next three years. Since domestic inflation surpassed world inflation, the exchange rate appreciated by almost 30 per cent in two years. Exporters and others had called for an abandonment of this controversial policy since 1980, but highly indebted conglomerates resisted devaluation – the private debt represented two-thirds of the total debt (Ffrench-Davis 1988: 18). As a result, there was a massive speculation against the peso, capital flight worsened and international reserves decreased. The fixed exchange rate was finally abandoned in mid-1982.

By 1982, it had become clear that excessive liberalization and indebtedness had made the Chilean economy very vulnerable. The country faced a serious financial crisis; foreign debt had tripled between 1978 and 1981 and many borrowers could not service their debts (Foxley 1983: 88; Corbo 1985: 108). Bankruptcies multiplied, output dropped by 15 per cent in 1982 and unemployment soared to 30 per cent in 1983. The worst economic crisis since the 1930s was in full swing. In response to pressures from international banks, the government nationalized a substantial proportion of the private debt.[4]

The economic crisis and popular protests forced the government to implement some expansionary policies and to retreat from radical neo-liberalism for a while; when the immediate pressures abated in 1985, orthodox policies were resumed. Although this led to rising unemployment and greater social problems, government economists did improve the country's credit-worthiness. In response, the IMF, the World Bank and the Inter-American Bank provided important financial resources. By 1989, the economy had recovered, partly through increases in investments and exports.

During the 1980s, the structural reforms of the 1970s were intensified. Throughout the period, the labour markets (low wages and high unemployment) constituted the main mechanism for adjustment (Meller 1990; Solimano 1990). In the early 1990s, Chile presented a better picture than many Third World debtors, but important social demands remained unsatisfied. The Chicago team consistently argued in favour of cutting excessive social spending and reorienting government subsidies to the poorest groups.[5] It has been estimated that, in the mid-1980s, 45 per cent of the population lived in conditions of poverty and 25 per cent were indigent (Torche 1987).

IMPACT OF REFORMS ON WOMEN

The economic reforms of the 1970s and 1980s successfully placed Chile on the path to sustained economic growth. Yet, these policies also resulted in capital concentration and a more regressive income distribution. The poorest 20 per cent of the population saw their relative share of total expenditures decline from 7.6 per cent in 1969 to 5.2 per cent in 1978 and then to 4.4 per cent in 1988. Per capita consumption returned to its 1970 level in 1981 but fell again after the 1982 crisis and has not recovered since (Raczynski and Romaguera forthcoming).

Universal access to social welfare programmes, achieved through decades of compromise between the state and various social groups, was replaced by a highly selective and targeted system favouring those with urgent needs – the extremely poor. Those who did not qualify for public assistance had to either pay for the services previously provided by the state, or do without them. Social spending for the poorest two deciles increased, while services for the middle and working classes were reduced. Policies for the poor, although authoritarian in their conception and implementation, attempted to channel a larger proportion of social expenditure to groups that had traditionally been marginalized (Graham 1993).

The principle of least government intervention and the promotion of market incentives and efficiency shaped a series of institutional 'modernizations' in the provision of social services. Reforms in the areas of education, housing, health and social security were implemented in the 1980s. These included such measures as privatization, the use of markets, a strict selection of beneficiaries and decentralization (Castañeda 1990).

As economic policies put heavy demands on the poor, and as social policies sought to keep subordinate groups passive, women displayed new forms of social visibility and inventiveness. Women were crucial participants in private and community initiatives supported by non-governmental organizations (religious institutions, private foundations and independent groups of professionals and workers) that were designed to supplement official policies. Simple, low-cost solutions were designed to encourage community participation and assist poor communities in urban and rural areas (Downs et al. 1989).

Non-governmental organizations assumed that grassroots actions would primarily be performed by men because of their labour and organizational experience. Women's role in these actions was at first conceptualized in the traditional definitions of the feminine, as an expression of concern for the fate of their spouses and families. But after a few years, it became apparent that men were not among the leaders or among the most committed participants of communal social programmes. Women were discovered to be crucial partners in the search for innovative political discourses and actions (González Meyer 1992). This is not surprising as many of the programmes taught women new forms of income generation, energy-efficient methods for the elaboration of food, the design and creation of kitchen gardens and the restoration of agricultural land in areas affected by desertification (Vergara 1989).[6]

In implementing social policies, these non-governmental organizations provided important economic and institutional resources that have now become a standard component of Chilean political life. They are now recognized by political parties and government agencies and the role of women has received some official attention. Despite these advances, it is too early to expect a significant break with the subsidiary tone in which 'women's issues' normally enter the public policy debate.[7]

Poverty and social policies

As neo-liberal reforms increased unemployment rates and impoverished the working classes, women became more vulnerable to poverty. In times of high unemployment separation rates, single motherhood and female-headed households all increase. Approximately 20 per cent of Chilean households are headed by women; the proportion is higher among the poor. Estimates indicate that in the late 1980s, more than 40 per cent of poor families were headed by women (FEMPRESS 1988). These households have higher rates of poverty due to gender-specific factors: women tend to be affected by higher rates of unemployment; childcare responsibilities conflict with full-time participation in the workforce; and occupational segregation offers women mainly unstable and low-paying jobs. Due to differences in life expectancy between the sexes, widows and older women are also vulnerable to poverty.

Trade liberalization increased the availability of imported consumer goods. Yet, many poor and unemployed women had to sell or pawn their household appliances (furniture, stove, washing and sewing machine, refrigerator, TV). Since men remained mostly identified by their activities outside the home, women had to redefine the boundaries of home and work. They brought jobs to the home and monitored changes in patterns of consumption, savings and other aspects of family life.

During this period, women assumed a more active role in the economy of subsistence, as survival strategies (domestic labour, barter, gifts, donations among neighbours, begging, stealing) enhanced their economic value. In the operation of fraternal soup kitchens, sometimes dozens of families co-operated in preparing and conserving food, in growing organic vegetables, and in adopting 'magic' cooking pots to save fuel. Women were put in charge of distributing the chores, collecting the money, buying the food and the fuel, cooking, and ensuring the continuity of the group (Velasco and Leppe 1989). Impoverished women had to switch from gas to firewood, from meat and vegetables to starch and legumes, and from the purchasing of goods and services to domestic production. Women organized the work of children, sometimes sending them to live with relatives or friends and sometimes receiving relatives and even strangers who could share the costs of living.[8]

Under the military regime, government economists stressed the need to distribute subsidies directly to individuals and households, rather than to occupational or community groups.[9] Excessive targeting transformed some preventive programmes into merely curative actions, and many vulnerable groups were left unprotected. For example, preventive health policies for women and children available in Chile since the 1950s, were discontinued. The undesirable effects of excessive targeting were also notable in nutritional programmes. By restricting benefits to children under six in extremely poor families, school children and youngsters out of school were excluded. Also, the children of low-income working mothers did not qualify for free nurseries provided for the poor (Vergara 1990; Raczynski and Romaguera forthcoming).

Critics have pointed out that under Pinochet, government subsidies for the poor were politically manipulated, stigmatized the recipients, and fostered paternalism and dependency. Some have referred to the military govern-ment's approach to social policy as the 'statization of poverty', because the poorest groups became increasingly dependent on state assistance, with public subsidies covering a substantial portion of their family budget. Up to a third of the families obtained half their subsistence income from the state (Tironi 1989). Although the value of individual subsidies was rather small, the social safety net for the poor was crucial in compensating for the general deterioration in the standards of living.[10] Subsidies and programmes for the poor were not sufficient to compensate for the regressive effects of economic policies on income distribution (Cortázar 1985).

Wages and employment

Replacing the Labour Code of 1931, the labour legislation passed in 1979 severely constrained centralized bargaining, limited the power of unions and made it relatively easy for employers to dismiss workers. Worker rights were curtailed, including some protective measures that favoured working mothers. Strikes and collective bargaining were suspended in 1973 (Angell 1991), and wages were de-indexed in 1982. These reasons combined with the very high unemployment rates (over 24 per cent between 1982 and 1985) that followed the implementation of tight fiscal and monetary policies to cause a severe deterioration in wages. By 1988, real wages were 5 per cent below their 1970 level. Unemployment remained over 24 per cent between 1982 and 1985. In contrast to the poor who had lost important government benefits, middle- and high-income groups were partly compensated for the costs of adjustment through income tax cuts in 1984, and public assistance to private debtors.

Low wages are particularly detrimental to the well-being of working women and their dependent families. Estimates for the 1960–85 period indicate that for all occupations and educational levels, women receive about 68 per cent of men's salaries (Hola 1988).[11] Although women's educational level is proportionately higher than men's in all segments of the Chilean labour markets, women remain concentrated in occupations typified as 'feminine', with lower average remunerations relative to men. A recent survey estimated that only 54 per cent of women in the workforce have labour contracts, 23 per cent are self-employed, and the rest work as domestic servants or in occasional jobs (*El Mercurio* 1993a).

Due in part to the high percentage of women in the informal sector, in small firms and in unstable jobs, the majority of female workers never joined the unions; and their problems did not receive much attention in labour organizations. Like political parties of the left, trade union ideology had traditionally emphasized class over gender issues. In the words of one prominent woman in the labour movement, unions used to be a predominantly masculine world, where 'leaders had trouble accepting that women could make a contribution, other than serving tea and lunch at their meetings' (Rozas 1986).

However, during the years of the military regime, the number of women in leadership positions and their activism in the labour movement increased. The enhanced presence of women in the labour market and the organizational crisis that affected unions during this period (union membership dropped to one-third of its highest level) may have facilitated women's participation in organized labour. Especially after the Women's Department in the Co-ordinadora Nacional Sindical was created in 1979, unions showed more openness in dealing with women's issues.

In Chile, the workforce participation rate is lower for women with lower incomes and educational levels (Raczynski and Serrano 1985: 48). According to the 1982 census, approximately 60 per cent of women with university education participate in the workforce, compared with only 30 per cent of women with secondary education, 20 per cent of women with primary education and 10 per cent of women with no schooling (Rossetti 1988: 157). This coincides with the figures provided by a 1993 survey, which showed that 64 per cent of upper-class women work, as compared with 41 per cent of middle-class women and 27 per cent of women in the lower income groups (*El Mercurio* 1993a).

In times of economic crisis, however, poor women are pressured to fully provide or at least complement the family income. Even meagre remuner-ations obtained in jobs with flexible schedules and located close to home are accepted to ensure family subsistence. Women must also intensify their domestic labour, which is valued between 20 and 30 per cent of the GDP (Pardo 1983).

During the 1970s and 1980s, declining standards of living, high rates of unemployment, and the rising proportions of female-headed households forced more and more women into the workforce. As a result, women's share of the national workforce grew from 22 per cent to almost one-third between 1970 and 1990. This is in contrast to a mere 2 per cent increase between 1950 and 1970.[12] Most of the increased participation occurred in the growing service sector. Employment in domestic service, which had declined during the 1960s, began to grow – from 17 per cent of working women in 1970, to 21 per cent in 1975, to 25 per cent in 1977 and to 28 per cent in 1982 (Muñoz Dalbora 1988).

Excluding domestic service, the proportion of female labour force in the informal sector fluctuated at around 30–35 per cent between 1980 and 1985. Many informal occupations constituted forms of underemployment. The self-employed or workers in small family enterprises coped as they could with the shortage of stable and more productive jobs caused by recession, cuts in the public payroll and de-industrialization. The safety valve provided by employ-ment in the informal sector may have been particularly important for women. In 1982, only 18 per cent of the male workforce was occupied in the informal sector, as compared with 35 per cent of female workers (Díaz and Hola 1988).

During the 1970s and 1980s, workshops and microenterprises for the collective provision of goods and services, known as 'Popular Economic Organizations' (OEPs) multiplied in urban centres. OEPs were mostly formed by poor and unskilled women. Those operated by formerly unionized unemployed workers had a higher concentration of men, but represented a considerably smaller proportion of the OEPs. Although these organizations allowed for some enrichment of the social world and solidarity networks of poor women, they faced numerous obstacles: highly competitive markets, financial restrictions, and legal and organizational problems. OEPs had a tendency to remain heavily dependent on the external support of non-governmental organizations.[13]

In the rural areas, the transformations brought about by export-promotion policies and the discontinuation of the agrarian reform generated a growing feminization of employment and an increased proletarization of rural women.[14] In part, this was caused by a higher demand for cheap female labour, since low wages helped the increase in agricultural exports. The instability of seasonal agricultural activities (export activities demand seasonal labour), the pressure on the poor to supplement their meagre incomes, and the expulsion of peasants from the land, all worked to push rural women to the paid workforce. When women entered jobs in the production and processing of agricultural exports, they faced a highly segmented labour market. Stable jobs are performed only by men, who tend to have a much more stable workforce participation rate even when engaged in seasonal work. While supervisory and management tasks are performed by men, women do the cleaning and packing (Valdés 1988).[15]

The decline in demand and trade liberalization decreased job opportunities for women. At the same time that women's search for jobs put pressure on the labour market, female unemployment rates were particularly high. Between 1980 and 1984, the female unemployment rate increased from 10.7 to 19 per cent; for men the increase was from 12.1 to 15.9 per cent (Hola 1988). In 1982, female industrial employment in skilled and semi-skilled occupations in the capital city was only half of its 1960 level (Gálvez and Todaro 1988; Muñoz Dalbora 1988).

Public sector layoffs (over 130,000 employees lost their jobs after 1973) most likely affected a significant number of women, since more than half of the women employed in the formal sector work for the state. This may have been particularly true in the more 'feminine' areas of education and health, where public expenditure cutbacks led to significant declines in both employee numbers and salaries. With the privatization of schools and their transfer to municipalities in 1987, about 8,000 teachers lost their jobs (PIIE 1989).

Massive emergency employment programmes were implemented in response to the threat of political destabilization posed by high rates of unemployment. For unemployed workers with little skills, Programa de Empleo Mínimo (PEM) was introduced in 1975. For unemployed workers who were more skilled and were heads of households, Programa Occupacional Para Jefes de Hogar (POJH) was created in 1982.[16] Participation in these programmes gave many marginalized women a rare opportunity to gain some financial independence and some labour-market experience – as many as 67 per cent of the women had never worked before (Hola 1988). However, these programmes likely reinforced occupational segregation based on gender.[17] Many of those hired by PEM or POJH replaced (at lower salaries and benefits) public employees dismissed from schools, childcare centres, hospitals and municipalities. PEM, the less remunerative and more stigmatizing of the emergency programmes, had the highest percentage of women (75 per cent of the participants were women, whereas 70 per cent of POJH participants were men).[18]

Another relatively unsuccessful government effort to deal with the high number of unemployed women was the creation of microenterprises. One programme was designed to benefit women registered in POJH. In the initial stages, the United Nations Fund For Women (UNIFEM) and municipal and central government agencies were to provide support through training, credit, technical assistance and marketing. As in the case of OEPs, however, participating women had little work experience and even less experience as entrepreneurs. They also confronted multiple economic and administrative difficulties – the economic conditions were recessionary, official assistance was insufficient and poorly coordinated, and domestic demands conflicted with labour responsibilities. Moreover, in only a few cases did these jobs provide income that was as high as the subsidy provided by the emergency employment programme. Analysts have concluded, therefore, that the creation of microenterprises among poor women does not present a good instrument for generating stable employment and adequate income, particularly in a recessionary context (Raczynski 1989).[19]

Social insurance programmes

Despite the growing importance of paid female labour and the typical double burden of housework on women, they remain heavily unprotected by social security schemes. Notwithstanding the increasing awareness (ILO 1993), social security systems still reflect the traditional concept of men as breadwinners and women as dependants whose benefits derive from their husband. Women generally receive lower pension benefits. This is due partly to differences in family situation, and partly to inequalities and sex discrimination in the labour market, which lead to lower earnings, more precarious conditions of employment and higher unemployment rates for women.

During the 1970s and 1980s, high rates of unemployment, a growing informal sector and inadequate enforcement of labour legislation resulted in a marked decline in the proportion of social security contributors. In 1988, only 56 per cent of the workforce and their families were covered by the system. Twenty years earlier, social security in Chile covered around 70 per cent of the population.[20]

In Chile, as in other countries, those without coverage were more prone to be women, since women are heavily represented in occupational categories that are not likely to be covered by social security – temporary or seasonal workers, self-employed, employees of small firms and domestic servants. The military government reformed social security in 1981, but this reform did not address the gender inequalities in the system.[21] Contributions, requirements and benefits were made uniform regardless of the sector, category or occupation of workers. Social security reform also eliminated retirement by seniority and established minimum retirement ages. Although women can still retire (voluntarily) five years earlier (at age 60) than men, the current system discriminates against women in the calculation of pension benefits. Women's rights advocates have emphasized the need to compensate for women's double workload by reducing the female retirement age. However, this form of favourable discrimination is criticized for worsening the current financial disequilibrium of social insurance (Mesa-Lago 1989).

The percentage of women covered by social security is related to the concentration of women in occupations with a high degree of social insurance coverage (civil service, garment industry, banking and commerce). Women's coverage tends to be higher in the case of health benefits (as dependants of an active worker are covered) and survivor pensions (due to differences in life expectancy) than in the case of old age pensions (ibid.). In the late 1980s, only 14 per cent of Chilean women of retirement age were retired. This low rate is partly due to the relatively low level of female participation in the workforce, particularly among older women (Arellano 1989).

In general, since pensions are primarily calculated on the basis of earnings, female pensions can be expected to be lower than male pensions. Actuarial calculations currently in use do not spread the risks evenly among all participants of the scheme. Because of higher life expectancy (73 years for women, 68 years for men), women retiring at the same age and with the same capital as men, receive a lower pension.

Since social security benefits deteriorated after 1974, an increase in coverage is currently considered to be a main priority. The needs of older women who have not been able to pursue a full lifetime career are only beginning to be a policy concern. Indeed, under authoritarian rule, the pensions that deteriorated most were paid to widows and the elderly, a group with a high female representation.[22]

However, it should also be noted that several changes in Chile's social insurance programmes did benefit women. Subsidies that did not require contributions were increased: welfare pensions, family welfare allowance and health care for indigents. Because these compensatory programmes targeted the poor who had traditionally been unprotected, they had a considerable redistributive impact. The family welfare allowance, in particular, benefited pregnant women and children who had lost social security coverage and all those who had never been covered. In the past, pregnant women and children not affiliated with the social security system were excluded from the family allowance programme (Vergara 1990).[23]

Health

Chile has had a long tradition of granting women access to health services. From the 1930s, public health policies concentrated on providing health care and supplementary feeding for pregnant women and children. Universal programmes included pregnancy and post-natal care, well-baby checkups, nutritional education and intervention, and family planning.[24] Until 1985, approximately 90 per cent of the population had access to various state preventive and curative programmes (ibid.).

The military government sought to maintain the emphasis on health care for mothers and children[25] at the same time that it reduced public health expenditure. Government actions concentrated almost exclusively on primary care targeted at the most vulnerable groups (pregnant women and children suffering from or at high risk of malnutrition). Day nurseries, childcare centres for undernourished children and nutrition rehabilitation centres for children under 2 years of age successfully built upon a tradition of primary health care. While preventive care for mothers and children remained free of charge, and while the state assumed the responsibility of payment over all maternity-leave subsidies for working mothers, other segments of the population experienced a deterioration in their standards of health care and access to health services.[26]

The transfer of primary health care to municipalities and the private sector eroded the quality of medical infrastructure (hospitals, beds, etc.), services and the preventive nature of health programmes.[27] This led to more emergency consultations, longer waiting lists for hospitalization, a higher incidence of some infectious diseases, and higher rates of malnutrition among school-age children. More alcoholism, drug addiction and mental health problems were also detected (Hardy 1989; Raczynski and Romaguera forthcoming).

Critics of the official emphasis on curative medicine created a set of grassroots health organizations, known as the 'Solidarity Health System'. Pointing to the inadequacies of government reforms, which focused on the transferring of primary health care to the municipalities without actually embracing the goal of health for all, these organizations emphasized quality of life as a guiding principle and an integrated approach to public health.[28]

The proponents of alternative health care approaches argued that participatory schemes were better able to identify the specific needs of women and their families, and transfer medical know-how to the community. Several initiatives were undertaken at the local level with high female participation rates. Some received financing from the church and international organizations; others established mechanisms of cooperation between the local authorities, health professionals and monitors trained among community members.[29]

Politics

For most of this century, gender issues have been invisible in the political and policy spheres. Political divisions among the left, the centre and the right were essentially construed as a reflection of class cleavages in Chile. Gender demands were not a part of the ideological discourse of political parties, the main institutional mediator between the state and society.[30]

As a result, the laws in Chile are notoriously retrograde. They do not allow divorce and limit women's maternal rights, their property rights and their rights to engage in commerce. Common law unions are not legally valid. A married woman must obey her husband, who has rights over the person and the property of his wife. Married women are considered to be 'relatively incapable', and they can only exercise their rights and contract obligations when represented or authorized by their husbands (Malic and Serrano 1988).

Traditionally, labour laws were less discriminatory toward women than civil and penal codes and granted working mothers a series of rights. These included maternity leaves (6 weeks before birth and 12 weeks after birth), childcare facilities and job protection for pregnant women.[31] However, because labour legislation was not fully implemented and gender was not a concern for policy-makers, working women continue to experience multiple disadvantages.

The exclusion of gender demands in party politics did not prevent government officials from promoting the political mobilization of women based on their traditional role as mothers. In the 1950s, mothers' clubs were first sponsored by presidents' wives and organized at the local level. In the 1960s, these grassroots organizations became formally institutionalized as part of government programmes for popular sectors.

The military government showed particular interest in promoting women's collaboration in the regime's campaign to depoliticize the country. Traditional views of gender relations were used to reinforce ideological appeals for order, respect for authority and discipline. An 'army' of more than 50,000 middle-class volunteer women was recruited, and existing mechanisms for the organization of poor women were expanded. Directed and inspired by General Pinochet and his wife, volunteers worked in the training and political indoctrination of millions of women. Social programmes were also channelled through CEMA-Chile, which administered 10,000 mothers' clubs, with 431,000 members (in 1982); the Secretaría Nacional de la Mujer, a state agency, reached 2,300,000 participants in courses organized between 1975 and 1983 (Lechner and Levy 1986; Del Gatto 1989). The regime's official rhetoric placed women in a privileged social position. Yet, the economic and social policies reinforced subordination.

In fact, growing numbers of women mobilized against the military government. Women's groups organized for the defence of human rights and supported actions sponsored by the poor (emergency programmes for unemployed workers, community health and education programmes, and legal and economic protection for the politically persecuted). Certainly, the growing awareness of women's issues in contemporary Chile was nurtured by cross-national trends in which the significance of gender is being 'discovered' in debates on social stratification, economic development and social justice. In Chile, as elsewhere, the need to incorporate women's concerns and participation in policy formulation and implementation is particularly emphasized in the case of social policies (UNICEF 1989; Raczynski and Serrano 1992).

In the 1980s, with the formulation of demands for democracy and gender equality, Chileans put an end to the 'feminist silence' which had prevailed since the early 1950s (Kirkwood 1986). Political parties began to incorporate gender issues in their platforms but there were tensions over the degree of autonomy of women's leadership. Only two parties allowed for organizational changes in their structure to increase women's share of power. In the legislative elections of 1989, only nine women were elected. The appointment of an all-male cabinet by President Aylwin angered many leaders of what had become a fairly coordinated and active series of women's movements.

After the transition to democracy, gender issues could no longer be officially ignored, for women had developed a visible political agenda that included the need for a divorce law, legal equality for married women, punishment for domestic and marital violence, reproductive rights and the elimination of prejudiced and sexist practices in the workplace, school curricula and domestic life. The new regime acknowledged that the mobilization of organized women had made contributions in the struggle for democratization. Also recognized was the need to modify the discriminatory nature of the legal system, taking into consideration women's participatory and organizational capacities in the policies that targeted them specifically.

With this goal, a new state agency with ministerial rank was created soon after President Aylwin took office. Changes have so far been less dramatic than many expected. As traditional cultural and institutional practices continue to obstruct progress in the direction of gender equality, some of the initiatives and the thrust towards organizational unity that women developed during the 1980s have lost their initial impetus.

CONCLUSION

Pinochet's authoritarian regime dismantled social and political channels of participation for all citizens. Economic reforms in the direction of increased trade liberalization, privatization, and greater monetary and fiscal stability imposed heavy costs on the most vulnerable segments of the population.

As a vulnerable group in general, women came to bear the brunt of the costs of Pinochet's reforms. Social policies were part of the domain controlled by government economists, who systematically ignored the structural basis of class, gender and regional stratification. These policies were conceptualized as a component of macroeconomic management; and the reduction in benefits, services and subsidies were a sign of government withdrawing from economic intervention.

Under authoritarian rule, economic policies were detrimental to the interests of women. Paradoxically, however, women managed to express their demands more forcefully than in the past. Although women's demands for enhanced economic and political participation were officially ignored or submerged in ideological appeals to their role as guardians of patriotic and domestic traditions, within the democratic opposition, women carved a new political identity. But the space they conquered and the visibility their agenda received were somewhat ephemeral.

Democratic politics does not by itself guarantee progress towards gender equality. Political parties and traditional politicians challenge the autonomy and legitimacy of women's leadership and are reluctant to recognize that gender is indeed linked to power and social justice. Moreover, it cannot be taken for granted that welfare policies benefit women, as if citizens were not gendered. The gradual evolution of Chile's complex welfare state, in the context of a competitive party system, left important gaps in the provision of women's needs.

Even under democratic conditions, traditionally 'gender-blind' conceptions of social stratification only perpetuate the inability of policy-makers to identify relevant sources of inequality and foster failure in altering the subordinate social position of women. Decentralization of public policies and the political activism of organized women are significant steps; yet it is only through major changes in social institutions that greater equality between the sexes will be achieved.

NOTES

1 I am grateful to Dagmar Raczynski, Aysegul Baykan and Carmelo Mesa-Lago for their friendly advice.
2 The conglomerates that emerged out of the privatization of public enterprises dominated the economy until the financial crisis of 1982. After 1985, many large enterprises became controlled by multinational corporations and foreign banks (Rozas and Marín 1989).
3 Land under cultivation increased significantly after 1977. Fruit and forestry became the two most dynamic export activities in the 1980s. Fruit exports came to represent more than 12 per cent of total exports and Chile is now the most important exporter of grapes in the southern hemisphere (Cruz 1988: 92).
4 Government responsibility for the debt increased from 36 per cent in 1981 to 84 per cent in 1988 (Edwards and Edwards 1987: 80; Ffrench-Davis 1989: 69). The Central Bank lost more than 45 per cent of its reserves and played a key role in bailing out financial institutions and private debtors through the conversion of debts into pesos, subsidies and preferential exchange rates (Meller 1990: 9).
5 Despite targeting social spending on the poor, many of the economic policies (tax

reform, privatization, labour-market reforms) had regressive effects. The regressive nature of government policy was especially prominent in the rescue operations undertaken during the financial crisis of the early 1980s, which were generous to middle- and higher-income groups.

6 Because information, services and benefits provided by the central government are usually too standardized, remote, expensive or inadequately understood, poor women often become passive beneficiaries. Given the opportunity, women could be more actively involved in the design and application of programmes affecting them and their families (Raczynski and Serrano 1992; Errázuriz 1992).

7 Authorities in the Aylwin administration have reinforced the state's role in the provision of social services, and changes have been introduced to improve equity and social participation in the design and implementation of social policies. However, the transition to a democratic regime in 1990 did not reverse the trends towards decentralization, privatization and the targeting of social expenditures.

8 See Montecinos and Spessart (1977); Schkolnik and Teitelboim (1988b); Díaz and Hola (1988); Raczynski and Serrano (1985).

9 Only households falling below a certain minimum level were entitled to receive public assistance. A selection mechanism established at the municipal level considered an index of employment, education, housing and household equipment.

10 Programmes targeting the poor partly explain improvements in infant mortality rates, nutrition and life expectancy, despite the increases in absolute poverty and income inequality (Raczynski and Oyarzo 1981). Since beneficiaries were selected by the same instrument, access to one programme facilitated access to others (emergency employment, welfare pensions, nutritional programmes, basic housing programmes) (Raczynski and Romaguera forthcoming).

11 Among individuals with a university education, women's earnings are only 49 per cent of men's earnings. Women with eight or fewer years in school earn 59 per cent of what men receive in the same educational category (M.E. Valenzuela 1991).

12 Between 1976 and 1985, the female workforce increased at an annual rate of 3.4 per cent, while the population of females of working age increased at 2.2 per cent. In 1970, only 0.9 per cent of women were looking for their first jobs; in 1982, that rate was 4 per cent. In the same period, the proportion of women looking for their first jobs more than doubled that of men (Hola 1988; Muñoz Dalbora 1988).

13 It has been estimated that between 10 and 15 per cent of the poor were direct participants or beneficiaries of OEPs. In the mid-1980s, almost 90 per cent of OEPs consisted of solidarity groups providing subsistence support.

14 Although official statistics underestimate the participation of women (partly because they are based on surveys conducted in months of low female participation), some believe that the number of salaried women in temporary agricultural employment is now similar to the number of women in manufacturing activities.

15 Discrimination against rural women has been persistent in recent history. The land reforms of the 1960s and early 1970s eliminated many stable jobs for women in the hacienda system. Not having legal access to property, women were discriminated against in the distribution of land and were forced to increase their (unpaid) family labour.

16 In 1982, when the unemployment rate reached its peak, emergency programmes employed up to 13 per cent of the workforce, with wage rates equivalent to 25 per cent (PEM) and 40 per cent (POJH) of the minimum wage. PEM and POJH provided a semi-permanent protection in exchange for labour. The low wages were in some cases comparable with the minimum wage because participants were eligible for other government subsidies (Graham 1991).

17 Other aspects criticized are the large amount of resources used in relatively unproductive projects, the little concern for the promotion of workers' skills,

independence and participation. The employment programmes were politically manipulated as part of the authoritarian apparatus at the disposal of local authorities. Workers resented the conditions of the programmes and employers discriminated against participants, labelling them as unreliable and lazy.

18 PEM and POJH, discontinued in 1987, rank well compared with the resources, stability and administrative features exhibited by other programmes of its kind in Latin America (Graham 1993).

19 Microenterprises may, however, prove important as they improve opportunities for personal development, communication and social solidarity, particularly in the case of poor women (Raczynski 1989).

20 Per capita expenditure in social security decreased 40 per cent in 1974–6. In 1981–2 there was an increase due mainly to the cost of implementing the social security reform, but spending fell again in the 1983–9 period (Raczynski and Romaguera forthcoming).

21 Reformers focused on the same justifications used in previous, unsuccessful attempts to reform the system: financial crisis, equity problems and administrative efficiency. The social security reform reduced the role of the state, replacing the pay-as-you-go system with a compulsory private insurance system based on individual capitalization accounts, administered by corporations operating in the financial market.

22 Of the various social security programmes, pensions (often modest and insufficient) constitute the main one. In 1981, they were 18 per cent lower than in 1970. The monthly per capita real value of pensions remained below the 1970 level in each year between 1974 and 1989 (Raczynski and Romaguera forthcoming).

23 Welfare pensions (only one-third of the minimum pensions) were destined for people 65 years or older who were without means of subsistence, and for handicapped adults who did not have social security coverage.

24 The SNS, created in 1952, provided free care to about 65 per cent of the population, primarily indigent and blue-collar workers and their dependants. It administered 90 per cent of all hospitals. SERMENA, created in the mid-1960s, served approximately 20 per cent of the population, mostly white-collar workers. Higher income families relied on private, independent providers (Raczynski and Romaguera forthcoming).

25 There was continuity in implementing family planning programmes until 1979 when government officials began to favour population expansion (Raczynski and Serrano 1985).

26 In 1988, almost 100 per cent of urban and rural clinics had been decentralized and were being managed by municipalities. In 1990, 16 per cent of the population, mainly higher income groups, was affiliated to a newly created system of private health insurance plans (ISAPRES). The public sector (through FONASA) continued to cover the needs of 70 per cent of the population.

27 In the 1970s and 1980s, there were shortages of medicine and personnel and a deterioration in medical infrastructure due to a decline in capital investment in health (which fell from 10 per cent of total expenditure in 1970 to 2–4 per cent in 1974–88).

28 These groups proved highly vulnerable. With a high turnover rate of participants, scarce and unstable personnel and resources, they were difficult to coordinate and maintain. However, observers and participants valued them for their symbolic as well as expressive functions. Some characterize these experiments in community participation as a valuable learning experience for health professionals and bureaucrats involved in policy design and implementation (Serrano 1989; Infante 1989; Marshall and Pérez 1989).

29 Comprehensive programmes included the diagnosis of local needs, the imple-

mentation of prevention programmes, community organization and development, health education (basic nursing, the administration of medicines, violence against women), opportunities for self-expression and recreation, sanitation, nutrition (including family vegetable gardens), alcoholism, housing and urban development.

30 The invisibility of gender is particularly striking in a country where women enjoy high levels of education and where a ready supply of domestic help frees middle-class women to pursue careers in a variety of professions and activities (Kirkwood 1986).

31 Coverage of state services for pre-school children (0–6 years old) increased from 12 per cent in 1983 and to 33 per cent in the early 1990s (Raczynski and Serrano 1985: 38; *El Mercurio* 1993b).

12

THE 1982 REFORMS AND THE EMPLOYMENT CONDITIONS OF MEXICAN WOMEN

Richard P.F. Holt

INTRODUCTION

In August 1982, the Mexican economy was in grave economic circumstances. The foreign debt exceeded 40 per cent of the gross domestic product (GDP), inflation approached 100 per cent, the foreign exchange reserves were nearly depleted, and the government was unable to honour external financial obligations (Teichman 1988: 154, 1989: 163). After intense negotiations, an agreement with the International Monetary Fund (IMF) in November 1982 provided some relief against foreign creditors (Rojas 1991: 168–79). In return, Mexico accepted the demands of the United States and the IMF to steer a new economic course.[1]

The new economic model has led to policies quite different from those pursued in the past. To enhance economic efficiency and integrate Mexico into international markets, the government emphasized reducing the foreign debt by restructuring domestic industries for export production. The reforms adopted by the government included the removal of trade barriers, incentives for new foreign investment, governmental fiscal constraint, stable exchange rates and controlled inflation. According to its supporters, the new economic plan would create new jobs and benefit the Mexican populace at all levels (Teichman 1988, 1989; Rojas 1991).

There are questions, however, as to whether all Mexicans have in fact gained from these reforms. In particular, it appears that, at best, the reforms have had a mixed impact on women. On the one hand, women have increased their workforce participation rates in such non-traditional areas as manufacturing (Brydon and Chant 1989; Lopez and Pollack 1989; Selby *et al.* 1990); and job opportunities for women have expanded in the export-processing zones (the maquiladoras). On the other hand, women have been pushed into the unstable informal economy and stand a greater chance of being poor.

The purpose of this chapter is to analyse the impact of post-1982 economic reforms on the employment conditions of Mexican women. Following a brief overview of the reforms, empirical data will be provided to analyse their effects on women's workforce participation and employment conditions. The chapter will end with some comments on how the North American Free Trade Agreement (NAFTA) might affect the employment opportunities for women in Mexico.

ECONOMIC REFORMS SINCE 1982

For over half a century the Mexican government has played an important role in national development. As early as 1940, government policies were used to transform an agrarian economy into an industrial one. In addition, the government was careful to balance the interests and well-being of different groups as market capitalism developed. The policy of promoting social programmes in conjunction with private domestic industrialization came to an end, however, with the 1982 debt crisis and the presidency of Miguel del la Madrid (1982–8).[2] At this point, the Mexican government dramatically changed its role in economic development.

President Madrid agreed with the IMF's assessment in holding previous policies responsible for Mexico's debt problem, and in recommending a new economic direction.[3] This entailed reduced expenditure on social programmes as well as a shift of emphasis from domestic investment and development to private production for export. In many ways, the plan was quite simple. The government would liberalize the Mexican economy by selling off many of its own enterprises, reducing or eliminating trade barriers, increasing the public sector prices to better reflect market forces and getting rid of government investment plans. Along with this, Mexico planned to carry out policies that would tie its markets into the world economy and transform itself from an importer of manufactured goods to an exporter of such goods.[4]

This industrial reconversion has led to mixed economic results for Mexico. It did succeed in forcing fiscal constraint. Public spending decreased from 41.8 per cent of GDP in 1982 to 29.7 per cent in 1991 (*CEPAL News* 1992a). Average per capita social expenditure dropped 19 per cent from 1982–5 to 1986–8 (*CEPAL News* 1992a). Also successful was the strategy of export promotion. The share of manufactured products in total exports increased from 11.3 per cent in 1980 to 47.2 per cent in 1989 (United Nations 1991a).

Other statistics are not as impressive, however. The GDP growth rate declined from an average annual rate of 6.8 per cent in 1975–80 to 0.7 per cent in the 1980–6 period. Economic growth increased to 2.5 per cent in 1988, and to 4.5 per cent in 1992. But in 1993, Mexico's economy slowed down again with second quarter growth falling to 0.3 per cent (United Nations 1991b; *The Economist* 1993b: 40–1). In 1987, the unemployment rate was 18 per cent and the underemployment rate was estimated to be in the 25–40 per cent range. These rates remained stable until 1993 when unemployment increased slightly due to layoffs in the auto industry.[5] Consumer purchasing power has

declined by more than 35 per cent since 1982 and gross domestic investment
has decreased as economic reforms have led to deindustrialization in the
country (Barkin 1990: 101; United Nations 1990).

More importantly, however, industrial reconversion has engendered a
reorganization of production that has affected all social groups, particularly
women. The next section will discuss the effects on Mexican women's labour-
market activities.

EMPLOYMENT CONDITIONS OF WOMEN SINCE THE 1982 DEBT CRISIS

During the last two decades, the proportion of Mexican women entering the
workforce has increased significantly. As Table 12.1 indicates, women
increased their workforce participation at a faster rate relative to men in the
1980–8 period.[6] Table 12.2 sheds more light on rising workforce participation
rates by distinguishing among three different age-groups. Looking at prime-
age Mexicans (those between 20 and 59 years old), it is evident that there is a
sharp jump in female workforce participation as opposed to a slight decline
in the male participation in the workforce.

Tables 12.3 and 12.4 provide further evidence that women have been
entering the Mexican workforce in large numbers during the 1980s. Women's
workforce participation in non-agricultural paid employment has increased

Table 12.1 Percentage distribution of economically active* population by gender

	1980	1988	Percentage change 1980–8
Female	18.2	22.8	4.6
Male	48.2	51.2	3.0

Sources: *Year Book of Labour Statistics* (1990: table 1, 1992: table 1).
* Those in the working-age population who are either employed or seeking employment in the
  formal sector.

Table 12.2 Female and male workforce participation rates by age

Age	1980	1988
	Female (%)	
10–19	32.1	35.5
20–59	31.1	37.2
60+	20.2	20.1
	Male (%)	
10–19	33.8	36.2
20–59	93.3	93.0
60+	73.2	68.1

Sources: *Year Book of Labour Statistics* (1990: table 1, 1991: table 1).

at a faster rate relative to men (Table 12.3), and significantly more women have found paid employment in manufacturing while fewer men have received paid manufacturing jobs (Table 12.4).

This increase in women's workforce participation rates is surprising. In the United States and other industrialized nations, when the economy becomes sluggish and wages fall, women are more likely to become discouraged workers.[7] That is, unemployed men are likely to continue looking for work while unemployed women are likely to spend more time with their families and taking care of household responsibilities. As a result, women drop out of the workforce more readily during economic downturns (Bellante and Jackson 1983: 74). What is curious about Mexico in the 1980s is that there has been an 'added-worker' effect;[8] when the primary worker of the family is laid off, another member enters the workforce in order to protect the family's standard of living.

It is important to notice that women's workforce participation rate has increased despite significant reductions in both the average and the minimum real wage rates in the urban areas between 1981 and 1989 (Table 12.5).[9] Real urban minimum wages in 1988 were half the level prevailing in 1981. None the less, women's workforce participation grew 25 per cent over the same period (see Table 12.1).

Table 12.3 General employment and paid employment in non-agricultural activities in Mexico (in thousands)

	1980	*1985*	*1990*	*Percentage change from 1980 to 1990*
General employment	5,825	6,700	8,899	52.78
Paid employment in non-agricultural activities in Mexico				
Female	1,309	1,898	2,482	89.6
Male	2,494	4,277	5,933	69.8
Total	4,802	6,175	8,415	75.2

Sources: *Year Book of Labour Statistics* (1988: tables 3 and 4, 1992: tables 3 and 4).

Table 12.4 Paid employment in manufacturing in Mexico (in '000s)

Year	*Total*	*Male*	*Female*
1981	2,280	1,776	505
1982	2,072	1,554	518
1983	2,089	1,554	495
1984	2,263	1,713	550
1985	2,387	1,801	585
1986	2,371	1,762	609
Percentage change from 1981 to 1986	4.0	−0.8	20.1

Source: *Year Book of Labour Statistics* (1991: table 5).

181

It is difficult to obtain consistent data for female–male wage differentials in Latin American countries. Psacharopoulos and Tzannatos (1992) show the Mexican gender differential to be lower than that in the more advanced countries (85.6 per cent in Mexico as opposed to 65–75 per cent in the industrialized nations for 1984). The wage data in Mexico (and other Latin American countries) are, however, mostly from the formal sector rather than the informal sector where women are concentrated. Also a large number of women employed in the formal sector work for the government, where gender wage differentials are much smaller than in the private sector.

Table 12.5 Average annual real wage index (1980=100)

Year	Real average wages	Real urban minimum wages
1981	103.5	101.9
1982	102.2	92.7
1983	80.7	76.6
1984	75.4	72.3
1985	76.6	71.1
1986	72.3	64.9
1987	72.8	61.7
1988	72.1	55.2
1989	75.8	50.8

Source: United Nations (1991a: 71–2).

The following sections will examine three sectors of the economy where women actively participate – the rural sector, the urban sector and the maquila industry. It will be argued that the debt crisis and the economic reforms of the 1980s have forced women to join the labour force to protect their families' incomes in each and every sector.

The rural sector

The economic reforms have resulted in major cutbacks in agricultural development programmes, causing massive migration from the countryside. Input subsidies and price supports have been reduced considerably and, with the privatization of banks, the private sector handles most credit decisions for agricultural development. Due to restrictive monetary policy and the perceived risk of small- and medium-size farms, banks have been unable or unwilling to extend credit to their owners (Barkin 1990). Lack of credit has consequently prevented farmers from increasing food production either for export or for the expanding domestic market.

Table 12.6 substantiates the above argument. The average annual growth rate of food production in Mexico dropped from 3.9 per cent in 1970–80 to 2.7 per cent in 1980–5. From 1986 to 1990 growth rates were negative (except for 1988); 1990 recorded 0 per cent growth. Table 12.7 shows that exports of

Table 12.6 Average annual growth rates of food production in Mexico

1970–80	1980–5	1986	1987	1988	1989	1990
3.9	2.7	−3.9	−0.9	6.3	−0.8	0.0

Source: United Nations (1991a: 79).

Table 12.7 Agricultural exports as a percentage of total exports in Mexico

1970	1980	1982	1985	1986	1987	1988	1989	1990
54.2	12.0	7.5	7.3	16.2	11.2	12.0	11.0	9.9

Source: United Nations (1991a: 79).

agricultural products stagnated during the 1980s. In 1970 agricultural exports represented 54.2 per cent of total exports, in 1980 they were 12 per cent and by 1990 they had been reduced to 9.9 per cent.

To aggravate the plight of farmers, trade liberalization has allowed foreign imports to replace many domestic agricultural products. Foreign agricultural capital, particularly from the United States, has also been able to take advantage of the best and most productive irrigation districts in northern Mexico for fruit and vegetable exports (Barkin 1990: 5–6). As economic reforms cut back subsidies and sources of credit for small- and medium-size farms, unemployment increased and wage rates and income levels dropped for the rural population (Barkin 1990: 70–97; United Nations 1991a: 471).

The above consequences have not gone unnoticed. In 1984, President Madrid set up Regional Employment Programs. Among other things, their objective was to create jobs for rural workers by providing labour-intensive projects such as road construction. In addition, there were Scholarships for Training Workers, the Ignacio Ramirez Scholarship Program and the Program for Involving Women in Development. From 1983 to 1988, these programmes employed 900,000 workers for short periods of time (Tamayo and Lozano 1991: 375–81). But they had very little to offer women. The number of women involved was very small and in many cases they were excluded due to such participation criteria as property ownership. The programmes also focused on welfare assistance for women instead of increasing opportunities for long-term employment (Tamayo and Lozano 1991: 375–81).

Under President Salinas, most of the above programmes came to an end. Markets, he claimed, would 'increase the output and productivity of the countryside' through the liberal restructuring of the economy (Office of the President, Mexico 1989). In his National Development Plan (1989–94), Salinas proposed to deal with extreme cases of poverty in the rural and urban areas through the National Solidarity Program (PRONASOL) (Tamayo and Lozano 1991: 381–3). But so far, no action has been taken to give this programme meaningful power or resources to deal with the increasing poverty in Mexico.

It is clear that since 1982 the Mexican government has ignored the regional dimensions of its industrial reconversion by not formulating any concrete policy toward the rural or the urban sector. The reconversion has simply focused on macroeconomic policies while ignoring how the policies change the social and economic conditions of the Mexican people. The increased unemployment of primary workers and cutbacks in public assistance have forced rural women to join the workforce in order to keep themselves and their families alive. In 1980 women represented 3.4 per cent of those formally working in the agricultural sector; by 1987 the percentage had jumped to 14 per cent (*Year Book of Labour Statistics* 1987: table 2, 1991: table 2). The increase is even more remarkable given the high levels of female (relative to male) rural–urban migration (see below).

Because of women's need to join the workforce and the limited job opportunities provided by the declining agricultural sector, many have been forced to migrate in search of work to the urban areas of Mexico or to the United States (Selby *et al.* 1990; Lopez and Pollack 1989). Rural–urban migrants in Mexico have been predominantly female in the 1980s. The average annual ratio of women to men migrating to the urban areas in the 1980s was 107 to 100 (ibid.). As a result, women outnumber men in urban areas by a ratio of 105 to 100 but are outnumbered in the rural areas 97 to 100 (United Nations 1991b: 71–9). The residency rates have also changed. In 1970, 40 per cent of women in Mexico lived in rural areas whereas in 1987 only 33 per cent did (ibid.).

The government has done very little to stop the migration (Cornelius 1991: 89–131). According to officials, the new economic reforms will provide economic opportunities in the rural areas, allowing both men and women to stay at home with their families. But in effect, the policies support migration, particularly to the United States, as a way of easing some of the unemployment burden facing the rural population (Barkin 1990: 117; Tamayo and Lozano 1991).

The urban sector

The economic reforms have affected the urban population as well. As mentioned earlier, the real urban minimum wage rate has dropped. From 1980 to 1986, real per capita income of urban workers in the informal sector decreased by 20.4 per cent, while for those in the formal sector the decline amounted to 16.4 per cent (*CEPAL News* 1990, 1992b).[10] It can be argued that most of the increased poverty in the 1980s was felt by women for a variety of reasons. More women migrated to the cities relative to men; women outnumbered men in the urban areas; and women were being pushed into low-paying jobs in the informal sector (see below).

Similar to their rural counterparts, urban women have responded to the economic changes by joining the workforce (Selby *et al.* 1990: 175). Table

12.8 shows the extent to which women have entered the urban workforce during the 1980s. In 1977, 26 per cent of urban wives were in the workforce; 13 per cent of them were active in the formal sector, and the other 13 per cent held informal sector jobs. By 1987, a much higher percentage (41) of married women were in the workforce. As a group, however, they lost ground. Only 11 per cent were in the formal sector; the other 30 per cent were engaged in informal sector activities.

Table 12.8 allows us to compare women in lower and higher income quintiles. The economic crisis has forced women in the lower quintiles to enter the informal sector at an increasing rate; their opportunities in the formal sector have decreased mostly due to insufficient training. Women in the upper quintiles have also been entering the workforce, but seem to have gained in the formal sector because of their higher relative education (ibid.). What stands out in both income categories is that more women enter the workforce in times of economic crisis.[11]

Table 12.8 Wives in workforce by quintile of household income in Mexico

Households	Quintiles 1–3 (%)	Quintiles 4–5 (%)	Total (%)
1977			
Wives in the workforce	18	39	26
Informal sector	5	26	13
Formal sector	13	13	13
1987			
Wives in the workforce	33	51	41
Informal sector	30	31	30
Formal sector	3	20	11

Source: Selby *et al.* (1990: 174).

The increased workforce participation of women has affected fertility rates. The family unit has always played an important role in protecting women from poverty (ibid.: 163–77); larger families have higher incomes because they can send more people to work (Lopez and Pollack 1989: 37–79). However, increased education and housing costs, and reduced urban subsidies have significantly affected the cost of having children. At the same time, the ability of children to augment the family income has decreased as job opportunities shrink and wage rates fall (Selby *et al.* 1990: 163–77). The increased opportunity cost of having children has also been a factor. Since work and raising children have similar demands on time, as women enter the workforce they choose to have fewer children (Selby *et al.* 1990; Lopez and Pollack 1989: 37–45; United Nations 1991b).[12]

Table 12.9 shows that women tend to be more heavily concentrated in clerical and service jobs than in other categories. The clerical and service jobs can be broken down into two categories. Education plays an important role in allowing women to enter in this sector and to decide which segment of it they can participate in. The white-collar positions require a few years of schooling or training and offer some stability and job mobility. They employ mostly younger, single women. The low-level service jobs require less education or training but are less stable. During recessions, many women in low-level service segments of the formal sector lose their jobs and are forced into the informal sector. Women with some education do better, staying in the formal sector longer, even during recessions (Selby et al. 1990: 163–78). Since 1982, cutbacks in education expenditure – public expenditure for education decreased from 3.4 per cent of GDP in 1982 to 2.0 per cent in 1988 (United Nations 1991a) – and women's increased workforce participation to protect their family's standard of living, have affected their ability to stay in the formal sector of the economy.

There are no time-series studies from the 1980s that examine the effects of cutbacks in education expenditure on the ability of women to enter the formal sector. However, cross-sectional studies covering the same period suggest that less educated women enter the workforce early and usually join the informal sector. More educated women are more likely to find work in the formal sector (see Selby et al. 1990).

Table 12.9 Women per 100 men in different (formal) occupational groups, 1980s

Administrative	Clerical	Production	Agriculture
18	70	20	14

Source: United Nations (1991b: table 8).

To sum up, the number of urban women entering the workforce has increased since 1982. Cutbacks in public education make it more difficult for women to augment the human capital necessary for entering the formal sector of the economy. But, given the recent national debates on NAFTA, a third alternative for working women has attracted attention, namely, the expanding maquila industry.

The maquila industry

The Mexican export-processing plants, called maquiladoras, represent one of the largest manufacturing export assembly operations in the world. They are concentrated near the northern border, and consist mostly of American-owned factories (Sklair 1989: 1–23). The number of maquiladoras has expanded rapidly since their inception in 1965. During their expansion in the 1960s and 1970s, government pursuit of import-substitution policies limited the economic role of the maquila industry. Since the economic reforms of the 1980s, however, the industry has been presented as a model for Mexico's future. President Salinas has made it clear that the maquiladoras play an important role in his industrialization plan (Weintraub 1991: 155–68).

The maquila industry has been exceptionally attractive to foreign businesses since 1982 because of the devaluation of the peso, major government investment incentives, and the possibility of a new trade agreement with the United States. The devaluation of the peso has reduced the average hourly operative wage from $1.32 in 1982 to $0.80 in 1988 (Sklair 1989: 72), and the strategy of encouraging investment has been successful. By the end of 1991, Americans had invested over $21.4 billion in Mexico (*US Department of State Dispatch* 1992). And as Table 12.10 indicates, the number of plants increased from 585 in 1982 to 1,179 in 1988; employment increased from 127,048 to 329,413 in the same period. In 1991, 2,000 plants employed nearly 500,000 workers (US Department of Labour 1991: 8).

Unfortunately, this growth has not had any spillover benefits to other manufacturing industries. Table 12.11 compares the employment of the maquila industry with other manufacturing firms in Mexico. Employment outside of the maquiladoras has declined throughout the 1980s. But for the export-processing industries there has been a significant increase in employment and women have benefited from this growth.

Table 12.10 Maquila industry by plants and employees

Year	Plants	Employees
1982	585	127,048
1983	600	150,867
1984	672	199,684
1985	760	211,968
1986	890	249,833
1987	1,125	305,253
1989(Jan.)	1,279	329,413

Source: Sklair (1989: 68).

Table 12.11 Indices of employment in manufacturing in Mexico

1982	1983	1984	1985	1986	1987	1988	1989
Persons employed in manufacturing excluding the maquiladoras							
103.0	93.1	92.2	94.3	90.5	87.4	87.5	89.1
Percentage variation							
	−9.6	−1.0	2.3	−4.0	−3.4	0.1	1.8
Persons employed in the maquiladoras							
122.0	151.0	167.0	177.3	207.6	254.0	310.1	362.5
Percentage variation							
	23.8	10.6	6.2	17.1	22.4	22.1	16.9

Source: United Nations (1989: 70).

A great deal of attention has been given to the maquila industry as a major source of employment for women who are entering the workforce for the first time. As Table 12.12 indicates, the number of women working in the export-processing zones more than doubled in the 1982–8 period. The strict sexual division of labour within the export-processing zones should, however, be taken into account (Sklair 1989: 156–92). Many of the jobs offered to women are low-level, blue-collar positions which do not provide expanded job opportunities. Technicians and white-collar positions which do provide such opportunities are almost exclusively occupied by men (US Department of Labour 1990: 59).

Table 12.12 also shows that, despite the increased number of women employed in the maquila industry, their employment share has dropped consistently. From 1979 to 1982 women represented roughly 77 per cent of workers in the industry, but in 1983 the ratio of men to women began to rise; by 1988, the employment share of women in the industry was 64.2 per cent.

The declining share of women's employment can be explained through the change in the composition of maquiladora plants. During the 1980s, the maquiladoras shifted their emphasis from light to heavy manufacturing. As a result, more technical and white-collar workers have been hired, who, as previously argued, are predominantly male (ibid.).

Available wage data for the maquila industry are not broken down by gender. One could argue, however, that since women hold the low-level, unskilled positions, they could be earning closer to the minimum wage rate than technicians and white-collar workers. Table 12.13 shows that real minimum wages in the high-cost areas, which include the maquiladoras, declined more than 40 per cent in the 1980s.

Table 12.12 Female and male operatives* in the maquilas, 1975–88

Year	Male	Female	Per cent female employed
1975	12,575	45,275	78.3
1976	13,686	50,984	78.8
1977	14,999	53,188	78.0
1978	18,205	60,837	76.8
1979	21,981	73,837	77.1
1980	23,140	78,880	77.3
1981	24,993	85,691	77.4
1982	23,990	81,393	77.2
1983	32,004	93,274	74.5
1984	48,215	117,290	70.9
1985	53,812	120,042	69.0
1986	64,812	139,082	68.2
1987	84,525	164,100	66.0
1988 (Jan.)	95,524	171,603	64.2

Source: Sklair (1989: 167).
* Operatives are defined as those working on the shop floor.

Table 12.13 Mexican daily (real) minimum wage rates for production workers in high-cost areas, 1982–9

| Year | In average 1989 units | |
	Pesos	Dollars
1982	17,818	6.56
1983	14,819	5.07
1984	13,709	5.34
1985	13,506	5.24
1986	12,142	3.62
1987	11,335	3.38
1988	9,926	3.72
1989	9,207	3.79

Source: US Department of Labor (1990: 93).

The economic reforms seem to have led to two effects for women who work in the maquila industry. First, despite declining real wage rates, women have entered the industry in record numbers. Secondly, there has been a shift from light industry to heavy manufacturing which has increased men's employment share.

CONCLUSION

This chapter has looked at the employment conditions of women following the 1982 reforms in Mexico. Special attention has been paid to changes in the rural and urban sectors as well as in the maquila industry. Declining wages and the high unemployment rates forced women to increase their workforce participation rates faster than their male counterparts. Unlike the more developed countries, however, higher female workforce participation has not greatly benefited Mexican women. They have been forced to migrate to the urban areas in order to protect their family incomes. In addition, while married women have been working more, they have been pushed into the less desirable jobs of the informal sector.

In June 1991, the United States, Mexico and Canada began negotiations on NAFTA. In many ways NAFTA is a continuation of the liberalization policies that have been going on in Mexico since 1982. The text of the draft agreement calls for the elimination of tariffs either immediately or over a period of years. Non-tariff barriers such as import licences and quotas are also going to be eliminated. In addition, the investment climate needs to remain open to international investors (*US Department of State Dispatch* 1992).

The Mexican government has followed these policies over the last decade hoping that foreign investment would provide the necessary resources for the expansion of manufacturing along with the related back-up services, education and infrastructure. In reality, gross domestic investment has declined by an average annual rate of 4.9 per cent from 1980 to 1987, leading to a reduction in manufacturing employment outside the zones (United Nations 1990: 10). In other words, NAFTA is not likely to solve Mexico's economic problems.

Unless the Mexican government changes its policies, it will continue to see female migration from the rural areas to the urban barrios and the United States as women search for work. With cutbacks in education and training programmes women will be forced to enter or stay in the informal sector of the economy. Economic growth in all sectors and regions necessitates reforms that not only support free trade and open markets but also provide domestic resources for internal investment. This can only succeed if the government recognizes that industrial reconversion does not by itself create the dynamic growth the country needs and that domestic reforms and assistance are essential.

NOTES

1 See Leeds and Thompson (1987) for an excellent review of the negotiations between Mexico and the United States.
2 Teichman (1988) gives an excellent explanation of the role of the state in Mexico's economic development. See especially the chapter on 'State interests and the politics of patronage and stabilization' (127–42).
3 See Tamayo and Lozano (1991: 375–81) for a brief review of some of Madrid's policies during his presidency.
4 With President Carlos Salinas de Gortari (1988–94) reforms took on a new intensity. Failure to attract the necessary capital inflows persuaded Salinas to provide confidence for foreign investors (Loser and Kalter 1992) by opening up negotiations on the North American Free Trade Agreement (NAFTA) in June 1991. This, he believed, would prove Mexico's commitment to maintaining an open and stable economy, ensuring easy access to United States markets for export manufacturing (Kalter 1992: 3–13).
5 Accurate employment figures for Mexico are hard to obtain. The US Labor Department reports the following: 'While unemployment figures are particularly difficult to come by, with 8 or 9 per cent as a generally accepted figure under the more narrow Mexican definition of unemployment as "persons actively looking for work," most observers would place the unemployment figure at a higher 18 to 20 per cent figure. Underemployed Mexicans, the largest numbers to be found in the informal economy, and "seeking employment" are generally estimated to be numbered at 25 to 40 per cent of the work force' (US Department of Labour 1991: 10).
6 Women increased their workforce participation at a much higher rate during the 1970s for two reasons. First, the United Nations and the World Bank urged the Mexican government to institute support programmes, allowing women to enter occupations that were previously inaccessible to them. Secondly, the economy was growing at higher rates, providing more job opportunities. The continued increase in the workforce participation rate of women in the 1980s is significant in light of cutbacks in education and training as well as the deep economic recession.
7 See Mincer (1962: 63–97); Cain (1966); Nakamura (1969: 787–805).
8 For a discussion on women's workforce participation rates in Latin America see Psacharopoulos and Tzannatos (1992).

190

9 The increased workforce participation of women, in turn, leads to a further decline in urban wages (United Nations 1991a: 488).

10 The percentage of households under the poverty line has increased in the urban areas from 20 per cent in 1970 to 23 per cent in 1986 (*CEPAL News* 1990; Selby *et al.* 1990: 175).

11 Economic conditions have affected household behaviour in other ways. Until the 1980s there was a decrease in the average household size; but that trend has changed. For example, in 1970 the average household size was 4.9. By 1987 it was 5.5. Families are finding that economies of scale are the best way to handle the decline in family's income. What distinguishes the 1980s downturn is that multiple families are being forced under one roof (Selby *et al.* 1990: 173–5).

12 Numerous studies show the existence of direct correlation between education and workforce participation in the formal sector of the economy for women in Mexico (United Nations 1983: 111–36). In addition, the longer women stay in school, the smaller the families they seem to prefer, which affects their fertility rate (Lopez and Pollack 1989: 37–45).

13

STATE POLICY AND THE RESTRUCTURING OF WOMEN'S INDUSTRIES IN NICARAGUA

Nan Wiegersma[1]

INTRODUCTION

The International Monetary Fund (IMF), the World Bank and the United States Agency for International Development (AID) have advocated policies that encourage the restructuring of industry for export processing, privatization and foreign ownership. Because of their debt positions and credit needs, the Central American governments in general, and Nicaragua in particular, have had no choice but to restructure in compliance with the policies of these international agencies and bilateral donors.

During the 1980s, the Nicaraguan economy had suffered great hardship due to the civil war and to the United States' support for the Contras who opposed the Sandinista government. The country was in disastrous economic circumstances by the mid-1980s, the war taking its toll on production and trade. Despite the economic contraction, the government continued its spending, which resulted in runaway inflation. Nicaragua's default on international commercial loans only worsened the situation.

To gain some control over a rapidly deteriorating situation, the Sandinistas were forced to restructure their economy in 1988. These policies were not effective; neither was the first set of reforms under the UNO government of Violeta Chamoro, elected in 1990. By the last half of 1991, however, a severe economic contraction finally stabilized the currency. The World Bank/IMF then agreed to restructure the international loans; United States aid was also forthcoming if Nicaragua consented to liberalize trade and privatize the economy.

In Nicaragua, as in other former socialist countries, these institutional changes have been particularly rapid and the human effects particularly debilitating. The Sandinista government had previously instituted an extensive set of labour services and benefits such as free noon-time meals, transportation, health services and paid pregnancy leaves. Privatization and restructuring have been tantamount to the elimination of these programmes.

Restructuring and privatization have most severely affected female workers. With the development of export processing, domestic industries that predominantly employ women have been completely shut down while industries with predominantly male employees remain open. A variety of agreements with former owners, new investors and the government have often kept male jobs intact. In addition, men have been given the opportunity to own 11–100 per cent of their companies (Anderson and Cuadra 1993: 11; *Acuerdo de Privatización* 1993).

An increase in export production by multinational enterprises in free trade zones is an important part of restructuring; in other countries this has increased female employment. However, with the transition from a mostly socialist to a predominantly capitalist economy Nicaragua has experienced decreased female employment. Textile and garment factories have been shut down in their domestic form as companies start up in the export-processing zone, *Zona Franca*. At the same time, privatization has transformed state industries; between July 1991 and July 1993 all state-owned garment factories in the zone were privatized. In the process, many older female workers were laid off, younger women were hired, and working conditions changed tremendously.

Trade liberalization and export promotion have also exposed Nicaragua to increased outside competition. Price competition on the world market, mostly due to Asian technological breakthroughs in thread and textile production, has forced policy-makers either to increase investments substantially or liquidate parts of their industries. Also, the reduction of import taxes puts at risk domestic industries that employ mainly female labour (CEPAL 1990: 152).

With its neo-liberal (free-market) ideology, the current Nicaraguan government decided to change its tax and industrial structures more rapidly and more drastically than the rest of Central America. The UNO government liquidated the largest segment of the domestic textile and garment industry in 1991–2. Although export-processing production is simultaneously expanding, the employment gains in the export-oriented zone fall short of the layoffs effected by the liquidation of domestic firms. As a result, women's employment in textile manufacturing dropped by several thousands in the 1991–2 period, and was only just beginning to recover in 1993.

This chapter investigates how restructuring has affected employment opportunities for Nicaraguan women. It focuses primarily on the garment and textile industry, which has been a major source of female industrial employment in Nicaragua. The next section presents the methodology used for this study as well as a recent history of women's workforce participation in Nicaragua. The restructuring rationale is then set forth. This is followed by analyses of the impact of restructuring and privatization on female workers. Finally, the role of labour unions in restructuring is examined.

WOMEN AND THE STRUCTURE OF INDUSTRY IN NICARAGUA

Methodology

To compare women's overall employment position inside and outside Nicaragua's *Zona Franca*, this chapter uses an 'industry study' approach, investigating the different institutional formations, wages and working conditions for enterprises inside and outside the zone. This is done for both state and private enterprises. An industry study was chosen in the light of the problems encountered with alternative methods. Time series and cross section approaches to the impact of export processing and industrial restructuring on workers contain inconsistencies brought about by involving false comparisons of different sizes and types of industry (Jenkins 1990). An industry study can specify the differences in industry size and institutional setting in making comparisons.

Interviews and questionnaires have been used to obtain information from government officials, managers of industries and from workers themselves. Fifteen initial and follow up interviews were conducted with enterprise managers and personnel directors using a Spanish version of a 1990 ECLAC study (Bishop *et al.* 1990).[2] Twenty initial and fifteen follow-up interviews were also conducted with textile–garment operatives who worked in the zone as well as outside the zone (in both formal and informal sector enterprises). The interviews were conducted between July 1991 and July 1993.

The garment industry is a natural choice for comparing enterprises inside and outside the free trade zones because it has a long history; by the 1980s, Central American countries had experienced several decades of textile–garment production for domestic and regional markets. These industries had been encouraged by high import taxes associated with the import substitution policies of the 1960s and 1970s and by the development of the Central American Common Market in the 1970s. Moreover, unlike electronics, the garment industry has not previously been associated with export processing.[3] Also, the new international division of labour has transformed the garment industry, creating new institutional structures.

Background

The employment trends for women in Nicaragua reflect both urbanization and industrialization. Nevertheless, the majority of women who have participated in the workforce have continued to work in the service sector, and are employed in such jobs as domestic work and vending. In 1971, three-quarters of employed women worked in the service sector. This proportion declined to 61 per cent by 1977, due to an increase in women's participation in agricultural export production and manufacturing. With limited growth in the agricultural and manufacturing sectors under the Sandinistas, the percentage of women employed in the service sector increased again, reaching 67 per cent by 1985 (Table 13.1). Since 1988, structural adjustment programmes (under the Sandinista and UNO governments) have led to the further restructuring of the workforce. Women have increasingly turned to services and the informal sector, and away from manufacturing as more than 10,000 industrial jobs have vanished.

During the 1950s and 1960s, the big surge in industrialization created job opportunities for Nicaraguan men and women alike. With the development of garment, textiles and food processing industries, women's share in manufacturing employment grew to approximately one-fifth of the industrial workforce by 1971. Despite this growth in numbers, the share remained stable until the late 1980s (Pérez-Aleman et al. 1989). Although the share of women in agriculture and services shifted somewhat with the Sandinista administration and with the war-time economy, industrial employment for women was relatively stable until the recent structural adjustment policies eliminated more than 4,000 jobs in textiles as well as a large number in other industries (Table 13.1).

Women's participation in large-scale industry is more significant than these figures might suggest. Along with the development of national industry from the 1950s to the 1970s, an urbanized female working class emerged with specific household characteristics. Only half of all women working in manufacturing were married; one-third of them were heads of households; and 14 per cent were single (Pérez-Aleman et al. 1989: 31).

The civil war of the 1980s encouraged women's workforce participation, but female employment in large manufacturing establishments did not increase very much because of limited opportunities. In general, large

Table 13.1 Nicaraguan women workers, in thousands and percentages, 10 years and older

	1971	1977	1985
Women as a percentage of the workforce	21.7	30.0	32.9
Women as a percentage in industry	21.5	30.0	32.3
Total number of women in the workforce:	108.1	234.4	340.6
Agriculture	8.8	47.6	42.8
Industry	18.6	43.1	69.0
Services	86.7	143.7	228.8
Percentage of women in:			
Agriculture	8.1	20.3	12.5
Industry	17.3	18.4	20.3
Services	74.6	61.3	67.2

Source: Garcia and Gomáriz (1989).

industries performed poorly under Sandinista rule and the sexual division of labour remained fairly rigid despite the young men going off to war.

By 1985, nevertheless, one-third of females aged 10 years and older were in the workforce. Twenty per cent of them were in industry, 13 per cent in agriculture and the rest in services. The sectors with increasing participation during the Sandinista period were government, services and small-scale industry. Women entered the workforce in increasing numbers during this period because a large part of the male workforce was involved in the war, more members of the family were forced to look for jobs due to the economic crisis, and there was a large increase in the number of female-headed households in the cities (Perez-Aleman *et al.* 1990: 1–33)

A combination of circumstances in the 1980s shifted the focus of industrial enterprises to production for the domestic economy, and away from exports. Sandinista ideology favoured production for the internal markets. Moreover, the United States' trade embargo, the war, and Nicaragua's defaulting on foreign loans made international commerce very difficult. Some clothing and shoes continued to be produced for export during the 1980s, but most of the plants in Nicaragua's Mercedes Free Trade Zone were shifted to produce exclusively for the domestic economy.

Although the number of women in large-scale manufacturing industries did not increase substantially during Sandinista rule, working conditions changed considerably for workers in general and for women in particular. Manufacturing workers were given access to free medical care through the social security system. Employees were granted free transportation and noon-time meals. Particularly important to women was the change in labour legislation that gave them paid pregnancy leave and the right to return to their jobs afterwards.

At the time of changeover from the Sandinista administration to UNO in 1990, women were the largest part of the workforce in commerce and services (especially health and education). They were also a significant part of the industrial workforce. Nevertheless, the structural adjustments of the late 1980s and early 1990s have greatly affected women's job opportunities. Vast numbers have become unemployed and/or moved back into an already overcrowded informal sector. The hardest hit were the large-scale garment–textile industries in Managua, which employed about 10 per cent of the female industrial workforce. Also affected was another 10 per cent who participated in small household apparel shops and cooperatives. Nation-wide, women in the garment–textile industry made up approximately one-quarter of the employed female industrial workforce.

In the continuing depression, estimates of unemployment and under-employment are as high as 50 per cent in the daily newspapers. A social science research organization, FIDEG, puts the unemployment figure in the Managua area at about 20 per cent and the underemployment at 34 (FIDEG 1992: 32). A high unemployment rate is the 'medicine' that Nicaragua has had to endure in order to defeat the runaway inflation which had gathered steam under the Sandinistas and during the first year of the UNO government. The current managed depression is a policy which the World Bank, the IMF and the United States AID insisted upon; investment was impossible as long as inflation persisted. Unfortunately, three years after inflation was defeated, there are still few signs of economic growth.

In the important realm of large-scale industry, many companies were returned to their pre-1979 owners with agreements about workers' right to own 25 per cent of their companies. Other industries were sold by the state to multinational corporations. Production of rum, beer and cola, with a predominantly male workforce, has been stable as these do not show a strong downward turn during depressions. Unique among the large companies are the garment–textile enterprises employing large percentages of women which have been closed down in their domestic institutional form (see Table 13.2).

Table 13.2 Workers in the garment–textile industry in the Managua region

	1989	1991	1993
Export-processing zone	1,500	500	2,000
Outside the zone	4,500	2,000	500
Total	6,000	2,500	2,500

Sources: Interviews with Secretaria de la Mujer, CST Labour Unions; and *Zona Franca* management.

THE RESTRUCTURING RATIONALE

In response to international trends, restructuring of industry proceeded apace in the rest of the Caribbean and Central America during the ten years of Sandinista rule. It made use of the availability of low wages throughout the region as specialization continued to subdivide markets further. Nicaraguan industries had to restructure to be incorporated into this global assembly or factory (Kamel 1990). Under the UNO leadership, Nicaragua has adjusted by drawing down the textile–garment industries as well as small national firms. Shutdown orders have been accompanied by changes in import taxes in 1991; increased taxes on raw materials and decreased taxes on finished goods have squeezed small domestic, private industries.

Adjustment has led to the contradictory situation whereby the same industries that are being shut down in their national form are being constructed in *Zona Franca* with a very different institutional structure. The economic rationale for this transition is as follows:

1 The domestic textile industry has equipment which is 20–30 years old and must be replaced in any event.

2 Although textiles were operating with old equipment in other Central

American countries, they were maintained with spare parts which were not available in Nicaragua during the blockade.[4]

3 The special tax advantages of the free trade zone can bring in the investment money for the garment industry which the government and domestic capitalists cannot afford.

4 There is low demand for garments and textiles in the domestic market because of a continuing depression and because used clothes from the United States – given away or sold in the 1980s and early 1990s – replaced a segment of the domestic market.

5 When capitalists returned to run their former companies, they chose not to upgrade facilities or produce for the domestic market. This choice was at least partly due to such social benefits as paid pregnancy leaves, which had accrued to women under the Sandinista government. Returning capitalists were aware that female workers received more benefits than male workers.

The problem with this transition is that thousands of women have lost their jobs in the old industries, but the anticipated job openings in the new export-processing zone will not increase beyond 3,000 in the near future. In addition, the new jobs will not go to women over thirty-five who were laid off, nor will they go to former workers who are not from the north-eastern part of the city. Thousands of women, most of them single mothers, have been without formal sector jobs for years and the informal sector is vastly overcrowded.

RESTRUCTURING OF THE GARMENT–TEXTILE INDUSTRY AND GENDER DISCRIMINATION

The government and the unions see the textile and apparel sector as including all of the garment, textile and shoe production factories in the Managua area. Women, whose work histories include both formal and informal sector experience (Table 13.3), see the industry as broader, including sewing in the home and vending. On the other hand, most of these same women see the geographic limits of their labour market in narrow terms, since they must rely on public or employer-provided transportation. These two different views of reality have impacted on policy in various ways.

First, government advertisements have encouraged women to invest their severance pay in small shops in their neighbourhoods, mistakenly assuming that these businesses do not already exist. Additional small businesses, if successful, would cut into the earnings of the already established sewers and vendors.

Secondly, even if the industries that were established in the free trade zone had kept pace with those that were shut down in the city, the new jobs would not be filled with the unemployed workers from the old industries. It cannot be assumed that workers from one side of the city can afford transportation, or can relocate to the other side of the city, to take advantage of the new job openings. The vast majority of workers with experience in the new industries were the younger workers hired from Enaves, the former enterprise in the zone, and other factories located in that area.

Shifting the formal workforce from one location in the city to another is extremely disruptive of family life, especially for women who are the family care givers. The one worker in our study who found employment and was attempting to make the move from the north-western part of the city to the north-eastern suburbs is quite atypical. She had to leave her young children with family members as she tried to work her way through the bureaucratic maze necessary to sell her house in her barrio and purchase a house north-east of the city. Most former garment and textile workers will find it difficult to move their families from their native barrios.

The buildup of the Mercedes Free Trade Zone for export production is an important part of the UNO restructuring plan for Nicaragua. There were initially five clothing firms operating in the zone in the 1970s, producing for the United States market. These firms were taken over by the government during the 1980s and were operated by the Sandinistas under one management in a company called Enaves. Production for the military and for the home market was combined with some export production during this period. Approximately 2,000 workers produced shoes, clothing and aluminium products.

By the time of our initial interviews in 1991, Enaves was producing very little, being prepared for privatization. By the end of 1991, it was employing less than 400 workers. Three private firms were setting up operations but as yet had few workers; hence the estimate of 500 apparel workers in the zone for 1991 given in Table 13.2.

In the next period, 1992–3, the new small enterprises in the zone grew larger and the newly privatized enterprises grew rapidly since structure and equipment already existed. The United States market was again open to Nicaraguan exports, and by the middle of 1993 the zone's workforce had grown to 2,500. Unfortunately, this increased employment in no way made up for the workers laid off from the textile and apparel mills outside the zone.

The first large textile mill, Texnicsa, closed its doors in August 1991, laying off more than 900 workers. More than 70 per cent of those who lost their jobs were women with children to support. The remaining domestic textile garment factories had closed by 1993. According to Sandra Ramos of the Women's Secretariat of the Confederation of Sandinista Workers, of the 6,000 workers in this sector in 1989, only 1,500 still had jobs by the end of 1992 (interviews September–November 1992). The last textile company to close, an enterprise which had originally been scheduled to remain open, Fanatex, shut its doors in 1993 while negotiating a new ownership agreement with the cotton workers, and reportedly also negotiating with a Taiwanese firm (see Table 13.3) (author's interviews with CST and zone management).

Production cooperatives and neighbourhood garment makers and vendors

Table 13.3 Formal/informal sector shifts in worker location (eleven re-interviewed workers with work histories)

Code name	Age	Work history (years)	1991	1993
Julia	35	18, Enaves	Enaves	Velcas
Anna	37	10, Enaves	Enaves	Clothes vending
Claudia	48	18, Enaves	Enaves	Unemployed
Carmen	30	5, Enaves	Enaves	Velcas
Maria	40	4, Enaves	Enaves	Sporadically unemployed
Christina	49	10, Enaves 3, Contemi	Ronaco	Ronaco
Isabel	35	Clerical work, mayor's office	- Sewing/vending	Office clerk, political party
Rosalia	28	8, Texnicsa 1, Tricatex 1, Enaves	Unemployed	Fortex
Sandra	35	Clothes sewing	Clothes sewing/ vending	Clothes sewing/ vending
Georgina	36	1, Enaves	Clothes vending	Clothes vending
Ruth	38	8, Incasa (1971–8)	Clothes sewing	Clothes sewing

Source: Worker interviews.
Enaves: state-operated clothing factory in the Free Trade Zone, 1979–92.
Velcas: new private factory carved out of Enaves.
Ronaco: new garment factory in the zone since 1991.
Fortex: Taiwanese-owned factory carved out of Enaves.
Contemi, Tricatex, Incasa: private garment companies.
Texnicsa: Shut-down textile factory.

continued operation during this period of shutdown. Every locale in Managua seems to have at least one *costerera* or sewer/tailor and there are a number of sewing production cooperatives. In addition, and sometimes in combination with the above role, women sell clothing in their neighbourhoods and on market stalls. It is reasonable to assume that this informal sector included as many garment workers as in the formal sector, even before the shutdowns. Interviews among cooperatives, sewers and vendors showed that women with experience and reputation often make above the factory wage, even in the worst of economic times. On the other hand, the greatest poverty exists among workers in the informal sector and newcomers into the informal sector in the depressed economic climate of 1991–3 did very poorly (worker interviews and FIDEG 1991: 56).

IMPACT OF PRIVATIZATION ON WORKING WOMEN

The gender bias in the current Nicaraguan economic programme, partially a post-war phenomenon, exists in all types of industries as well as in government. With demilitarization, the few women who had worked in 'male' industries like beer, rum, cola and petroleum during the war lost their jobs as the soldiers came back. Moreover, the restructuring and cutbacks in government affected women in much larger percentages than men. According to Betina Reyes of the Ministry of Finance, over 70 per cent of government layoffs were women (interview July 1991). The health and education fields were hard hit and the vacant government offices testify to the great effects on the clerical workforce. My interviews show examples of middle-class women who, after rising to some prominence in universities and government service, have been pushed aside to make room for male leadership.

When compared to state industries, workers in private industries in the *Zona Franca* have experienced reductions in their rights and social services. The first workers to make the transition to the new regime of export production were happy about the higher hourly wages (Table 13.4). They soon realized, however, that their real incomes had not increased as transportation, cafeteria and health centre were no longer a part of the services package. Another important change is that workers are no longer paid when there is a problem with the production process, such as poor raw materials or slack demand (worker interviews).

The new employers are hiring workers at an average age that is six years younger than in the old enterprises. Meanwhile, a new industry in the zone, jewellery, sought even younger workers (Table 13.5). The new entrepreneurs are thus avoiding the problems of older workers whose eyes are no longer sharp and who may have other physical disabilities. As is customary in export-

Table 13.4 Salaries of workers in Mercedes Free Trade Zone (in cordoba, per month)*

Company	Number of employees	Operators (female)†	Floor supervisors inspectors (female)†	Mechanics (male)†
*1991**				
Enaves	400	260–350	968	500
Pronto	114	250–370	440	–
Ronaco	70	400–620	1,500	1,400
*1993**				
Cresen	107	720–780‡	–	–
Fortex	880	450–900§	2,000	900
INCAR (Neptune)	60	750–1,000	1,500–2,000	–
Pronto	80	600	–	–
Ronaco	131	400–620	1,500	1,400
Velca	500	700–800**	2,000	1,000

Source: Management and worker interviews.
* C$5 = US$1 in 1991; C$6 = US$1 in 1993.
† There is usually a strict sexual division of labour.
‡ Includes lunch and transportation payment.
§ C$400 for the trial (training) period.
** Piece workers sometimes make less.

processing zones, employers in Nicaragua are careful not to hire pregnant women. One manager reported that his workers had to undergo a physical examination which included a pregnancy test (manager interviews).

The more leisurely pace in the remaining state industries also contrasted, in 1991, with the pressure put on workers and supervisors to perform at a very rapid rate in private enterprises.[5] Rapid production is enforced by standard rates, quotas and/or payment by piece rates. Many workers have to stay until evening in order to finish the 'production standard'. According to one worker in the new jewellery industry, some workers stayed up to three hours late in order to make their quotas (worker interviews).

Table 13.5 Ages of workers in Mercedes Free Trade Zone

Company	Number of workers	17–25	26–35	Over 35	Average age
1991					
Enaves	400	15%	60%	25%	33
Pronto	114	65%	30%	5%	25
Ronaco	70	30%	70%	–	28
1993					
Cresen	107	99%	1%	0%	20
Fortex	880	40%	40%	20%	25
Neptune (Incar)	60	5%	75%	20%	30
Pronto	80	80%	20%	–	25
Ronaco	131	30%	70%	–	28
Velca	500	20%	65%	15%	30

Source: Management and worker interviews.

As the free trade zone developed over the 1991–3 period, older female workers were laid off and replaced by the very large pool of younger women looking for work in the garment–textile industry. Three of our interviewees were among the two-thirds of Enaves employees who were not rehired by the two private firms that bought Enaves property. Meanwhile, one woman whom we had interviewed as a laid-off textile worker was hired by the Taiwanese-owned Fortex as a cutter at near the basic salary, despite her many years of experience in the textile industry.

Older women who had worked for Enaves and were not rehired entered the informal sector, sewing or taking care of grandchildren. Thirty-five was the cut off age for hiring sewers at the new Fortex firm. Since about 30 per cent of the old Enaves workers were thirty-five or older, and the new employers had a preference for younger workers, it was not surprising that two-thirds of the old workers were not rehired.[6]

LABOUR UNIONS' GENDER BIAS IN RESTRUCTURING

In this period of market adjustment and privatization, it is not just the government and businesses that seem unwilling to deal with the problems of converting and updating industries that formally employed large percentages of women. Unions have also been gender biased in their cooperation with government and businesses.

As part of the Sandinista Front, women had organized for change. The first national women's organization, later known as AMNLAE,[7] was formed in 1977. It grew in the 1980s to a national membership of 25,000 women, working politically to advance their social, political and economic rights. AMNLAE was successful in organizing women around issues such as health and day care, as well as the legalization of paid pregnancy leave. A Women's Secretariat was also set up within the Sandinista trade union organization (CST). The Secretariat has been very active during the recent period of cutbacks in women's employment, specifically in protecting women's indemnification rights. From 1993, the organization has also been participating in women's labour actions in the new export-processing industries, recently supporting a spontaneous strike against Fortex.

The fact remains, however, that the compromises between the UNO government and the Sandinista union leadership (CST) favour men. In industries that predominantly hire men, for example the sugar industry, there were strikes and political actions across the country when settlements with former owners had disadvantaged workers. It seemed that because the textile and garment industries were 'women's industries', the response of the Sandinista unions was muted. Female union members in these industries were disadvantaged for reasons indicated above and because of union leaders' assumptions about their priorities.

During the closing down of textile and garment industries in 1991 and 1992, unions appeared to react differently to job losses suffered by women and by men. Women were encouraged to leave their jobs and struggle only for severance pay, while unions struggled so that men could keep their jobs. In the beginning of 1990, 70 per cent of those employed in a shoe factory in the free trade zone were female (CONAPRO 1992: 25). In November of the same year, the factory employed mostly men (management interviews). Meanwhile, women who had been employed by the factory demonstrated for severance pay (*Barricada* 1992: 6).

The gender differences in the UNO–Sandinista agreements became clearer as the process of privatization progressed. Workers were supposed to receive 25 per cent of the ownership of enterprises in the process, although, depending on the agreement, a larger or smaller percentage was possible. There were no women on the negotiating committee which developed the property settlements between the government and the unions, and we were not able to find any female workers who became stockholders in their enterprises in the zone. Enaves was sold to two private companies. Workers, primarily female, received severance pay but none received stocks.

CONCLUSION

Although the trend for women's job opportunities in industry throughout Latin America, and particularly in Central America, has shown significant gains in the past few decades, women in Nicaragua have lost ground in the 1990s. A free-market government policy, post-war unemployment trends and the particular economics of female industries have been factors leading to this decline.

Both the UNO government and the unions have favoured male workers, as the assumed family heads, in the current period. A depressed economy and restructuring with gender bias have significantly worsened working women's prospects. Female workers have been adversely affected in general, but middle-aged women have suffered the most. The new industrial job openings in the export sector have been going to younger workers and they will not, at any time in the near future, make up for the job losses in female industries.

Even if employment in the export industries shortly reaches or exceeds the 6,000 mark of 1989, approximately half of the women laid off in the 1989–92 period will not get jobs in this sector due to age discrimination and the inability to commute or relocate. They will most likely retire early or find marginal employment in an already overcrowded informal sector. The most distressing loss of jobs from a humanitarian point of view is the joblessness at the bottom of the economic ladder. The thousands of women in the garment and textile fields, the majority of whom are single mothers, have no way to feed their children. Many have been forced to resort to prostitution (Ibarra 1992: 2). Women have become the clear victims of Nicaragua's economic crisis and restructuring.

NOTES

1 I would like to thank Elizabeth Miller and Patricia Mulligan for their research assistance. I am also indebted to Carmen Diana Deere and the New England Women and Development Group for their comments on an earlier draft. This study was financed by a Fulbright fellowship and a graduate research grant from Fitchburg State College.
2 Five of the author's interviews can be listed here. (i) Orosco, Ligia – Investigator, Confederation of Sandinista Workers (CST) – on 23 June 1993; (ii) Ramos, Sandra – Director of the Women's Secretariat of the CST, Managua – on 19 September and 24 October 1991 as well as on 6 May 1992; (iii) Reyes, Betina – Management of the Ministry of Finance and originator of the government's employment reduction programme, Managua – on 18 August 1991; (iv) Zamora, Sergio – Director of the *Zona Franca*, Managua and former Director of Cartago Free Trade Zone in Costa Rica, Managua – on 29 August and 15 November 1991; and (v) Zuniga, Carlos – Public Relations Director, *Zona Franca*, Managua – on 23 June 1993.

3 The industry's march to a new international industrial format began with 'Operation Bootstrap' in Puerto Rico as far back as 1940 (Safa 1985: 85–6). Puerto Rico's diversification in the 1960s and wage increases in the 1970s diverted international investment to other countries in the region. The Caribbean Basin Initiative (1980s) did not include Nicaragua until the early 1990s. Open United States quotas for apparel imports from Central America have recently encouraged East Asian exporters, who face filled quotas for their own countries, to invest in this region.

4 Debt, financial crisis and a dramatic decline in terms of trade for Central American agricultural exports in the late 1970s severely contracted the regional and domestic markets for industrial goods. These factors as well as the political strife of the 1980s made the textile and garment industries unable to deal with the technological changes that have modernized the competition in other parts of the globe. A 1990 CEPAL study found that with the exception of thread production in El Salvador and some computerized technology in Costa Rican textiles, Central American industries are not well equipped to deal with the 1993 import tax reductions. The majority of these plants will either have to invest in modernized technology or liquidate (CEPAL 1990: 18, 52, 178–9).

5 The new companies are modelled after firms in export-processing zones around the world where workers experience more health problems related to eyesight and tension.

6 This age discrimination did not hold true for inspectors, who were older in the new firms. They were more experienced workers, probably chosen from the forewomen and inspectors at Enaves.

7 AMNLAE refers to the Luisa Amanda Espinosa Nicaraguan Women's Association, named after the first woman Sandinista to die in the Sandinista revolution.

BIBLIOGRAPHY

Acuerdo de Privatización, CST y CORNAP (1993) Managua, Nicaragua, February.
Africa South & East (1993) 'Maize goes through the roof', January/February: 22.
Altvater, E., Hubner, K., Lorentzen, J. and Rojas, R. (eds) (1991) *The Poverty of Nations: A Guide to the Debt Crisis from Argentina to Zaire*, London: Zed Books.
Anderson, S. and Cuadra, S. (1993) 'Workers in the privatization of state companies: challenge to succeed', *Barricada International*, May: 11–13.
Andersson, Per-Ake (1990) *Zambia's Experience with Structural Adjustment in the 1980s*, Gothenburg: School of Economics and Commercial Law, University of Gothenburg.
Andors, P. (1988) 'Women and work in Shenzhen', *Bulletin of Concerned Asian Scholars*, 20 (3): 22–41.
Angell, A. (1991) 'Unions and workers in Chile during the 1980s', in P. Drake and I. Jaksic (eds), *The Struggle for Democracy in Chile, 1982–1990*, Lincoln and London: University of Nebraska Press.
Anuarul statistic al Republicii Socialiste România 1971 (n.d.) Direţia centrală de statistică.
Anuarul statistic al Republicii Socialiste România 1981 (n.d.) Direţia centrală de statistică.
Anuarul statistic al României 1991/Romanian Statistical Yearbook 1991 (n.d.) Bucharest: Comisia naţională pentru statistică.
Arellano, J.P. (1985) *Políticas sociales y desarrollo. Chile 1924–1984*, Santiago: CIEPLAN.
—— (1989) 'La seguridad social en Chile en los años 90', Santiago: Colección Estudios CIEPLAN, 27.
Armstrong, A. (1987) 'Women as victims: a study of rape in Swaziland', in A. Armstrong (ed.), *Women and Law in Southern Africa*, Harare: Zimbabwe Publishing House.
Aslanbeigui, N. and Summerfield, G. (1989) 'Impact of the responsibility system on women in rural China: an application of Sen's theory of entitlements', *World Development*, 17 (3): 343–50.
Bacon, W. M., Jr. (1981) 'Queens, concubines and wives: women in Romanian politics', unpublished paper presented at the American Association for Southeast European Studies, Columbus, Ohio.
Balassa, B. (1985) 'The role of foreign trade in the economic development of Korea', in W. Galenson (ed.), *Foreign Trade and Investment: Economic Development in the Newly Industrializing Asian Countries*, Madison: University of Wisconsin Press, 141–75.

—— (1988) 'The lessons of East Asian development: an overview', *Economic Development and Cultural Change*, 36 (3): S274–S290.

Banda, G. (1991) 'Adjusting to adjustment in Zambia: women's and young people's responses to a changing economy', Oxfam Research Paper no. 4, Oxford.

Banister, J. (1991) 'China population changes and the economy', in *China's Economic Dilemmas in the 1990s*, Washington, DC: Joint Economic Committee, USGPO, 234–52.

Banugire, F.R. (1989) 'Employment, incomes, basic needs and structural adjustment policy in Uganda, 1980–87', in B. Onimode (ed.), *The IMF, the World Bank, and the African Debt: The Social and Political Impact*, London: Zed Books.

Barkin, D. (1990) *Distorted Development: Mexico in the World Economy*, Boulder, CO: Westview Press.

Barricada (1992) 'Exigen indemnization a COIP', 2 April: 6.

Bathily, A. (1989) 'Senegal's structural adjustment programme and its economic and social effects: the political economy of regression', in B. Onimode (ed.), *The IMF, the World Bank, and the African Debt: The Social and Political Impact*, London: Zed Books.

Becker, G. S. (1975) *Human Capital*, New York: Columbia Press.

Beijing Review (1988) 'New challenges to women's employment', 31 October: 18.

—— (1989a), 'Zhao Ziyang's comments on coastal area's development strategy', 8 February: 19.

—— (1989b), 'Fruit of the open policy', 32(34) 21–27 August: 11–13.

Bellante, D. and Jackson, M. (1983) *Labor Economics: Choices in Labor Markets*, New York: McGraw-Hill.

Bello, W. and Rosenfeld, S. (1990) *Dragons in Distress: Asia's Miracle Economies in Crisis*, San Francisco: Institute for Food and Development Policy.

Beneria, L. and Roldan, M. (1987) *The Crossroads of Class and Gender*, Chicago: University of Chicago Press.

Bishop, M., Long, F. and St. Cyr, J. (1990) *Export Processing Zones and Women in the Caribbean*, Varadero, Cuba: United Nations Economic Commission for Latin America and the Caribbean (ECLAC).

Brand, V., Mupedziswa, R. and Gumbo, P. (1993) 'Women informal sector workers and structural adjustment in Zimbabwe', in P. Gibbon (ed.), *Social Change and Economic Reform in Africa*, Uppsala: Nordiska Afrikainstitutet.

Browning, G. K. (1987) *Women and Politics in the USSR: Consciousness Raising and Soviet Women's Groups*, New York: St Martin's Press.

Brunet-Jailly, J. (1991) 'Health financing in the poor countries: cost recovery or cost reduction?', World Bank Working Paper no. 692, Washington, DC.

Brydon, L. and Chant, S. (1989) *Women in the Third World: Gender Issues in Rural and Urban Areas*, New Jersey: Rutgers University Press.

Buckley, M. (ed.) (1992) *Perestroika and Soviet Women*, Cambridge: Cambridge University Press.

Burkhardt, M. and Zierke, I. (1990) 'Die Gestaltung der Lebenszeit und die Einführung neuer Technologien', *Wirtschaftswissenschaft*, 38 (1).

Buzatu, S. (1988a) 'Edificarea socialismului în România, tărîm istoric al emancipării şi afirmării depline a femeii în societate', *Anele de istorie*, XXXIV (3): 75–90.

—— (1988b) 'Edificarea socialismului în România, tărîm istoric al emancipării şi afirmării depline a femeii în societate', *Anele de istorie* XXXIV (4): 45–60.

Byrd, W. and Lin, Q. (eds) (1990) *China's Rural Industry: Structure, Development, and Reform*, Oxford: Oxford University Press.

Cain, G.G. (1966) *Married Women in the Labor Force*, Chicago: University of Chicago Press.

Campbell, B.K. (ed.) (1989) *Political Dimensions of the International Debt Crisis*, New York: St. Martin's Press.

Castañeda, T. (1990) *Para combatir la pobreza. Política social y descentralización en Chile durante los '80*, Santiago: Centro de Estudios Públicos.

—— and Park, F. (1992) 'Structural adjustment and the role of the labor market,' in V. Corbo and S. Suh (eds), *Structural Adjustment in a Newly Industrialized Country: The Korean Experience*, Baltimore: Johns Hopkins University Press, 228–55.

Ceauşescu, N. (1973) *Romania on the Way of Building Up the Multilaterally Developed Socialist Society*, Vol. 8, Bucharest: Meridiane Publishing House.

CEPAL (1990) *Reconversión Industrial en Centroamerica*, 8 October.

CEPAL News (1990) 'Poverty in Latin America in the 1980s', X, August: 1–2.

CEPAL News (1992a) 'Social equity and changing production patterns: an integrated approach', XII, May: 1–3.

CEPAL News (1992b) 'Latin American poverty profiles', XII, December: 1–3.

Chapkis, W. and Enloe, C. (eds) (1983) *Of Common Cloth: Women in the Global Textile Industry*, Washington, DC: Transnational Institute.

Chen, P.S.J. (1978) 'Development policies and fertility behaviour: the Singapore experience of social disincentives', in *Southeast Asian Affairs 1978*, Singapore: Institute of Southeast Asian Studies: 245–56.

Chetley, A. (1990) *A Healthy Business? World Health and the Pharmaceutical Industry*, London: Zed Books.

Chilivumbo, A. and Kanyangwa, J. (1984) *The Case of the SIDA Lima Programme*, Lusaka: SIDA.

Chinemana, F. and Sanders, D. (1993) 'Health and structural adjustment in Zimbabwe', in P. Gibbon (ed.), *Social Change and Economic Reform in Africa*, Uppsala: Nordiska Afrikainstitutet.

Chipulu, P. (1990) 'North-western area development project', Nutrition Working Paper, Lusaka.

Chirot, D. (1979) 'Social change in communist Romania', *Social Forces*, LVII (2): 457–99.

Cho, Haejong (1987) 'Korean women in the professions', in E. Yu and E.H. Phillips (eds), *Korean Women in Transition At Home and Abroad*, Los Angeles: Center for Korean–American and Korean Studies, California State University, 47–70.

Cho, Hyong (1987) 'The position of women in the Korean work force', in E. Yu and E.H. Phillips (eds), *Korean Women in Transition At Home and Abroad*, Los Angeles: Center for Korean–American and Korean Studies, California State University, 85–102.

Cho, O. (1987) 'Women in transition: the low income family', in E. Yu and E.H. Phillips (eds), *Korean Women in Transition At Home and Abroad*, Los Angeles: Center for Korean–American and Korean Studies, California State University, 71–84.

Cho, U. and Koo, H. (1983) 'Economic development and women's work in a newly industrializing country: the case of Korea', *Development and Change*, 14 (4): 515–31.

Cho, Y. and Cole, D.C. (1992) 'The role of the financial sector in Korea's structural adjustment', in V. Corbo and S. Suh (eds), *Structural Adjustment in a Newly Industrialized Country: The Korean Experience*, Baltimore: Johns Hopkins University Press, 115–37.

Chu, D.K.W. (1987) 'China's special economic zones: expectations and reality', *Asian Affairs*, 14 (2): 77–89.

CONAPRO (Confederacion Nacional de Profesionales) (1992) *Radiografía del Desempleo en las Obreras Industriales del la Rama Textil Vestuario,* Managua: CONAPRO.

Constituţia Romăniei/The Constitution of Romania 1991 (1991) Bucharest: Monitorul Oficial.

Corbo, V. (1985) 'Chilean economic policy and international economic relations since 1970', in G.M. Walton (ed.), *The National Economic Policies of Chile, 1975–1982,* Greenwich, CT: Jai Press.

Corbo, V. and Nam, S. (1992a) 'Recent evolution of the macroeconomy', in V. Corbo and S. Suh (eds), *Structural Adjustment in a Newly Industrialized Country: The Korean Experience,* Baltimore: Johns Hopkins University Press, 35–67.

—— and Nam, S. (1992b) 'Recent experience in controlling inflation', in V. Corbo and S. Suh (eds), *Structural Adjustment in a Newly Industrialized Country: The Korean Experience,* Baltimore: Johns Hopkins University Press, 95–114.

—— and Suh, S. (eds) (1992) *Structural Adjustment in a Newly Industrialized Country: The Korean Experience,* Baltimore: Johns Hopkins University Press.

Cornelius, W. A. (1991) 'Labor migration to the United States: development outcomes and alternatives in Mexican sending communities', in S. Diaz-Briquets and S. Weintraub (eds), *Regional and Sectoral Development in Mexico as Alternatives to Migration,* Boulder, CO: Westview Press.

Cornia, G.A. and deJong, J. (1992) 'Policies for the revitalisation of human resources development', in G.A. Cornia, R. van der Hoeven and T. Mkandawire (eds), *Africa's Recovery in the 1990s: From Stagnation and Adjustment to Human Development,* New York: St Martin's Press.

Cortázar, R. (1985) 'Distributive results in Chile, 1973–1982', in G.M. Walton (ed.), *The National Economic Policies of Chile, 1975–1982,* Greenwich, CT: Jai Press.

Creese, A.L. (1990) 'User charges for health care: a review of recent experience', SHS Paper no. 1, Geneva: World Health Organization.

Croll, E. (1983) *Chinese Women Since Mao,* London: Zed Books.

Cruz, J.M. (1988) 'La fruticultura de exportación. Una experiencia de desarrollo empresarial', Santiago: Colección Estudios CIEPLAN, 25.

CSO (Central Statistical Office) (1991) *Women and Men in Zambia,* CSO: Lusaka.

Daines, V. and Seddon, D. (1993) 'Confronting austerity: women's responses to economic reform', in M. Turshen and B. Holcomb (eds), *Women's Lives and Public Policy: The International Experience,* Westport, CT: Greenwood Press.

Davin, D. (1976) *Woman-Work: Women and the Party in Revolutionary China,* Oxford: Oxford University Press.

Dawn (1992) 'Panel on debt and trade: the trouble with SAPs', *Dawn Informs,* 92 (3): 1, 2.

DeJong, J. (1991) 'Nongovernmental organizations and health delivery in sub-Saharan Africa', World Bank Working Paper no. 708, Washington, DC.

Delano, M. and Traslaviña, H. (1989) *La herencia de los Chicago boys,* Santiago: Las Ediciones del Ornitorrinco.

Del Gatto, D. (1989) 'Canales institucionales de participación de la mujer en Chile', Santiago: Instituto de la Mujer.

Deliman, E. (1977) *Femeia: personalitate politică în societatea noastră socialistă,* Bucharest: Editura politică.

Department of Statistics, Singapore (1983) *Economic & Social Statistics Singapore 1960–1982,* Singapore.

Census of Population, Singapore (various years) Singapore: Department of Statistics.

—— (1991) *Census of Population 1990 Advance Data Release,* Singapore: SNP Publishers.

Deutscher Bundestag (1989) Drucksache 11/5948 Bonn.

Development Digest (1982) *Women and Technology,* XX: 1.

Deyo, F.C. (ed.) (1987) *The Political Economy of the New Asian Industrialism*, Ithaca, NY: Cornell University Press.
—— (1989) *Beneath the Miracle: Labor Subordination in the New Asian Industrialism*, Berkeley: University of California Press.
—— (1991) 'Singapore: developmental paternalism', in S.M. Goldstein (ed.), *Minidragons: Fragile Economic Miracles in the Pacific*, Boulder, CO: Westview Press, 48–87.
Díaz, X. and Hola, E. (1988) 'La mujer en el trabajo informal urbano', in Centro de Estudios de la Mujer (CEM), *Mundo de mujer. Continuidad y cambio*, Santiago: Ediciones CEM.
Diaz-Briquets, S. and Weintraub, S. (eds) (1991) *Regional and Sectoral Development in Mexico as Alternatives to Migration*, Boulder, CO: Westview Press.
DIW (Deutsches Institut für Wirtschaftsforschung) (ed.) (1990) 'Quantitative Aspekte einer Reform von Wirtschaft und Finanzen in der DDR', *Wochenbericht*, no. 17.
—— (1991) 'Gesamtwirtschaftliche und unternehmerische Anpassungsprozesse in Ostdeutschland', *Wochenbericht*, no. 51–2.
Doeringer, P. B. and Piore, M.J. (1971) *Internal Labor Markets and Manpower Analysis*, Lexington, MA: Heath Lexington Books.
Dornbusch, R. and Park, Y. (1992) 'The external balance', in V. Corbo and S. Suh (eds), *Structural Adjustment in a Newly Industrialized Country: The Korean Experience*, Baltimore: Johns Hopkins University Press, 68–94.
Downs, C., Solimano, G., Vergara, C. and Zuñiga, L. (eds) (1989) *Social Policy from the Grass-Roots. Nongovernmental Organizations in Chile*, Boulder, CO: Westview Press.
Due, J.M. (1991) 'Policies to overcome the negative effects of structural adjustment programs on African female-headed households', in C.H. Gladwin (ed.), *Structural Adjustment and African Women Farmers*, Gainesville: University of Florida Press.
Dumoulin, J., Kaddar, M. and Velasquez, G. (1991) *Accès aux médicaments et financement: analyse économique et financière de base*, Geneva: World Health Organization.
EAF (Evangelische Aktionsgemeinschaft für Familienfragen) (ed.) (1990) 'Familienpolitik in der DDR und der Bundesrepublik Daten Maβnahmen im Vergleich', *Familienpolitische Informationen*, no. 3.
The Economist (1991) 'Zambia. Out of maize', 5 October: 58.
—— (1993a) 'The miseries of modeldom', 20 February: 48.
—— (1993b) 'What goes up can come down', September: 40–1.
—— (1993c) 'China speeds on to market', 20 November: 35–6.
Edwards, S. and Edwards, A.C. (1987) *Monetarism and Liberalization. The Chilean Experiment*, Cambridge, MA: Ballinger Publishing Co.
Edwards, S. and Larrain, F. (eds) (1989) *Debt, Adjustment and Recovery: Latin America's Prospects for Growth and Development*, Oxford: Basil Blackwell.
EIU (Economist Intelligence Unit) (1992) *Zambia: Country Profile 1992–93*, London: Business International Limited.
—— (1993) *Zambia, Zaire. Country Report*, No. 1, London: Business International Limited.
El Mercurio (1993a) International Edition, 'Chile necesita a sus mujeres!', 21–27 October: 8.
—— (1993b) International Edition, 23–29 September: 3.
Elson, D. (1989) 'The impact of structural adjustment on women: concepts and issues', in B. Onimode (ed.), *The IMF, the World Bank and the African Debt*, Vol. 2, London: Zed Press, 57–74.
—— (ed.) (1991) *Male Bias in the Development Process*, Manchester: Manchester University Press.

—— (1992) 'From survival strategies to transformation strategies: women's needs and structural adjustment', in L. Benería and S. Feldman (eds), *Unequal Burden: Economic Crises, Persistent Poverty, and Women's Work*, Boulder, CO: Westview Press.

Elson, D. and Pearson, R. (1981) 'The subordination of women and the internationalization of factory production', in K. Young, C. Wolkowitz and R. McCullagh (eds), *Of Marriage and the Market*, London: CES Books.

Enciclopedia României (1938) Vol. I, *Statul*, Bucharest: Imprimeria Naţională.

—— (1939) Vol. III, *Economia Naţională*, Bucharest: Imprimeria Naţională.

Endean, E.M. (1991) 'China's foreign commercial relations', in *China's Economic Dilemmas in the 1990s*, Washington, DC: Joint Economic Committee, USGPO, 741–69.

Enders, U. (1986) 'Kinder, Küche, Kombinat Frauen in der DDR', *Aus Politik und Zeitgeschichte*, no. 6–7.

Engels, F. (1973) [orig. 1884] *The Origin of Family, Private Property and the State*, New York: Pathfinder Press.

Errázuriz, M.M. (1992) 'El gobierno local como espacio para la acción con mujeres: Promesa que requiere reflexión', in D. Raczynski and C. Serrano (eds), *Políticas Sociales, Mujeres y Gobierno Local*, Santiago: CIEPLAN.

Fawcett, J.T. and Khoo, S. (1980) 'Singapore: rapid fertility transition in a compact society', *Population and Development Review*, 6 (4): 549–79.

FEMPRESS (1988) *Demandas de las mujeres*, Santiago: FEMPRESS/ILET.

Fernandez-Kelly, M.P. (1983) *For We Are Sold, I and My People: Women and Industry in Mexico's Frontier*, Albany, NY: SUNY Press.

Fewsmith, J. (1986) 'Note: special economic zones of the PRC', *Problems of Communism*, November–December: 78–85.

Ffrench-Davis, R. (1988) 'Ajuste, renegociaciones de la deuda y financiamiento externo negativo: Chile, 1982–87', Santiago: Apuntes CIEPLAN, 72.

—— (1989) 'Conflicto entre la deuda y el crecimiento en Chile,' Santiago: Colección Estudios CIEPLAN, 26.

FIDEG (Fundacion International para Desafio Económico Global) (1991) *El Impaco de las Politicas de ajuste sobre la mujer en Nicaragua: Reflexiones de un Estudio de Caso*, Managua, Nicaragua.

—— (1992) *Coyuntura Eonómica: Conditiones de Vida de la Poblacion en Managua*: 32.

Fischer, M. E. (1985) 'Women in Romanian politics: Elena Ceauşescu, pronatalism, and the promotion of women', in S. Wolchik and A. G. Meyer (eds), *Women, State, and Party in Eastern Europe*, Durham: Duke University Press.

—— (1989) *Nicolae Ceauşescu: A Study in Political Leadership*, Boulder, CO: Lynne Rienner.

Fong, M. (1993) *The Role of Women in Rebuilding the Russian Economy*, Washington, DC: World Bank.

Foreign Broadcast Information Service (1988a) 2 August: 41–2.

—— (1988b) 'Factories employing more women suffer losses', 30 February: 39.

—— (1988c) 'More women working in technology fields', 22 August: 34–5.

—— (1988d) 'Chinese women struggle for equality', 31 August: 41–2.

—— (1988e) 'Paper urges solving women employment problem', 25 August: 42–3.

—— (1989) *East Europe Daily Report Supplement, 14th Congress of the Romanian Communist Party*, 12 December: 69–70.

—— (1991) 'Government designs fund to cover maternity costs', 1 July: 48.

—— (1993) *East Europe Daily Report*, 17 August: 34.

Foster, S. (1991) 'Supply and use of essential drugs in sub-Saharan Africa: some issues and possible solutions', *Social Science & Medicine*, 32 (11): 1201–18.

Foxley, A. (1983) *Latin American Experiments in Neoconservative Economics*, Berkeley, University of California Press, 1983.

Freund, P. (1986) 'Health care in a declining economy: the case of Zambia', *Social Science and Medicine*, 23 (9): 875–88.

Friedrich-Ebert-Stiftung (ed.) (1987) *Frauen in der DDR. Auf dem Weg zur Gleichberechtigung?*, Bonn: Neue Gesellschaft.

Funk, N. and Mueller, M. (eds) (1993) *Gender Politics and Post Communism*, New York: Routledge.

Galenson, W. (ed.) (1985) *Foreign Trade and Investment: Economic Development in the Newly Industrializing Asian Countries*, Madison: University of Wisconsin Press.

—— (1992) *Labor and Economic Growth in Five Asian Countries: South Korea, Malaysia, Taiwan, Thailand, and the Philippines*, New York: Praeger Press.

Gálvez, T. and Todaro, R. (1988) 'La segregación sexual en la industria', in Centro de Estudios de la Mujer (CEM), *Mundo de mujer. Continuidad y cambio*, Santiago: Ediciones CEM.

Garcia, A.I. and Gomáriz, E. (1989) *Mujeres Centroamericanas, ante la crisis*, Vol. I, San Jose, Costa Rica: FLACSO.

Gazeta Wyborcza (1992) 'Norma Spodnic w Parliamentach', 16 July: 1

Geisler, G. (1992) 'Who is losing out? Structural adjustment, gender, and the agricultural sector in Zambia', *Journal of Modern African Studies*, 30 (1): 113–39.

—— and Narrowe, E. (1990) *Not So Good but Quite Ambitious: Women and Men Coping with Structural Adjustment in Rural Zambia*, Stockholm: SIDA.

——, Keller, B. and Chuzu, P. (1985) *The Needs of Rural Women in Northern Province: Analyses and Recommendations*, Lusaka: Government Printer.

Gelb, A. (1990) 'TVP workers' incomes, incentives, and attitudes', in W. Byrd and Q. Lin (eds), *China's Rural Industry: Structure, Development, and Reform*, Oxford: Oxford University Press, 280–98.

Gendler, G. and Gildingersh, M. (1992) 'Unemployment in St. Petersburg', *RFE/RL*, no. 40: 57–9.

Gibbon, P. (1993) 'Introduction: economic reform and social change in Africa', in P. Gibbon (ed.), *Social Change and Economic Reform in Africa*, Uppsala: Nordiska Afrikainstitutet.

——, Havnevik, K. and Hermele, K. (1993) *A Blighted Harvest? The World Bank and African Culture in the 1980s*, Trenton: Africa World Press.

Gilberg, T. (1990) *Nationalism and Communism in Romania: The Rise and Fall of Ceauşescu's Personal Dictatorship*, Boulder, CO: Westview Press.

Gilson, L. and Sen, P.D. (1993) 'Assessing the potential of health sector NGOs: policy options', in *Report of the Workshop on the Public/Private Mix for Health Care in Developing Countries*, London: London School of Hygiene and Tropical Medicine.

Gloyd, S. (1992) 'Manipulation of health policy through foreign assistance: a case study from Mozambique', Paper presented at the annual meeting of the African Studies Association, Seattle, WA, 23 November.

Goldstein, S.M. (1991) 'The Minidragons: economic miracles and political change', in S.M. Goldstein (ed.), *Minidragons: Fragile Economic Miracles in the Pacific*, Boulder, CO: Westview Press, 8–21.

Gómez, S. and Echenique, J. (1988) *La agricultura chilena. Las dos caras de la modernización*, Santiago: FLACSO.

González Meyer, R. (1992) 'Organismos no gubernamentales, políticas sociales y mujer. El caso de Chile', in D. Raczynski and C. Serrano (eds), *Políticas Sociales, Mujeres y Gobierno Local*, Santiago: CIEPLAN.

Gorbachev, Mikael (1987) *Perestroika – New Thinking for Our Country and the World*, New York: Harper & Row.

Gottschang, T. (1992) 'The economy's continued growth', *Current History*, September: 268–72.

Graham, C. (1991) 'From emergency employment to social investment. Alleviating poverty in Chile', Washington, DC: Brookings Occasional Papers.

—— (1993) 'Gender issues in poverty alleviation: recent experiences with demand-based programs in Latin America, Africa, and Eastern Europe', International Labour Office, Geneva.

Green, R.H. (1991) 'Africa, 1975–95: the political economy of boom, decline, conflict, survival – and revival?', UNCTAD Nongovernmental Liaison Service Occasional Papers no. 4.

Grunwald, J. and Flamm, K. (1985) *The Global Factory: Foreign Assembly in International Trade*, Washington, DC: Brookings Institute.

Gruppe Frauenforschung am Zentralinstitut für Hochschulbildung (1990) 'Wozu Forschungen über Frauen im Hochschulwesen?', unpublished manuscript.

Gruzdeva, E.B. and Chertikhina, E. S. (1987–88) 'The occupational status and wages of women in the USSR', *Soviet Sociology*, 26: 67–81.

GRZ (Government of the Republic of Zambia) (1981) *Women's Development Programmes: Report to the 1981 GRZ/SIDA Mission on Agricultural Sector Support*, Lusaka: SIDA.

—— (1989) *Fourth National Development Plan, 1989–93*, Lusaka: Government Printer.

—— (1990) *Social Action Programme for 1990–1993*, Lusaka: Consultative Group for Zambia.

Guillaume, A. (1991) 'Women, children, and health in Côte d'Ivoire', in M. Turshen (ed.), *Women and Health in Africa*, Trenton: Africa World Press.

GUS (1988) *Statystyka Polski, Studia i Prace*, no. 17, Warsaw.

Guzman Stein, L. (1983) 'La mujer en la producción', *Ciencia Social*, 25: 9–26.

—— (1984) 'La industria de la maquila y la explotación de la fuerza de trabajo de la mujer', *Desarollo y Sociedad*, 12: 101–10.

Hansen, K.T. (1980) 'The urban informal sector as a development issue: poor women and work in Lusaka, Zambia', *Urban Anthropology*, 9 (2): 199–225.

—— (1989a) 'The black market and women traders in Lusaka, Zambia', in J.L. Parpart and K.A. Staudt (eds), *Women and the State in Africa*, Boulder, CO: Lynne Rienner, 143–60.

—— (1989b) *Distant Companions: Servants and Employers in Zambia, 1900–1985*, Ithaca: Cornell University Press.

—— (1994) 'Dealing with clothing: second-hand clothes and the construction of identity in Zambia's third republic', *Public Culture*, 6 (3): 503–24.

Hardy, C. (1989) *La Ciudad Escindida*, Santiago: Programa de Economía del Trabajo.

Harris, N. (1989) 'Aid and urbanization', *Cities*, 6 (3): 174–85.

Hayes, M.D. (1984) *Latin America and the U.S. National Interest: A Basis for U.S. Foreign Policy*, Boulder, CO: Westview Press.

Heise, L. (1993) 'Violence against women: the missing agenda', in M. Koblinsky, J. Timyan and J. Gay (eds), *The Health of Women: A Global Perspective*, Boulder, CO: Westview Press.

Hellen, J.A. (1968) *Rural Economic Development in Zambia, 1890–1964*, Munich: Weltforum Verlag.

Hola, E. (1988) 'Mujer, dominación y crisis', in Centro de Estudios de la Mujer (CEM), *Mundo de mujer. Continuidad y cambio*, Santiago: Ediciones CEM.

Holst, E. and Schupp, J. (1991) 'Frauenerwerbstätigkeit in den neuen und alten Bundesländern-Befunde des socio-ökonomischen Panels', DIW Discussion Paper no.37.

213

Howe, R. (1993) 'Zambia: The score so far. Democracy 2, economic recovery 1', *The Courier*, 138 (March/April): 31.

Huber, J.H. (1993) 'Ensuring access to health care with the introduction of use fees: a Kenyan example', *Social Science & Medicine*, 36 (4): 485–94.

IAB (Institut für Arbeitsmarkt- und Berufsforschung) (ed.) (1991) *IAB-Kurzbericht*, Nuremberg.

Ibarra, E. (1992) 'Más obreras a la prostitución', *La Prensa*, 27 March, 3.

Infante, A. (1989) 'Primary health care in a local community', in C. Downs, G. Solimano, C. Vergara and L. Zuñiga (eds), *Social Policy from the Grass-Roots. Nongovernmental Organizations in Chile*, Boulder, CO: Westview Press.

Infas (Institut für angewandte Sozialwissenschaft) (1991) Frauen in den neuen Bundesländern im Prozeß der deutschen Einheit, Bad Godesberg.

Infratest (1991) Arbeitsmarkt Monitor für die neuen Bundesländer, Schnellbericht: Daten für Juli 1991, Munich.

ILO (International Labour Organisation) (1976) *Women Workers and Society: International Perspectives*, Geneva.

—— (1981) *Zambia: Basic Needs in an Economy under Pressure*. Addis Ababa.

—— (1993) 'Social security and social protection: equality of opportunity between men and women', Paper presented at Tripartite Meeting of Experts on Social Security and Social Protection: Equality of Opportunity between Men and Women, Geneva, 30 March–5 April.

ILO/UNCTC (1988) *Economic and Social Effects of Multinational Enterprises in Export Processing Zones*, Geneva.

International Monetary Fund (1993) *International Financial Statistics* (CD-ROM version), September, Washington, DC.

Iorga, N. (1911) *Feimeile în viaţa neamului nostru*, Valenii-de-Munte: Neamul Românesc.

Janova, M. (1992) 'Women's participation in political power in Europe: an essay in East-West comparison', *Women's Studies International Forum*, 15 (1): 115–28.

Jelavich, B. (1983) *History of the Balkans*, Vol. II, *Twentieth Century*, Cambridge: Cambridge University Press.

Jenkins, R. (1990) 'Comparing foreign subsidiaries and local firms in LDCs: theoretical issues and empirical evidence', *Journal of Development Studies*, 26 (2): 205–28.

Jespersen, E. (1992) 'External shocks, adjustment policies and economic and social performance', in G. A. Cornia, R. van der Hoeven and T. Mkandawire (eds), *Africa's Recovery in the 1990s: From Stagnation and Adjustment to Human Development*, New York: St Martin's Press.

Kahn, J. (1993) 'Cultural violence against women: an uphill battle for China against the new slave trade', *The Dallas Morning News*, 19 May.

Kalter, E. (1992) 'The Mexican strategy to achieve sustainable economic growth', in Claudio Loser and Eliot Kalter (eds), *Mexico: The Strategy to Achieve Sustained Economic Growth*, Washington, DC: International Monetary Fund.

Kamel, R. (1990) *The Global Factory*, Philadelphia: American Friends Service Committee, 1.

Kanji, N., Hardon, A., Harnmeijer, J.W., Mamdani, M. and Walt, G. (1992) *Drugs Policy in Developing Countries*, London: Zed Books.

Kaser, M. C. and Radice, E. A. (1985) *The Economic History of Eastern Europe, 1919–1975*, Vol. 1, *Economic Structure and Performance Between the Two Wars*, Oxford: Clarendon Press.

Kazilimani, E. (1993) 'Mozambique – from destruction to development: the health sector', *WIPHN News*, 14 (winter).

BIBLIOGRAPHY

Kelley, A.C., Williamson, J.G. and Cheetham, R.J. (1972) *Dualistic Economic Development: Theory and History*, Chicago: University of Chicago Press.

Kennedy, E. and Peters, P. (1992) 'Household food security and child nutrition: the interaction of income and gender of household head', *World Development*, 20 (8): 1077–85.

Kim, K.S. and Roemer, M. (1979) *Growth and Structural Transformation*, Cambridge, MA: Harvard University Press, Harvard East Asian Monographs, 86.

King, R. R. (1980) *History of the Romanian Communist Party*, Stanford: Hoover Institution Press.

Kirkwood, J. (1982) 'Ser política en Chile: Las feministas y los partidos', Santiago: FLACSO.

—— (1986) 'Feminismo y participación política', in M.A. Meza (ed.), *La otra mitad de Chile*, Santiago: Instituto para el Nuevo Chile, Centro de Estudios Sociales Ltda (CESOC).

Kligman, G. (1988) *The Wedding of the Dead: Ritual Poetics and Popular Culture in Transylvania*, Berkeley: University of California Press.

—— (1992) 'The politics of reproduction in Ceauşescu's Romania: a case study in political culture', *East European Politics and Society*, VI (3): 364–418.

Kommsomolskaya Pravda (1993) 'The position of women in Russia', 26 May: 2.

Koo, H. (1984) 'The political economy of income distribution in South Korea: the impact of the state's industrialization policies', *World Development*, 12 (10): 1029–37.

—— (1987) 'Women factory workers in Korea', in E. Yu and E.H. Phillips (eds), *Korean Women in Transition At Home and Abroad*, Los Angeles: Center for Korean–American and Korean Studies, California State University, 103–12.

Korean Statistical Association (1991) *Korea Statistical Yearbook, 1991*, Seoul: Korean Statistical Association.

Kotz, D. (1992) 'The direction of the Soviet economic reform: from socialist reform to capitalist transition', *Monthly Review*, 44: 14–34.

Krause, L.B., Koh, A.T. and Lee, Y.T. (1987) *The Singapore Economy Reconsidered*, Singapore: Institute of Southeast Asian Studies.

Kumar, S. and Lee, Y.T. (1991) 'The growth triangle – ASEAN's challenge in the 90s', Paper presented at the IPS-ISEAS Roundtable, Singapore, June.

Kuratowska, Z. (1991) 'Present situation of women in Poland', unpublished paper presented at Regional Seminar on the Impact of Economic and Political Reform on the Status of Women in Eastern Europe and the USSR, Vienna.

Kuznets, P.W. (1988) 'An East Asian model of economic development: Japan, Taiwan, and South Korea', *Economic Development and Cultural Change*, 36 (3): S11–S43.

Kwack, S.Y. (1990a) 'The economic development of the Republic of Korea, 1965–1981', in L.J. Lau (ed.), *Models of Development: A Comparative Study of Economic Growth in South Korea and Taiwan*, San Francisco: ICS Press, 65–125.

—— (1990b) 'The economy of South Korea, 1980–1987', in L.J. Lau (ed.), (1990) *Models of Development: A Comparative Study of Economic Growth in South Korea and Taiwan*, San Francisco: ICS Press, 217–36.

The Lancet (1990) 'Structural adjustment and health in Africa', 335: 885.

Lapidus, G. W. (1978) *Women in Soviet Society*, Berkeley: University of California Press.

—— (1977) 'Sexual equality in Soviet policy: a developmental perspective', in A.B. Atkinson (ed.), *Women in Russia*, Stanford: Stanford University Press.

Lau, L.J. (ed.) (1990) *Models of Development: A Comparative Study of Economic Growth in South Korea and Taiwan*, San Francisco: ICS Press.

Lee, B.S. (1993) 'Sex differentials in labor force participation in Korea', Korea Development Institute Working Paper no. 9304, Seoul.

Lee, C.H. and Naya, S. (1988) 'Trade in East Asian development with comparative reference to Southeast Asian experiences', *Economic Development and Cultural Change*, 36 (3): S123–52.

Lee, K., Urata, S. and Choi, I. (1992) 'Industrial organization: issues and recent developments', in V. Corbo and S. Suh (eds), *Structural Adjustment in a Newly Industrialized Country: The Korean Experience*, Baltimore: Johns Hopkins University Press, 204–27.

Leeds, R. and Thompson, G. (1987) *The 1982 Mexican Debt Negotiations: Response to a Financial Crisis*, Washington, DC: The Johns Hopkins Foreign Policy Institute.

Legal Status of Singapore Women (1986) Singapore: Asiapac Books and Educational Aids.

Lehmann, S. G. (forthcoming) 'Cost and opportunities of marketization: an analysis of Russian employment and unemployment', in R. Simpson and I. H. Simpson (eds), *Sociology of Work*, Vol. 4, Greenwich, CT: JAI Press.

Levy, S. and Lechner, N. (1986) 'CEMA-Chile y Secretaría Nacional de la Mujer', in M. A. Meza (ed.), *La otra mitad de Chile*, Santiago: Instituto para el Nuevo Chile, Centro de Estudios Sociales Ltda (CESOC).

Lim, C.Y. (1988) *Policy Options for the Singapore Economy*, Singapore: McGraw-Hill.

Lim, L.Y.C. (1990a) 'Singapore in Southeast Asia', *Journal of Southeast Asia Business*, 6 (4): 65–74.

—— (1990b) 'Women's work in export factories: the politics of a cause,' in I. Tinker (ed.) *Persistent Inequalities: Women and World Development*, New York: Oxford University Press, 101–19.

—— and Pang, E.F. (1986) *Trade, Employment and Industrialisation in Singapore*, Geneva: International Labour Organisation.

—— and Pang, E.F. (1991) *Foreign Direct Investment and Industrialisation in Malaysia, Singapore, Taiwan and Thailand*, Paris: OECD.

Loewenson, R. (1993) 'Structural adjustment and health policy in Africa', *International Journal of Health Services*, 23 (4): 717–30.

Lopez, C.M. and Pollack, M.E. (1989) 'The incorporation of women in development policies', *CEPAL Review*, 39: 37–45.

Loser, C. and Kalter, E. (1992) *Mexico: The Strategy to Achieve Sustained Economic Growth*, Washington, DC: International Monetary Fund.

Maccoby, E. E. and Jacklin, C.M. (1974) *The Psychology of Sex Differences*, Stanford: Stanford University Press.

McConnell, C.R. and Brue, S.L. (1992) *Contemporary Labor Economics*, 3rd edn, New York: McGraw-Hill.

Maier, F. (1991a) 'Erwerbstätigkeit von Frauen: Geschlechtsspezifische Umbrüche im Arbeitsmarkt und Beschäftigungssystem', in A. Westphal *et al.* (eds), *Wirtschaftspolitische Konsequenzen der deutschen Vereinigung*, Frankfurt: Campus.

—— (1991b) 'Geschlechterverhältnisse der DDR im Umbruch: Zur Bedeutung von Arbeitsmarkt und Sozialpolitik', *Zeitschrift für Sozialreform*, 37: 648–62.

Malic, D. and Serrano, E. (1988) 'La mujer chilena ante la ley', in Centro de Estudios de la Mujer (CEM), *Mundo de mujer. Continuidad y cambio*, Santiago: Ediciones CEM.

Malysheva, M. (1992) 'The politics of gender in Russia', *Women in Literature and Society*, Occasional Bradford Vocational Papers no. 7: 75–85.

Marcel, M. (1989) 'Privatización y finanzas públicas: El caso de Chile, 1985–88', Santiago: Colección Estudios CIEPLAN, 26.

Marshall, M.T. and Pérez, L.M. (1989) 'Experiences in community education and health in Latin America', in C. Downs, G. Solimano, C. Vergara and L. Zuñiga (eds), *Social Policy from the Grass-Roots. Nongovernmental Organizations in Chile*, Boulder, CO: Westview Press.

Meller, P. (1990) 'Revisión del proceso de ajuste de la década del 80', Santiago: Colección Estudios CIEPLAN, 30.

Merkel, I. (1990) 'Frauenpolitische Strategien in der DDR', in S. Gensior, F. Maier and G. Winter (eds), *Soziale Lage und Arbeit von Frauen in der DDR, Arbeitspapier 1990–6 des Arbeitskreises Sozialwissenschaftliche Arbeitsmarktforschung*, Paderborn.

Mesa-Lago, C. (1989) 'The current situation, limitation and potential role of social security schemes for income maintenance and health care in Latin America and the Caribbean: focus on women', Paper presented at the Conference on Coping with Social Change: Programs that Work, Acapulco, Mexico, June.

Mesa Mora, V. (1989) *La Maquila Y La Mujer Trabajadora en Costa Rica*, San Jose, Costa Rica: Comité Interconfederal Femenino.

Mincer, J. (1962) *Aspects of Labor Economics* Princeton, NJ: Princeton University Press.

Mingione, E. (1991) *Fragmented Societies: A Sociology of Economic Life Beyond the Market Paradigm*, London: Basil Blackwell.

Ministry of Labour, Singapore (1989) *Singapore Yearbook of Labour Statistics*, Singapore.

Ministry of Labour, South Korea (1991) *Yearbook of Labour Statistics*, Seoul.

Ministry of Trade and Industry, Singapore (1986) *The Singapore Economy: New Directions Report of the Economic Committee*, Singapore.

—— (1991) *Economic Survey of Singapore 1990*, Singapore.

Mirovitskaya, N. (1993a) 'Women and the post-socialist reversion to patriarchy', *Surviving Together*, Summer.

—— (1993b) 'The double burden weighs heavier on rural Russian women', *Surviving Together*, Fall: 27–30.

Montecinos, V. (1988) 'Economics and power. Chilean economists in government: 1958–1985', unpublished PhD Dissertation, University of Pittsburgh.

—— and Spessart, S. (1977) 'La busqueda de trabajo y los mecanismos de sobrevivencia de los desocupados en el Gran Santiago, 1976', International Labour Organisation–Regional Employment Program for Latin America and the Caribbean, Santiago, Documento de Trabajo 117.

Moore, H.L. (1988) *Feminism and Anthropology*, Minneapolis: University of Minnesota Press.

Moscow Times (1993) 'Women's party seeks to boost female representation', 23 October: 3.

Moses, J.C. (1977) 'Women in political roles', in A.B. Atkinson (ed.), *Women in Russia*, Stanford: Stanford University Press.

Moskoff, W. (1978) 'Sex discrimination, commuting and the role of women in Romanian development', *Slavic Review*, XXXVII (3): 440–56.

—— (1981) 'Child care in Romania: a comparative analysis', *East European Quarterly*, XV (3): 391–97.

—— (1982) 'The problem of the "double burden" in Romania', *International Journal of Comparative Sociology*, XXIII (1–2): 79–88.

Muller, M. (1982) *The Health of Nations: A North-South Investigation*, London: Faber & Faber.

Muños, J.F. (1991) 'Crece inversion atraida por CINDE', *La Nacion*, 5 August: 8A.

Muñoz Dalbora, A. (1988) 'Fuerza de trabajo femenina: Evolución y tendencias', in Centro de Estudios de la Mujer (CEM), *Mundo de mujer. Continuidad y cambio*, Santiago: Ediciones CEM.

Muntemba, D. (1989) 'The impact of IMF-World Bank programmes on women and children in Zambia', in B. Onimode (ed.), *The IMF, the World Bank, and the African Debt: The Social and Political Impact*, London: Zed Books.

Muntemba, M. (1987) 'The impact of the IMF/World Bank on the people of Africa with special reference to Zambia and especially on women and children', Paper presented to a conference of the Institute for African Alternatives on the Impact of the IMF and World Bank Policies on the Peoples of Africa, City University, London, 7–10 September.

Mupanga, E. (1993) 'Chiluba: repeating old mistakes', *New African*, June: 37.

Nakamura, M., Nakamura A. and Cullen D. (1969) 'Job opportunities, the offered wage, and the labor supply of married women', *American Economic Review*, 69: 5.

Nash, J. and Safa, H. (1986) *Women and Change in Latin America*, Massachusetts: Bergin & Garvey.

National Mirror (1993a) 'Concerned peasant, "fertilizer too expensive"', 18– 24 January.

—— (1993b) 'Farmers in Samfya cry foul over maize prices', 3–9 May.

—— (1993c) 'High prices dangerous: unions warn of food riots', 15–21 February.

National Statistical Office, Republic of Korea (various years) *Annual Report on the Economically Active Population Survey*, Seoul.

Nelson, D.N. (1985) 'Women in local politics in Romania and Poland', in S. Wolchik and A. G. Meyer (eds), *Women, State, and Party in Eastern Europe*, Durham: Duke University Press.

The New York Times (1993) 'Peasants of China discover new way to weed out girls', 21 July: A1.

Nickel, H. M. (1988) 'Effects of technological development on the occupational qualifications of women: greater equality or inequality between the sexes?', unpublished paper presented in Salamanca, Spain.

—— (1990) 'Geschlechtertrennung durch Arbeitsteilung', *Feministische Studien*, 8 (1).

Nkanagu, T. (1985) 'African experience in sickness insurance and health protection under social security', *International Social Security Review*, X: 119–40.

Ochs, C. (1990) 'Nicht alles, was die Partei der Frau zusammenbraute, gehört gleich in den Gully der Vereinigung', *WSI Mitteilungen*, no.5.

Office of the President, Mexico (1989) *National Development Plan*, Mexico: Government of Mexico.

Ogbu, O. and Gallagher, M. (1992) 'Public expenditures and health care in Africa', *Social Science and Medicine*, 34 (6): 615–24.

The One Percent Sample Survey (1987) China State Statistical Bureau.

Orescu, S. (1985) 'Multilaterally developed Romania: an overview', in V. Georgescu (ed.), *Romania: 40 Years (1944–1984)*, New York: Praeger Press.

Ortega, E. (1987) *Transformaciones agrarias y campesinado. De la participación a la exclusión*, Santiago: CIEPLAN.

Oshima, H.T. (1986) 'The transition from an agricultural to an industrial economy in East Asia', *Economic Development and Cultural Change*, 34 (4): 783–809.

—— (1988) 'Human resources in East Asia's secular growth', *Economic Development and Cultural Change*, 36 (3): S103–22.

Ott, N., Radtke, H., Thiel, W. and Wagner, G. (1990) 'Kindererziehung und Erwerbsarbeit. Marktwirtschaftliche Möglichkeiten einer erziehungsfreundlichen Erwerbsarbeit in Deutschland', DIW Discussion Paper no.7.

Owa, J.A., Osinaike, A.I. and Costello, A.M. de L. (1992) 'Letter to the Editor', *The Lancet*, 340 (8821): 732.

Palmer, I. (1991) *Gender and Population in the Adjustment of African Economies: Planning for Change*, Geneva: International Labour Office.

Palmer, R. (1977) 'The agricultural history of Rhodesia', in R. Palmer and N. Parsons (eds), *The Roots of Rural Poverty in Central and Southern Africa*, Berkeley: University of California Press, 221–54.

Pang, E.F. (1988) 'Structural change and labour market developments: the comparative experiences of five ASEAN countries and Australia', in E.F. Pang (ed.), *Labour Market Developments and Structural Change: The Experience of ASEAN and Australia*, Singapore: Singapore University Press, 1–12.

—— (1988) 'Development strategies and labour market changes in Singapore', in E. F. Pang (ed.), *Labour Market Developments and Structural Change: The Experience of ASEAN and Australia*, Singapore: Singapore University Press, 195–242.

Pankova, M. (1992) 'Discrimination of Russia's women', *Nezavisimaya Gazeta*, 19 December: 6.

Panorama International (1991) 'Centroamérica no da la talla', 19 August: 8–9.

—— (1992) 'Industria textil es el sector más dinámico', 21 September: 41.

Papalia, D. E. and Tennent, S. (1975) 'Vocational aspirations in preschoolers, a manifestation of early sex role stereotyping', *Sex Roles*, 1: 2.

Pardo, L. (1983) 'La dueña de casa y su aporte al PGB', *Revista de Economía*, 15, Santiago: Universidad de Chile.

Parpart, J.L. and Staudt, K.A. (1989) 'Women and the state in Africa', in J. L. Parpart and K.A. Staudt (eds), *Women and the State in Africa*, Boulder, CO: Lynne Rienner.

Pearce, R. (1989) *Food Consumption Subsidies in Zambia*, Oxford: Food Studies Group, International Development Centre, Oxford University.

Pepper, S. (1986) 'China's special economic zones: the current rescue bid for a faltering experiment', *University Field Services Staff International Report*, no. 14.

Pérez-Aleman, P., Martinez, D. and Widmair, C. (1989) *Industria Genero Y La Mujer en Nicaragua*, Managua: Instituto Nicaraguense de la Mujer.

——, Martinez, D. and Widmair, C. (1990) *Women in Nicaragua, A Profile: 1990*, Managua: The Canadian International Development Agency (CIDA).

Philip, G. (ed.) (1988) *The Mexican Economy*, London: Routledge.

PIIE (1989) *Ruptura y construcción de consensos en la educación chilena*, Santiago.

Prates, S. (1982) 'The impact of women and the family of economic stabilization policies in Latin America', *Development Research Digest*, Summer: 7.

Prices and Income Commission (1990) 'The social effects of structural adjustment programmes on vulnerable groups', Workshop paper, Lusaka.

Psacharopoulos, G. and Tzannatos, Z. (1991) *Women's Employment and Pay in Latin America*, Washington, DC: The World Bank.

—— (1992) *Latin America Women's Earnings and Participation in the Labor Force*, Washington, DC: The World Bank.

Putnam, R.D. (1976) *The Comparative Study of Political Elites*, Englewood Cliffs, NJ: Prentice-Hall.

Puzyrewski, T. (1989) *Polmart 1989: A Management Blueprint for Poland's Reform*, Somnis, CA: Macroman.

Pyle, J.L. (1990) *The State and Women in the Economy: Lessons from Sex Discrimination in the Republic of Ireland*, Albany: SUNY Press.

—— and Dawson, L.M. (1990) 'The impact of multinational technological transfer on female work forces in Asia', *The Columbia Journal of World Business*, XXV (4): 40–8.

Raczynski, D. (1989) 'Apoyo a pequeñas unidades productivas en sectores pobres: Lecciones de política', Santiago: Colección Estudios CIEPLAN, 27.

—— and Oyarzo, C. (1981) 'Por qué cae la tasa de mortalidad infantil en Chile?', Santiago: Colección Estudios CIEPLAN, 6.

—— and Romaguera, P. (forthcoming) 'Chile: poverty, adjustment and social policies in the 1980s', in N. Lustig (ed.), *Confronting the Challenge of Poverty and Inequality in Latin America*.

—— and Serrano, C. (1985) *Vivir la pobreza. Testimonios de mujeres*, Santiago: CIEPLAN.

—— and Serrano, C. (1992) 'Abriendo el debate: Descentralización del Estado, mujeres y políticas sociales', in D. Raczynski and C. Serrano (eds), *Políticas Sociales, Mujeres y Gobierno Local*, Santiago: CIEPLAN.

Radio Free Europe Research, East European Leadership List (1989) 27 October: 37–42.

Radio Free Europe Research, Situation Report (1981) Romania/6 (25 March): 17–22.

Radtke, H. (1990) 'Wissenschaftlich-technischer Fortschritt und Persönlichkeitsentwicklung der Frau', *Wirtschaftswissenschaft*, 38 (1).

Rady, M. (1992) *Romania in Turmoil*, London: IB Taurus and Co.

Rendel, M. (1981) *Women, Power and Political Systems*, New York: St Martin's Press.

Report on the Labour Force Survey of Singapore (various years) Singapore: Research and Statistics Department, Ministry of Labour.

Republic of Zambia (1985) *1980 Population and Housing Census of Zambia*, Analytical Report, Vol. III: Major Findings and Conclusions, Lusaka: Central Statistical Office.

—— (1990) *1990 Census of Population, Housing and Agriculture*, Preliminary Report, Lusaka: Central Statistical Office.

Reuters (1994) 'China's economy grows . . . ', 8 January.

Rimachevskaya, N. (1991) 'Socio-economic changes and the position of women in the Union of Soviet Socialist Republics', unpublished paper presented at the Regional Seminar on the Impact of Economic and Political Reform on the Status of Women in Eastern Europe and the USSR.

Roberts, H. L. (1969) *Rumania: Political Problems of an Agrarian State*, Chicago: Archon Books.

Rocznik Statystyczny Polski (Poland's Statistical Yearbook) (various years) Glowny Urzad Statystyczny.

Rodan, G. (1989) *The Political Economy of Singapore's Industrialization: National State and International Capital*, New York: St Martin's Press.

Roemer, M.I. (1987) 'Health system financing by social security', *International Journal of Health Planning and Management*, 2: 109–24.

Rojas, R. (1991) 'Mexico's five years of debt crisis', in E. Altvater, K. Hubner, J. Lorentzen and R. Rojas (eds), *The Poverty of Nations: A Guide to the Debt Crisis from Argentina to Zaire*, London: Zed Books.

Romania, Facts and Figures (1979) Bucharest: Editura stiinţifică şi enciclopedič.

Rossetti, J. (1988) 'La educación de las mujeres en Chile contemporáneo', in Centro de Estudios de la Mujer (CEM), *Mundo de mujer. Continuidad y cambio*, Santiago: Ediciones CEM.

Rothschild, J. (1974) *East Central Europe Between the Two World Wars*, Seattle: University of Washington Press.

Rothschild, K. (1993) 'Like a Lehrstück by Brecht: Notes on the German reunification drama', *Cambridge Journal of Economics*, no. 17.

Rozas, M. (1986) 'A pesar del miedo estamos abriendo un surco . . .', in M.A. Meza (ed.), *La otra mitad de Chile*, Santiago: Instituto para el Nuevo Chile, Centro de Estudios Sociales Ltda (CESOC).

Rozas, P. and Marín, G. (1989) *El 'mapa de la extrema riqueza' 10 años después*, Santiago: Ediciones Chile America, CESOC.

Rudolph, H. (1990) 'Brot und Rosen zu DM-Preisen? Frauenarbeit im wirtschaftlichen Umbruch', *Frauenforschung*, no.4.

Sachs, J. and Lipton, D. (1990) 'Poland's economic reform', *Foreign Affairs*, 69 (3): 47–66.

—— and Lipton, D. (1990) 'Creating a market economy in Eastern Europe: the case of Poland', *Brooking Papers on Economic Activity*, 1: 75–147.

Safa, H.I. (1981) 'Runaway shops and female employment: the search for cheap labor', *Signs*, winter.

—— (1985) 'Female employment in the Puerto Rican working class', in J. Nash and H. Safa (eds), *Women and Change in Latin America*, South Hadley, MA: Bergin and Garvey.

Safilios-Rothchild, Constantina (1985) *The Policy Implications of the Roles of Women in Agriculture in Zambia*, Republic of Zambia, Planning Division Special Studies no. 20, Lusaka: National Commission of Development Planning and Ministry of Agriculture and Water Development.

Sahn, D.E. (1992) 'Public expenditures in sub-Saharan Africa during a period of economic reforms', *World Development*, 20 (5): 673–93.

Salaff, J.W. (1985) 'The state and fertility motivation in Singapore and China', in E. Croll, D. Davin and P. Kane (eds), *China's One-Child Family Policy*, New York: St. Martin's Press, 162–89.

—— (1986) 'Women, the family, and the state: Hong Kong, Taiwan, Singapore – newly industrialized countries in Asia', in L.B. Iglitzin and R. Ross (eds), *Women in the World, 1975–1985: The Women's Decade*, 2nd rev. edn, Santa Barbara, CA: ABC-CLIO, 162–89.

Sandhu, K.S. and Wheatley, P. (1989) *Management of Success: The Moulding of Modern Singapore*, Singapore: Institute of Southeast Asian Studies.

Sanfuentes, A. (1987) 'Chile: effects of the adjustment policies on the agriculture and forestry sector', *CEPAL Review*: 33.

Sanyal, B. (1991) 'Organizing the self-employed: the politics of the urban informal sector', *International Labour Review*, 130 (1): 39–56.

Saw, S.H. (1984) *The Labour Force of Singapore*, Census Monograph no. 3, Singapore: Department of Statistics.

Schkolnik, M. and Teitelboim, B. (1988a) 'Encuesta de empleo en el Gran Santiago: empleo informal, desempleo y pobreza', PET, Documento de Trabajo no. 69, Santiago.

—— (1988b) 'Pobreza y desempleo en poblaciones. La otra cara del modelo neo liberal', PET, Santiago.

Schoepf, B.G. and Engundu, W. (1991) 'Women and structural adjustment in Zaire', in C.H. Gladwin (ed.), *Structural Adjustment and African Women Farmers*, Gainesville: University of Florida Press.

Schultz, T.W. (1963) *The Economic Value of Education*, New York: Columbia University Press.

Schwerthoeffer, S. (1985) 'The nationalities policy: theory and practice', in V. Georgescu (ed.), *Romania: 40 Years (1944–1984)*, New York: Praeger Press.

Scitovsky, T. (1990) 'Economic development in Taiwan and South Korea, 1965–1981', in L.J. Lau (ed), *Models of Development: A Comparative Study of Economic Growth in South Korea and Taiwan*, San Francisco: ICS Press, 127–81.

Selby, H.A., Murphy, A.D. and Lorenzen, S.A. (1990) *The Mexican Urban Household: Organizing for Self-Defense*, Austin: University of Texas Press.

Sen, A. K. (1981) *Poverty and Famines: An Essay on Entitlement and Deprivation*, Oxford: Clarendon Press.

—— (1985) *Women, Technology and Sexual Divisions*, New York: United Nations.

—— (1989) 'Women's survival as a development problem', *Bulletin of the American Academy of Arts and Sciences*, 43 (2): 14–29.

—— (1990) 'Gender and cooperative conflicts', in I. Tinker (ed.), *Persistent Inequalities*, Oxford: Oxford University Press, 123–49.

Serrano, C. (1986) 'Chile, mujeres en movimiento', in M.A. Meza (ed.), *La otra mitad de Chile*, Santiago: Instituto para el Nuevo Chile. Centro de Estudios Sociales Ltda (CESOC).

221

—— (1989) 'Política social en salud a nivel local', Santiago: Colección Estudios CIEPLAN, 27.

—— (1992) 'Estado, mujer y política social en Chile', in D. Raczynski and C. Serrano (eds), *Políticas Sociales, Mujeres y Gobierno Local*, Santiago: CIEPLAN.

Shlapentokh, V. and Marchenko, T. (1992) 'Family values on the rise while women fall in Russia', *FI Feminist Issues*, 12 (2): 43–6.

Sicular, T. (1991) 'China's agricultural policy during the reform period', in *China's Economic Dilemmas in the 1990s*, Washington, DC: Joint Economic Committee, 340–64.

Silva Donoso, M. de la L. (1987) *La participación política de la mujer en Chile: las organizaciones de mujeres*, Buenos Aires: Fundación Friedrich Naumann.

Silva, P. (1987) *Estado, neoliberalismo y política agraria en Chile, 1973–1981*, Amsterdam: CEDLA.

The Singapore Woman (1988) Singapore: Aware.

Sklair, L. (1989) *Assembling for Development: The Maquila Industry in Mexico and the United States*, Boston: Unwin & Hyman.

Slay, B. (1993) 'Roundtable: privitization in Eastern Europe', *RFE/RL Research Report* II, 32: 47–57.

Solimano, A. (1993) 'Chile', in Lance Taylor (ed.), *The Rocky Road to Reform: Adjustment, Income Distribution, and Growth in the Developing World*, Cambridge, Mass.: MIT Press.

Song, B. (1990) *The Rise of the Korean Economy*, Oxford: Oxford University Press.

Song, D. and Ryu, B. (1992) 'Agricultural policies and structural adjustment', in V. Corbo and S. Suh (eds), *Structural Adjustment in a Newly Industrialized Country: The Korean Experience*, Baltimore: Johns Hopkins University Press, 138–70.

Stacey, J. (1983) *Patriarchy and Socialist Revolution in China*, Berkeley: University of California Press.

State Statistical Bureau of the People's Republic of China (1985) *China Urban Statistics*, London: Longman Group and Beijing: China Statistical Information & Consultancy Service Centre.

Statistical Yearbook of China (1991), Hong Kong: State Statistical Bureau.

Statistisches Amt der DDR (1990) *Statistisches Jahrbuch der DDR*, Berlin.

Statistisches Bundesamt (1990) *Statistisches Jahrbuch der BRD*, Wiesbaden.

Stewart, S. (1992) 'Working the system: sensitizing the police to the plight of women in Zimbabwe', in M. Schuler (ed.), *Freedom from Violence: Women's Strategies from around the World*, New York: UNIFEM.

Stolz-Willig, B. (1990) 'DM morgen, Wirtschaftsaufschwung übermorgen, Frauenpolitik . . . ?', *WSI Mitteilungen*, no. 5.

Stoneman, C. (1993) 'The World Bank: some lessons for South Africa', *Review of African Political Economy*, 58: 87–98.

Story, D. (1986) *Industry, the State, and Public Policy in Mexico*, Austin: University of Texas Press.

Stourdza, A. A. C. (1911) *La femme en Roumanie: sa condition juridique et sociale dans le passé et le présent*, Paris: V. Giard & E. Brière.

Straits Times (1985) 'In the frontline of retrenchment', 18 September.

Stren, R., et al. (eds) (1992) *An Urban Problematique: The Challenge of Urbanization for Development Assistance*, Toronto: Centre for Urban and Community Studies, University of Toronto.

Tamayo, J. and Lozano, A. (1991) 'Mexican perceptions on rural development and migration of workers to the United States and actions taken, 1970–1988', in S. Diaz-Briquets and S. Weintraub (eds), *Regional and Sectoral Development in Mexico as Alternatives to Migration*, Boulder, CO: Westview Press.

Taubman, P. and Wachter, M.L. (1986) 'Segmented labor markets', in O.C. Ashenfelter and R. Layard (eds), *Handbook of Labor Economics*, Vol. 2, Amsterdam: North-Holland, 1183–217.

Teichman, J.A. (1988) *Policy Making in Mexico: From Boom to Crisis*, Boston: Allen & Unwin.

—— (1989) 'The politics of the Mexican debt crisis', in Bonnie K. Campbell (ed.), *Political Dimensions of the International Debt Crisis*, New York: St Martin's Press.

Thébaud, A. (1986) 'Aid games', *Review of African Political Economy*, 36: 43–9.

Times of Zambia (1992) 'Stalls razed: market a health hazard', 15 November: 1.

Tiano, S. (1986) 'Women and industrial development in Latin America (Review Essay)', *Latin American Research Review*, 21 (3).

Tironi, E. (1989) *Es posible reducir la pobreza en Chile*, Santiago: Zig-Zag.

Torche, A. (1987) 'Distribuir el ingreso para satisfacer las necesidades básicas', in F. Larraín (ed.), *Desarrollo económico en democracia*, Santiago: Centro de Estudios del Desarrollo.

Touré, M.L., Drame, M.L., Van Damme, W. and Ignatio Packer, M. (1992) 'Letter to the editor', *The Lancet*, 340 (8824): 916.

Tsantis, A.C. and Pepper, R. (1979) *Romania: The Industrialization of an Agrarian Economy Under Socialist Planning*, Washington, DC: The World Bank.

Turshen, M. (1984) *The Political Ecology of Disease in Tanzania*, New Brunswick, NJ: Rutgers University Press.

—— (1989) *The Politics of Public Health*, New Brunswick, NJ: Rutgers University Press.

—— (ed.) (1991) *Women and Health in Africa*, Trenton: Africa World Press.

United Nations (1983) *Five Studies on the Situation of Women in Latin America*, New York, 157–70.

—— (1989) *1989 World Survey on the Role of Women in Development*, New York.

—— (1990) *Trade Policies, Investment and Economic Performance of Developing Countries in the 1980s*, New York.

—— (1991a) *The Statistical Yearbook for Latin America*, New York.

—— (1991b) *The World's Women: Trends and Statistics 1970–1990*, New York.

—— (1992a) *1991 Demographic Yearbook*, New York.

—— (1992b) *The Impact of Economic and Political Reform on the Status of Women in Eastern Europe*, New York.

UNDP (1991) *Human Development Report 1991*, New York: Oxford University Press.

—— (1993) *Human Development Report 1993*, New York: Oxford University Press.

UNICEF (1989a) The Americas and The Caribbean Regional Office, *The Invisible Adjustment. Poor Women and the Economic Crisis*, Santiago: Alfabeta Impresores.

—— (1989b) *The State of the World's Children 1989*, New York: Oxford University Press.

—— (1993) *The State of the World's Children 1993*, New York: Oxford University Press.

US Department of Labor (1990) *Worker Rights in Export Processing Zones: Mexico*, Washington, DC: Government Printing Office.

—— (1991) *Mexico Foreign Trade Trends, 1989–1990*, Washington, DC: Government Printing Office.

US Department of State Dispatch (1992) 'Gist: North American Free Trade Agreement', 3 (5) August: 28–9.

Valenzuela, A. (1991) 'The military in power: the consolidation of one-man rule', in P. Drake and I. Jaksic (eds), *The Struggle for Democracy in Chile, 1982–1990*, Lincoln: University of Nebraska Press.

Valenzuela, M.E. (1991) 'The evolving roles of women under military rule', in P. Drake and I. Jaksic (eds), *The Struggle for Democracy in Chile, 1982–1990*, Lincoln: University of Nebraska Press.

Valdes, X. (1988) 'Feminización del mercado de trabajo agrícola: Las temporeras', in Centro de Estudios de la Mujer (CEM), *Mundo de mujer. Continuidad y cambio*, Santiago: Ediciones CEM.

Valota, B. (1979) *Questione agraria e vita politica in Romania (1907–1922): tra democrazia contadina e liberalismo autoritario*, Milano: Cisaplino-Goliardica.

Valverde, L. (1993) 'Zona Franca: la nueva cara de Nicaragua', *Barricada*, 6 May: 1, 6.

Van der Heijden, T. (1992) 'Letter to the editor', *The Lancet*, 340 (8821): 732.

Velasco, B. and Leppe, A. (1989) 'Appropriate technologies: a way of meeting human needs', in C. Downs, G. Solimano, C. Vergara and L. Zuñiga, (eds), *Social Policy from the Grass-Roots. Nongovernmental Organizations in Chile*, Boulder, CO: Westview Press.

Vergara, C. (1989) 'The new context of social policy in Chile and the space for non-governmental organizations', in C. Downs, G. Solimano, C. Vergara and L. Zuñiga, (eds), *Social Policy from the Grass-Roots. Nongovernmental Organizations in Chile*, Boulder, CO: Westview Press.

Vergara, P. (1990) *Políticas hacia la extrema pobreza en Chile 1973–1988*, Santiago: FLACSO.

Vogel, E.F. (1991) *The Four Little Dragons: The Spread of Industrialization in East Asia*, Cambridge, MA: Harvard University Press.

Ward, K. (ed.) (1990) *Women Workers and Global Restructuring*, Ithaca, NY: ILR Press, Cornell University.

Waty, M. (1993) 'Etat des lieux sur la crise du financement des services de santé en Afrique: quelles perspectives pour le financement communautaire?', *Argent et Santé: expériences de financement communautaire en Afrique*, Paris: Centre International de l'Enfance.

Weekly Post (1993) 'Maize marketing disaster looms', 27 August–2 September: 11.

Weintraub, S. (1991) 'The maquiladora industry in Mexico: its transitional role', in Sergio Diaz-Briquets and Sidney Weintraub (eds), *Regional and Sectoral Development in Mexico as Alternatives to Migration*, Boulder, CO: Westview Press.

Whitehead, A. (1990) 'Food crisis and gender conflict in the African countryside', in H. Bernstein, B. Crow, M. Mackintosh and C. Martin (eds), *The Food Question? Profits versus People*, London: Earthscan Publications, 54–68.

Whitehead, M. (1992) 'The concepts and principles of equity and health', *International Journal of Health Services*, 22 (3): 429–45.

WHO (World Health Organization) (1988) *The World Drug Situation*, Geneva.

—— (1990) *The Work of World Health Organization 1988–1989: Biennial Report of the Director-General*, Geneva.

—— (1991) *Interregional Meeting on the Public/Private Mix in National Health Systems and the Role of Ministries of Health*, Geneva.

—— (1992) *Evaluation of Recent Changes in the Financing of Health Services*, Geneva: World Health Organization Technical Report Series.

Winkler, G. (ed.) (1990a) *Frauenreport '90*, Berlin: Verlag Die Wirtschaft.

—— (ed.) (1990b) *Sozialreport 1990*, Vol. 1., Berlin: Verlag Die Wirtschaft.

Wolchik, S. L. (1981) 'Ideology and equality, the status of women in Eastern and Western Europe', *Comparative Politics*, 13 (4): 445–78.

Wolf, M. (1985) *Revolution Postponed: Women in Contemporary China*, Stanford: Stanford University Press.

Women's Global Network for Reproductive Rights (1993) *Newsletter*, 43, April–June.

Wong, A.K. 1980. 'Economic development and women's place: women in Singapore', *Change International Reports*, London.
—— (1981) 'Planned development, social stratification, and the sexual division of labor in Singapore', *Signs*, 7 (2): 434–52.
The World Bank (1980) *Health Sector Policy Paper*, Washington, DC.
—— (1987) *Financing Health Services in Developing Countries: An Agenda for Reform*, Washington, DC.
—— (1990) *World Development Report 1990: Poverty*, New York: Oxford University Press.
—— (1991) *World Development Report 1991: The Challenge of Development*, New York: Oxford University Press.
—— (1992a) *China: Strategies for Reducing Poverty in the 1990s*, Washington, DC.
—— (1992b) *World Development Report 1992: Development and the Environment*, New York: Oxford University Press.
—— (1992c) *Romania: Human Resources and the Transition to a Market Economy*, Washington, DC.
—— (1993a) *The World Bank Annual Report 1991*, Washington, DC.
—— (1993b) *World Development Report 1993*, New York: Oxford University Press.
Year Book of Labour Statistics (various years) Geneva: ILO.
You, P.S. and Lim, C.Y. (eds) (1984) *Singapore: Twenty-five Years of Development*, Nan Yang Xing Zhou Lianhe Zaobao.
Young, S. (1992) 'Import liberalization and industrial adjustment', in V. Corbo and S. Suh (eds), *Structural Adjustment in a Newly Industrialized Country: The Korean Experience*, Baltimore: Johns Hopkins University Press, 171–203.
Yu, E. (1987) 'Women in traditional and modern Korea', in E. Yu and E.H. Phillips (eds), *Korean Women in Transition At Home and Abroad*, Los Angeles: Center for Korean–American and Korean Studies, California State University, 15–27.
—— and Phillips, E.H. (eds) (1987) *Korean Women in Transition At Home and Abroad*. Los Angeles: Center for Korean–American and Korean Studies, California State University.
Yudelman, S. (1987) *Hopeful Openings: A Study of Five Women's Development Organizations in Latin America and the Caribbean*, West Hartford, CT: Kumarian Press.
Zaharia, G. (1980) *Condiţia juridică a femeii în dreptul internaţional*, Iaşi: Editura Junimea.
Zentralinstitut für Berufsbildung der DDR (1989) 'Zur beruflichen Orientierung der Mädchen und Frauen unter den Bedingungen der umfassenden Intensivierung unter besonderer Berücksichtigung der Facharbeiterberufe', unpublished manuscript.
Zhongguo Funu Bao (1988a) 'Gaige de chu lu bu zaiyu rang funu hui jia', 17 June: 3.
—— (1988b) 'Shanghai funu dui ci yilu zhong zhong', 20 June: 2.
—— (1988c) 'Huanyuan lun', 19 September.
Zhongguo Shehui Tonji Ziliao (various years) Beijing: State Statistical Bureau.
Zwi, A. and Ugalde, A. (1989) 'Towards an epidemiology of political violence in the Third World', *Social Science & Medicine*, 28 (7): 633–42.

INDEX

abduction of women: in China 126
ABM (Arbeitsmarkt und
Beschäftigungssystem) 22–3
abortion: in China 125; in Germany 24;
in Romania 50, 55
absenteeism: in Poland 39
academic staff: in Germany 18; in
Poland 30–1
administrative work: in Germany 21,
22, 23
Africa: non-governmental
organizations 87–8, 91, 92; political
activity 90, 92; population growth 91;
poverty 77, 81; Sub-Saharan 77–92;
(Zambia 79, 80, 81, 86, 87, 95–111);
urbanization 96, 97
agriculture: in Chile 162, 164, 168; in
China 113, 115, 119, 122–3; in
Mexico 182–4; in Nicaragua 194–5,
196; in Romania 44, 45, 46, 48, 50–1;
in South Korea 145, 146–7, 148, 149,
150, 153, 155, 156–7; in Sub-Saharan
Africa 77–8; (Zambia 97, 98, 99–100,
101–5)
aid, international 78, 89, 91–2
AIDS 89
AMNLAE (Luisa Amanda Espinosa
Nicaraguan Women's Association)
203
antenatal care: in Chile 170–1; in Sub-
Saharan Africa 82
apprenticeships: in Germany 12, 15; in
Romania 45–6
Australia 79
Austria 79
Aylwin, Patricio 161, 173

Bamako Initiative 83

benefits, maternity: in China 122; in
Germany 16–17; in Nicaragua 196,
198; in Soviet Union/Russia 70
Benin 81
Berlin 22, 23
birthrate: in China 125; in Germany 24;
in Mexico 185; in Romania 55, 57; in
Singapore 135, 142, 143
Blandiana, Ana 43
bonuses: in China 121
Botswana 81, 82
Buchi, Hernan 161
Burkina Faso 79, 86
Burundi 81, 85
businesses, private: in Chile 169; in
Nicaragua 198; in Romania 55–6, 57;
in Russia 69, 71–2;
see also privatization
Buzatu, S. 49

Cameroon 82, 83, 87
Canada: government expenditure 79;
and NAFTA 189
capitalism: in Chile 161–3; in China
114–15, 116; in Germany 20–5; in
Mexico 179–80; in Nicaragua 192–3,
197–8; in Poland 35–42; in Romania
55–6; in Russia 68–72; in Singapore
129–44; in South Korea 145–58;
see also privatization
Ceauçescu, Elena 50
Ceauçescu, Nicolae 43, 49, 53
CEMA-Chile 172
Central African Republic 79
Centre for Gender Studies (Moscow)
70–1
Chad 81
Chamoro, Violeta 192